Maldives

Tom Masters

LEGEND

Administrative Boundaries
Tourism Zone Boundaries
Reef with islands

0   70 km
0   40 miles

DEPTHS & ELEVATION

0m+
80m
200m
600m
1000m
2000m
3000m
4000m+

approximate values

INDIAN OCEAN

IHAVANDHIPPOLHU ATOLL

NORTH THILADHUNMATHEE ATOLL

HAA ALIF

Dhidhdhoo

SOUTH THILADHUNMATHEE ATOLL

HAA DHAAL

Kulhuduffushi

NORTH MILADHUNMADULU ATOLL

SHAVIYANI

Funadhoo

SOUTH MILADHUNMADULU ATOLL

NOONU

Manadhoo

RAA

Ugoofaaru

MAAMAKUNUDHOO ATOLL

NORTH MAALHOSMADULU ATOLL

FAADHIPPOLHU ATOLL

LHAVIYANI

Naifaru

BAA

Eydhafushi

SOUTH MAALHOSMADULU ATOLL

GOIDHOO ATOLL

NORTH MALE ATOLL

Thulusdhoo

KAAFU

Malé International Airport

MALÉ

RASDHOO ATOLL

ALIFU

Mahibadhoo

ARI ATOLL

SOUTH MALE ATOLL

FELIDHOO ATOLL

VAAVA

Feldhoo

FAAFU

FUSHIFARU THILA (p155)
Manta rays, sharks, sweetlips and turtles abound at this diving site

MALÉ (p88)
The Maldives' modern face, this thriving, fascinating capital is quite unlike anywhere else in the country

THULHAADHOO ISLAND (p152)
The traditional art of incised lacquer decoration thrives here

RASDHOO MADIVARU (p136)
Incredible diving with the most fascinating of sharks at Hammerhead Point

ARI ATOLL (p134)
The world's biggest fish cruise a remote corner of this atoll from May to September

KUDARAH THILA (p138)
A spectacular thila formation that attracts divers from around the world

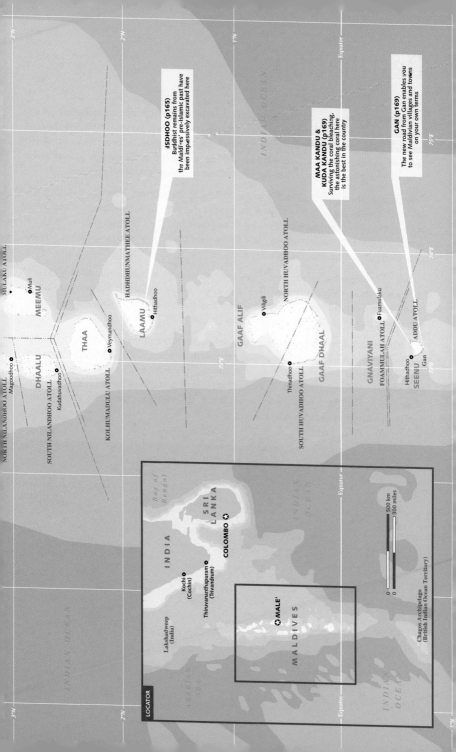

ISDHOO (p165)
Buddhist remains from the Maldives' pre-Islamic past have been impressively excavated here

MAA KANDU & KUDA KANDU (p169)
Surviving the coral bleaching, the astonishing coral here is the best in the country

GAN (p169)
The new road from Gan enables you to see Maldivian villages and towns on your own terms

LOCATOR

INDIAN OCEAN

Lakshadweep (India)

INDIA

Kochi (Cochin)

Thiruvananthapuram (Trivandrum)

Bay of Bengal

SRI LANKA

COLOMBO ✪

ARABIAN SEA

✪ MALE'

MALDIVES

Equator

INDIAN OCEAN

Chagos Archipelago (British Indian Ocean Territory)

0   500 km
0   300 miles

NORTH NILANDHOO ATOLL

MULAKU ATOLL

Magoodhoo

Muli

MEEMU

DHAALU

Kudahuvadhoo

SOUTH NILANDHOO ATOLL

THAA

Veymandhoo

KOLHUMADULU ATOLL

HADHDHUNMATHEE ATOLL

LAAMU

Hithadhoo

INDIAN OCEAN

GAAF ALIF

Viligili

NORTH HUVADHOO ATOLL

GAAF DHAAL

Thinadhoo

SOUTH HUVADHOO ATOLL

GNAVIYANI

FOAMMULAH ATOLL

Fuamulaku

Hithadhoo

SEENU

Gan

ADDU ATOLL

Destination

Perhaps the ultimate in long-haul luxury, the Maldives is currently enjoying incredible growth again, having bounced back from a series of disasters in the past few years including the coral bleaching wrought by El Niño and the horror of the 2004 tsunami. Indeed, so superior are its beaches, so cobalt blue its waters and so warm its welcome that the country has become a byword for paradise whether it be for honeymooners, sun worshippers or divers.

A geological eccentricity nestled in the middle of the Indian Ocean, the Maldives is a series of ancient coral reefs that grew up around the sides of towering prehistoric volcanoes. These immense structures have long since sunk into the ocean, leaving behind coral islands of incredible natural beauty, now themselves being colonised by travellers seeking unbridled pampering and romance.

This is life stripped down to simplicity – bright blue skies, all-year sunshine and fantastic diving and snorkelling in lagoons the temperature of bath water. The country embraces travellers from around the world allowing them the freedoms holidaymakers require without compromising the islands' deep Muslim faith one bit.

This is an exciting time to visit a country in developmental frenzy. Every few months brings newly opened resorts from top-end boutique brands to ecologically sound back-to-nature hotels. Not cheap even at the bottom end, this is a place for a holiday of a lifetime (and that phrase suddenly takes on a new meaning here). The Maldives demands the attention of anyone looking for a uniquely indulgent break, breathtaking nature and sheer beauty that stays with you long after your tan has faded.

JAMES LYON

Highlights

Plunge yourself into the deep blue – the Maldives is a world-class scuba-diving (p63) destination

CHRIS MELLOR

JAMES LYON

Admire the intricate Maldivian craft of lacquer work (p35)

Soak up the Indian Ocean sunset from your over-water villa (p48)

DENNIS WISKEN

Get some action with the many water sports (p53) available

Relish the sand between your toes at your resort's own amazing beach (p60)

Look but don't touch – the gorgeous corals (p40) have survived the bleaching

Cruise the atolls on a safari boat (p58)

MICHAEL AW

Explore the atolls in the traditional dhoni (boat; p29)

Get a glimpse of life beyond the resort, in Male' (p88)

JAMES LYON

JAMES LYON

Admire the majesty of the Grand
Friday Mosque (p93)

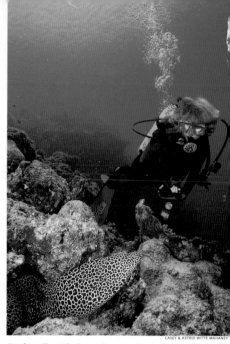

CASEY & ASTRID WITTE MAHANEY

Get friendly with the underwater locals (p72)

Indulge in the luxuries Maldivian resorts (p47) have to offer

MICHAEL AW

Contents

The Author   11

Getting Started   12

Snapshot   16

History   17

The Culture   25

Environment   37

Choosing a Resort   47

Snorkelling,
Diving & Surfing   61

Food & Drink   84

Male'   88
History   89
Orientation   89
Information   89
Dangers & Annoyances   92
Sights   92
Walking Tour   96
Male' for Children   98
Sleeping   98
Entertainment   102
Shopping   102
Getting There & Away   102
Getting Around   103
AROUND MALE'   103
Diving Sites   103
Viligili   103
Hulhule'   104
Hulhumale'   104
Other Islands   105

North & South
Male' Atolls   106
North Male' Atoll   106
Kaashidhoo   127

Gaafaru Falhu   127
South Male' Atoll   127

Ari Atoll   134
Thoddoo Island   134
Rasdhoo Atoll   134
Ari Atoll   137
Haa Alif   147

Northern Atolls   147
Haa Dhaal   148
Shaviyani   150
Noonu   150
Raa   150
Baa   152
Lhaviyani   155
Vaavu   159

Southern Atolls   159
Meemu   161
Faafu   161
Dhaalu   163
Thaa   165
Laamu   165
Gaaf Alif   165
Gaaf Dhaal   166
Gnaviyani   166
Addu Atoll   167

Directory   173
Accommodation   173
Business Hours   174
Children   174
Climate Chart   175
Courses   175
Customs   175
Dangers & Annoyances   175
Embassies & Consulates   176
Food   176
Gay & Lesbian Travellers   176
Holidays   176
Insurance   177
Internet Access   177
Legal Matters   177
Maps   177
Money   178
Post   179
Solo Travellers   180

Telephone	180	**GETTING AROUND**	**185**	**Language** 189
Time	180	Air	185	
Toilets	180	Boat	186	**Glossary** 191
Tourist Information	180	Car & Motorcycle	186	
Travellers with Disabilities	181			**Behind the Scenes** 193
Travel Permits	181	**Health** 187		
Visas	182	**BEFORE YOU GO**	**187**	**Index** 197
Women Travellers	182	Insurance	187	
		Recommended Vaccinations	187	**World Time Zones** 202
Transport 183		**IN THE MALDIVES**	**187**	
GETTING THERE & AWAY	**183**	Availability & Cost of Health Care	187	**Map Legend** 204
Entering the Country	183	Infectious Diseases	187	
Air	183	Traveller's Diarrhoea	187	
Sea	184	Environmental Hazards	188	

Regional Map Contents

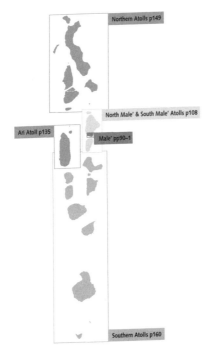

Northern Atolls p149

North Male' & South Male' Atolls p108

Ari Atoll p135

Male' pp90–1

Southern Atolls p160

The Author

TOM MASTERS

Tom Masters is a London-based travel writer. His latest foray for Lonely Planet took him across the Maldives, researching its incredible hotels and resorts by speedboat, quite a change from his usual stamping ground of Russia and Eastern Europe, but one that – it's fair to say – he didn't mind one bit. Going back to Siberia will never be the same.

CONTRIBUTING AUTHOR

Dr Trish Batchelor wrote the Health chapter. She is a general practitioner and travel-medicine specialist who works at the CIWEC Clinic in Kathmandu; she is also a medical advisor to the Travel Doctor New Zealand clinics. Trish teaches travel medicine through the University of Otago, and is interested in underwater and high-altitude medicine, and in the impact of tourism on host countries. She has travelled extensively through Southeast and East Asia and particularly loves high-altitude trekking in the Himalayas.

Getting Started

A country jealously guarding its cultural heritage and fragile ecology from the onslaughts of Western consumerism, the Maldives is almost exclusively a place for the package tourist. Despite most independent travellers' worst fears, coming on a package offers the best value for money, the easiest organisation and generally promotes preferential treatment – this is the way the Maldives is set up and everyone from the government to the resorts prefers you to travel this way. Fully independent travellers (FITs) are a rare species but, with good planning and some decent financial lubrication, this is an equally possible way to travel. However you arrive you'll find the same astonishing white beaches, surreally blue water and exceptional service.

WHEN TO GO

The Maldives specialises in winter sun for Europeans, making high season December to April, when the islands enjoy the dry monsoon with little rain and lower humidity while Europe shivers. February to April is the hottest period and resorts are almost all operating at capacity during this period. Mid-December to early January comes at even more of a premium due to Christmas and New Year and prices are even higher. Easter and the Italian holiday week in August also attract peak prices at most resorts, especially the Italian-oriented ones.

From May to November is the period when storms and rain are more likely. It's still warm, but skies can be cloudy and the humidity is higher. This is the low season, with fewer people and lower prices, with the exception of August.

Diving is good year-round, although a basic rule is that life on the reef is more varied and visibility better on the western side of any atoll from May to November and from the eastern side of any atoll December to April. This means you'd be wise to choose your resort accordingly.

The surfing season runs from March to October, which is great as this is when resorts are cheapest.

DON'T LEAVE HOME WITHOUT...

- Valid travel insurance
- Lots of sunscreen, sun block and after-sun
- A good pair of UV-blocking sunglasses
- A sun hat
- Flippers, mask and snorkel – if you'd like to do much snorkelling; most resorts charge for the hire of a kit
- Plasters – cutting your bare feet on coral or sharp shells is common
- Three-pin adaptors – the Maldives generally uses the UK-style electricity sockets (see p179)
- Lots of beach reading – don't rely on paperbacks left by other guests unless you're truly undiscerning
- All the medication and birth control you're likely to need
- Plastic bags for wet clothing and a waterproof jacket for the wetter months

There is no bad time to visit the Maldives, although if you're interested in spending time in Male' or any other inhabited islands, Ramazan (see p176) is a time to avoid as restaurants are closed and people aren't always at their most receptive.

COSTS & MONEY

The Maldives is no cheap destination – you'll hardly see a backpack the entire time you're here (and if you do it will be being carried for someone by a member of resort staff) – and the government prefers it this way, maximising revenue while keeping out the stoned hippies who so outraged local conservative values when they began to trickle through in the 1970s.

Even the folk here on budget packages are fairly well heeled, and don't fool yourself – even if you do get a cheap flight and accommodation deal, unless it's full board you'll spend almost as much again on food and drink during your stay.

While it's possible to say that costs are high, it's hard to be much more specific, mainly because two travellers can pay vastly different sums for the same deal at the same resort due to how they book – one travel agent may have an excellent deal on the room rate, another a far worse one, while an FIT will just have to pay whatever rate they are quoted directly by the resort reservations service.

Extremely roughly then, expect to pay at the very least $100 per person per day at the lower end for a room with full board. Midrange starts around $200 per day and extends up to $500, while for about $500 a day, you enter the heady heights of the Maldives luxury market, which currently seems to have no cap.

For those with a modest budget, the best deal is a full board or all-inclusive package (including certain drinks, both alcoholic and non) that includes flights and transfers. While it's still a lot of money, you'll spend almost nothing during your stay.

TRAVEL LITERATURE

While the Maldives has been covered in some detail by photography and nature guides, there's still precious little of any literary merit written about the place. This is perhaps unsurprising given the sun, sand and sea nature of most travel here, but the following titles are definitely worth a look.

Rudie H Kuiter's *Photo Guide to Fishes of the Maldives* is an indispensable book for divers and snorkellers, detailing some 700 species that live on the reefs of the country, all beautifully illustrated with photographs and descriptions of their habits.

The Maldive Mystery, by Norwegian explorer and ethnologist Thor Heyerdahl, is great for anyone wanting an overview of pre-Islamic Maldivian history and the numerous unanswered questions, although many of Heyerdahl's theories are now discredited.

Andrew Forbes' *Maldives – Kingdom of a Thousand Isles* is an odd mix of cultural overview, travel journal and resort guide. It's best employed as the first – the sections on history and traditional crafts are some of the most detailed available.

Divers' Guide to the Sharks of the Maldives, by Dr RC Anderson, is another fascinating title that describes the various shark species divers can encounter in the Maldives.

Dive Guide The Maldives, by Sam Harwood and Rob Bryning, is one of the best dive guides in print, with reviews of all the main diving and snorkelling sites in the country.

HOW MUCH?

Male'–airport ferry
US$1 or Rf10

Cappuccino US$3

Male' whale submarine
ticket US$75

Bed tax per person per
night US$8

Flat taxi fare in Male'
$2 or Rf15

Adrian Neville's *Male' – Capital of the Maldives* is a beautifully presented coffee-table book with great photos of Male' and its people.

Mysticism in the Maldives, compiled by Ali Hussain, documents superstitions, encounters with jinnis, supernatural phenomena and weird stuff. Published by Novelty, it's out of print but still available in a few shops.

Classical Maldivian Cuisine, by Aishath Shakeela, is a fascinating and informative book with delicious recipes for fish soup, fish, coconut and curried fish – order from www.maldiviancuisine.com.

INDEPENDENT TRAVEL

Independent travel in the Maldives is a challenge, but one risen to every year by many people, who decide that paradise on a package is not their idea of fun. As a fully independent traveller (FIT), you'll be a rarity, confusing hoteliers and transfer agents wherever you go when you tell them you don't have a tour operator. This is a great, if sometimes expensive, way to travel; although, while you're more independent than most package tourists, you still are not free to travel through the Maldives properly due to the extreme restrictions on foreigners outside of resorts.

Male' is a great place to start for FITs – allow a couple of days in town to shop around several travel agencies and arrange onward travel, accommodation and even excursions and diving. FITs who want to get on a safari boat will certainly have to make arrangements in Male' (see p58). Due to the system of discounts offered to travel companies, even the most resolutely independent traveller determined to see untouristed areas will benefit from the help of a good travel agent or operator.

Male' has over a quarter of the country's population, relatively few tourists and is quite an interesting place in its own right. If you eat in local teashops, visit the market and walk around in the evenings, you'll meet lots of locals. English is widely spoken and people will be more than willing to chat. There are a few inhabited nonresort islands (Viligili, Hulhumale', Thila Fushi and Himmafushi), which you could reach and return from in a day.

It's perfectly feasible to use Male' airport as a transport hub from which you can take speedboat, dhoni, air and seaplane transfers to visit different resorts – all at your own pace. However, this will be an expensive way to travel and planning will be essential, particularly in high season (December to April) when most resorts are fully booked and last-minute changes hard to arrange. Inner Maldives (p91) continues to come highly recommended as the travel agency best set up to meet the needs of FITs.

It's government policy to have tourists stay on island resorts or on boats within the 'tourism zone'. You need a travel permit to visit islands outside the tourism zone or to stay overnight on any nonresort island. To get a travel permit (see p181) you need a sponsor to invite you to the island concerned. If you want to visit islands that are occupied by Maldivians rather than tourists, you still have a few options.

Firstly, you can stay in a resort and make day trips. Most resorts offer 'island hopping' trips that visit local fishing villages, though these villages often have conspicuous souvenir shops and persistent sellers. Some resorts are quite close to village islands; you can charter a dhoni to visit the village without a big group. Resorts won't allow you to use catamarans, windsurfers or canoes to visit nearby islands, but if you explain what you want and you find a sympathetic ear, you may get help. You won't be allowed to stay in any village after 6pm.

The best resort to choose, if you want to visit local villages, is the Equator Village Resort (p171) on Gan, in the far south of the country. Gan is linked by causeways to four other islands with quite large villages and towns, including Hithadoo, the second largest settlement in the country after Male', and you can cycle, taxi or walk through all of them.

The second option is to arrange a safari-boat trip to the areas you're interested in and make it clear to the operator that you want to visit fishing villages. The operator will arrange permits for all the people on the boat, and because you stay overnight on the boat, the accommodation problem is solved. You will have to charter the whole boat, so you'll need some other like-minded passengers to share the expense.

INTERNET RESOURCES

The Internet is an extremely important resource for the Maldives – not only does it allow you to do virtual tours of nearly all resorts, it's also about the only forum for political debate in a country where the press and TV are tightly controlled by the state.

Friends of Maldives (www.friendsofmaldives.org) The website of the controversial British-based campaign group set up to protest against the Maldivian government's human rights record. It's a good if depressing read and tells potential travellers how to avoid putting money into the government coffers. See p47 for details.

Inner Maldives (www.innermaldives.com) One of the country's best travel agencies has a great website packed full of information, particularly good for FITs.

Maldives Culture (www.maldivesculture.com) Australian-based site with lots of background information, Maldives news archive and critical discussion of Maldivian issues.

Maldives Story (www.maldivesstory.com.mv) A government-backed history site that tells the story of the country's development from ancient history to the present day.

Minivan News (www.minivannews.com) Excellent UK-based website reporting news from the Maldives of the sort you won't get in the country.

Visit Maldives (www.visitmaldives.com) The official Maldives Tourist Promotion Board site has background information and data about virtually every resort, safari boat and tour operator in the country.

Snapshot

When hundreds of protesters occupied the main square in Male' in August 2004, it was the first time in any meaningful way the grievances of a nation were publicly aired after three decades of rule by the iron-fisted President Gayoom. The police brutality and repression that followed put paid to the long-standing Maldivian whitewashing of its own dictatorship in the name of tourism numbers – something the government is seeking to redress by hiring international PR firms to wipe down its image again. Don't be fooled by the idyllic photographs, the white sand and the dreamy blue sea; there's trouble in paradise, and it's official.

Despite this, it's perfectly ordinary for people visiting the Maldives to have no idea about the political background to their holiday. The tourism industry has been carefully engineered to avoid interaction between travellers and locals as much as possible, bringing in massive revenues without contaminating the population with liberal Western ideas. Despite the veneer of freedom, travellers have no real chance to visit islands independently or to even spend the night anywhere but in an (albeit rather lovely) resort.

A political survivor through and through, to appease his critics Gayoom has promised changes to the constitution and multiparty elections by 2008. However, the prospect of his giving up power voluntarily is remote – his family and allies run all aspects of the economy, they own resorts and reap much of the financial benefits of this country.

Increasingly discredited internationally and hated internally, Gayoom cannot last much longer: that much is clear to most. But it's anyone's guess what will follow him. While political parties are now legal, what will happen if one actually has the audacity to win an election remains to be seen. The leader of the main opposition group was arrested in 2005, later charged with terrorism and sedition and is believed to have been tortured in prison – and this before his party was even able to fight an election.

Rural poverty remains a further problem; the legacy of the 2004 tsunami may no longer be visible in the tourist resorts or Male', but visit an uninhabited island and evidence of the devastation is still easy to find. Furthermore there are an estimated 11,000 internally displaced people who have yet to rebuild their lives.

Even if the Maldives overcomes its internal unrest, there remain far bigger problems on the horizon, namely global warming. Just 1m above sea level, the Maldives is expected to disappear almost totally by the end of this century. Not for nothing did the government tourism board once famously consider using the slogan 'come and see us while we're still here'.

Travellers lucky enough to visit this wonderful country will discover a peaceful people with a rich and fascinating culture of survival in the middle of the ocean, as well as incredible natural beauty. It's been a tough few years for the Maldives, but this is no time to turn away from it. Go and spend a wonderful holiday here, meet the locals and don't be afraid to ask awkward questions; you can contribute to building freedom in a country denied it for too long.

FAST FACTS

Area: 90,000 sq km (above water 300 sq km)

Percentage of the country that is water: 99.9%

Number of atolls: 26

Population: 360,000

Percentage of population living in Male': 27%

GDP per capita: US$2509

Percentage of GDP spent on defence: 5.5%

Number of internally displaced people since the tsunami: 11,000

Inflation: 6.8%

Number of shark attacks since 1976: none

History

The history of the Maldives is that of a small, isolated and peaceful nation constantly trying to contain the desires of its powerful neighbours and would-be colonisers. It's also an incredibly hazy history for the most part – of which little before the conversion to Islam in 1153 is known. Indeed, the pre-Muslim period is full of heroic myths, mixed with conjecture based on inconclusive archaeological discoveries.

The Maldivian character has clearly been shaped by this tumultuous past: hospitable and friendly but fiercely proud and independent at the same time, it's safe to say that no conquering armies have got very far trying to persuade the Maldivian people of its benevolence.

More recently the history of the country has been defined by the dictatorship of Maumoon Abdul Gayoom, president for three decades and a man often jokingly referred to as the CEO of the Maldives, because he runs it like a giant tourist corporation. It's no joking matter though, as the police brutality and human rights abuses that have occurred under his rule are shocking and – perhaps worst of all – virtually ignored around the world.

EARLY DAYS

Some archaeologists, including the now much-dismissed Thor Heyerdahl, believe that the Maldives was well known from around 2000 BC, and was a trading junction for several ancient maritime civilisations including Egyptians, Romans, Mesopotamians and Indus Valley traders. The legendary sun-worshipping people called the Redin may have descended from one of these groups.

Around 500 BC the Redin either left or were absorbed by Buddhists, probably from Sri Lanka, and by Hindus from northwest India. HCP Bell, a British commissioner of the Ceylon Civil Service, led archaeological expeditions to the Maldives in 1920 and 1922. Among other things, he investigated the ruined, dome-shaped structures *(hawittas)*, mostly in the southern atolls, that he believed were Buddhist stupas similar to the dagobas found in Sri Lanka (Ceylon).

CONVERSION TO ISLAM

For many years, Arab traders stopped at the Maldives en route to the Far East – their first record of the Maldive islands, which they called Dibajat, is from the 2nd century AD. Known as the 'Money Isles', the Maldives provided enormous quantities of cowry shells, an international currency of the early ages. The cowry is now the symbol of the Maldives Monetary Authority. It must have been an almost magical land at the time – forget money growing on trees, in the Maldives it was washed up on the shore!

Abu Al Barakat, a North African Arab, is credited with converting the Maldivians to Islam in 1153. According to the legend, young virgin girls in Male' were chosen from the community and left alone in a temple as a sacrifice to Rannamaari, a sea jinni. One night Barakat took the place

Travels in Asia & Africa 1325-54, by Ibn Battuta, has been reprinted in paperback by Routledge Kegan Paul. Ibn Batutta, a great Moorish globetrotter, was an early visitor to the Maldive islands and wrote this history of the early Muslim period.

TIMELINE	1153	1558
	Islam officially adopted as the national religion	The Portuguese invade the Maldives from India

of a prospective sacrificial virgin and drove the demon away by reading from the Islamic holy book, the Quran. The Maldivian king at the time was sold on Islam, and ordered that the whole country convert.

A series of six sultanic dynasties followed, 84 sultans and sultanas in all, although some did not belong to the line of succession. At one stage, when the Portuguese first arrived on the scene, there were actually two ruling dynasties, the Malei (or Theemuge) dynasty and the Hilali.

THE PORTUGUESE

Early in the 16th century the Portuguese, who were already well established in Goa in western India, decided they wanted a greater share of the profitable trade routes of the Indian Ocean. They were given permission to build a fort and a factory in Male', but it wasn't long before they wanted more from the Maldives.

The Maldive Mystery, by Thor Heyerdahl, the Norwegian explorer of Kon-Tiki fame, describes a short expedition in 1982–83, looking for remains of pre-Muslim societies.

In 1558, after a few unsuccessful attempts, Captain Andreas Andre led an invasion army and killed Sultan Ali VI. The Maldivians called the Portuguese captain 'Andiri Andirin' and he ruled Male' and much of the country for the next 15 years. According to some Maldivian beliefs, Andre was born in the Maldives and went to Goa as a young man, where he came to serve the Portuguese. (Apart from a few months of Malabar domination in Male' during the 18th century, this was the only time that another country has occupied the Maldives; some argue that the Portuguese never actually ruled the Maldives at all, but had merely established a trading post.)

According to popular belief, the Portuguese were cruel rulers, and ultimately decreed that Maldivians must convert to Christianity or be killed. There was ongoing resistance, especially from Mohammed Thakurufaanu, son of an influential family on Utheemu Island in the northern atoll of Haa Alif. Thakurufaanu, with the help of his two brothers and some friends, started a series of guerrilla raids, culminating in an attack on Male', in which all the Portuguese were slaughtered.

This victory is commemorated annually as National Day on the first day of the third month of the lunar year. There is a memorial centre on the island of Utheemu to Thakurufaanu, the Maldives' greatest hero, who went on to found the next sultanic dynasty, the Utheemu, which ruled for 120 years. Many reforms were introduced, including a new judicial system, a defence force and a coinage to replace the cowry currency.

PROTECTED INDEPENDENCE

The Portuguese attacked several more times, and the rajahs of Cannanore, South India, (who had helped Thakurufaanu) also attempted to gain control. In the 17th century, the Maldives accepted the protection of the Dutch, who ruled Ceylon at the time. They also had a short-lived defence treaty with the French, and maintained good relations with the British, especially after the British took possession of Ceylon in 1796. These relations enabled the Maldives to be free of external threats while maintaining internal autonomy. Nevertheless, it was the remoteness of the islands, the prevalence of malaria and the lack of good ports, naval stores or productive land that were probably the main reasons neither the Dutch nor the British established a colonial administration.

1573	1834
Expulsion of the Portuguese	Moresby begins his celebrated charting of the Maldives

In the 1860s Borah merchants from Bombay were invited to Male' to establish warehouses and shops, but it wasn't long before they acquired an almost exclusive monopoly on foreign trade. The Maldivians feared the Borahs would soon gain complete control of the islands, so Sultan Mohammed Mueenuddin II signed an agreement with the British in 1887 recognising the Maldives' statehood and formalising its status as a protectorate.

The Story of Mohamed Thakurufaln, by Hussain Salahuddeen, tells the story of the Maldives' greatest hero, who liberated the people from the Portuguese.

THE 20TH CENTURY

In 1932 the Maldives' first constitution was imposed upon Sultan Shamsuddin. Until this time the Maldives had always had an unwritten constitution much like the British, and historical records show that

THE LEGEND OF THAKURUFAANU

As the man who led a successful revolution against foreign domination, and then as the leader of the newly liberated nation, Mohammed Thakurufaanu (sultan from 1573 to 1585) is the Maldives' national hero. Respectfully referred to as Bodu Thakurufaanu (*bodu* meaning 'big' or 'great'), he is to the Maldives what George Washington is to the USA. The story of his raid on the Portuguese headquarters in Male' is part of Maldivian folklore and incorporates many compelling details.

In his home atoll of Thiladhunmathee, Thakurufaanu's family were known and respected as sailors, traders and *kateebs* (island chiefs). The family gained the trust of Viyazoaru, the Portuguese ruler of the four northern atolls, and was given the responsibility of disseminating orders, collecting taxes and carrying tribute to the Portuguese base in Ceylon. Unbeknown to Viyazoaru, Thakurufaanu and his brothers used their position to foster anti-Portuguese sentiment, recruit sympathisers and gain intelligence on the Portuguese. It also afforded the opportunity to visit southern India, where Thakurufaanu obtained a pledge from the rajah of Cannanore to assist in an overthrow of the Portuguese rulers in the Maldives.

Back in Thiladhunmathee Atoll, Thakurufaanu and his brothers built a boat in which to conduct an attack on Male'. This sailing vessel, named *Kalhuoffummi,* has its own legendary status – it was said to be not only fast and beautiful, but to have almost magical qualities that enabled it to elude the Portuguese on guerrilla raids and reconnaissance missions.

For the final assault, they sailed south through the atolls by night, stopping by day to gather provisions and supporters. Approaching Male', they concealed themselves on a nearby island. They stole into the capital at night to make contact with supporters there and to assess the Portuguese defences. They were assisted in this by the local imam, who subtly changed the times of the morning prayer calls, tricking the Portuguese into sleeping late and giving Thakurufaanu extra time to escape after his night-time reconnaissance visits.

The attack on Male' was carefully planned and timed, and allegedly backed by supernatural forces – one story relates how a coconut tree mysteriously appeared in the Portuguese compound, and provided cover for Thakurufaanu as he crept close and killed Andiri Andirin with a spear. In the ensuing battle the Maldivians, with help from a detachment of Cannanore soldiers, defeated and killed some 300 Portuguese. Most versions of the story have the Portuguese drinking heavily on their last night, making it a cautionary tale about the evils of alcohol.

The Thakurufaanu brothers then set about re-establishing a Maldivian administration under Islamic principles. Soon after, Bodu Thakurufaanu became the new sultan, with the title of Al Sultan-ul Ghazi Mohammed Thakurufaanu Al Auzam Siree Savahitha Maharadhun, first Sultan of the third dynasty of the Kingdom of the Maldives.

1887	1932
Maldives becomes a self-governing British Protectorate	The country writes its first constitution, curbing the sultan's powers

pre-20th century Maldives was relatively progressive and democratic by the standards of the time. However, the imposition of the constitution marks the dawn of true Maldivian statehood. The sultan was to be elected by a 'council of advisers' made up of Maldivian elite, rather than being a hereditary position. In 1934, Shamsuddin was deposed and Hasan Nurudin became sultan.

WWII brought great hardship to the Maldives. Maritime trade with Ceylon was severely reduced, leading to shortages of rice and other necessities – many died of illness or malnutrition. A new constitution was introduced in 1942, and Nurudin was persuaded to abdicate the following year. His replacement, the elderly Abdul Majeed Didi, retired to Ceylon leaving the control of the government in the hands of his prime minister, Mohammed Amin Didi, who nationalised the fish export industry, instituted a broad modernisation programme and introduced an unpopular ban on tobacco smoking.

When Ceylon gained independence in 1948, the Maldivians signed a defence pact with the British, which gave the latter control of the foreign affairs of the islands but not the right to interfere internally. In return, the Maldivians agreed to provide facilities for British defence forces, giving the waning British Empire a vital foothold in the Indian Ocean after the loss of India.

In 1953 the sultanate was abolished and a republic was proclaimed with Amin Didi as its first president, but he was overthrown within a year. The sultanate was returned, with Mohammed Farid Didi elected as the 94th sultan of the Maldives.

BRITISH BASES & SOUTHERN SECESSION

While Britain did not overtly interfere in the running of the country, it did secure permission to re-establish its wartime airfield on Gan Island in the southernmost atoll of the country, Addu. In 1956 the Royal Air Force began developing the base, employing hundreds of Maldivians and resettling the Gan people on neighbouring islands. The British were informally granted a 100-year lease of Gan that required them to pay £2000 a year.

When Ibrahim Nasir was elected prime minister in 1957, he immediately called for a review of the agreement with the British on Gan, demanding that the lease be shortened and the annual payment increased. This was followed by an insurrection against the Maldivian government by the inhabitants of the southern atolls of Addu and Huvadhoo, who objected to Nasir's demand that the British cease employing local labour. They decided to cut ties altogether and form an independent state, electing Abdulla Afif Didi president.

In 1960 the Maldivian government officially granted the British the use of Gan and other facilities in Addu Atoll for 30 years (effective from December 1956) in return for the payment of £100,000 a year and a grant of £750,000 to finance specific development projects. Later, Nasir sent gunboats from Male' to quash the rebellion in the southern atolls. Afif fled to the Seychelles, then a British colony, while other leaders were banished to various islands in the Maldives. Afif later became the Seychelles foreign minister.

The Maldive Islands: Monograph on the History, Archaeology & Epigraphy is HCP Bell's main work. The Ceylon Government Press published it in 1940, three years after his death. Original copies of the book are rare, but Novelty Press has reprinted it and it's available from several tourist shops and bookshops in Male'.

A Description of the Maldive Islands for the Journal of the Royal Asiatic Society, by HCP Bell, the most renowned historian of the Maldives and former British commissioner in the Ceylon Civil Service, draws from his archaeological expeditions in 1920 and 1922.

1953	1965
The Republic of Maldives is declared and the sultanate abandoned	The Maldives finally gains full independence from Britain

In 1965 Britain recognised the islands as a completely sovereign and independent state, and ceased to be responsible for their defence (although it retained the use of Gan and continued to pay rent until 1976). The Maldives was granted independence on 26 July 1965 and later became a member of the UN.

THE REPUBLIC

Following a referendum in 1968 the sultanate was again abolished, Sultan Majeed Didi retired to Ceylon and a new republic was inaugurated. Nasir was elected president. In 1972, the Sri Lankan market for dried fish, the Maldives' biggest export, collapsed. The first tourist resorts opened that year, but the money generated didn't benefit many ordinary inhabitants of the country. Prices kept going up and there were revolts, plots and banishments as Nasir clung to power. In 1978, fearing for his life, Nasir stepped down and skipped across to Singapore, reputedly with US$4 million from the Maldivian national coffers.

A former university lecturer and Maldivian ambassador to the UN, Maumoon Abdul Gayoom, became president in Nasir's place. Hailed as a reformer, Gayoom's style of governing was initially much more open, and he immediately denounced Nasir's regime and banished several of the former president's associates. A 1980 attempted coup against Gayoom, involving mercenaries, was discovered and more banishment occurred. What had started as a forward-looking, reform-minded regime was already beginning to look very suspect.

Gayoom was re-elected in 1983 and continued to promote education, health and industry, particularly tourism. He gave the tiny country a higher international profile with full membership in the Commonwealth and the South Asian Association for Regional Co-operation (SAARC). The focus of the country's economy remained the development of tourism, which continued throughout the 1980s.

Norwegian explorer and ethnographer Thor Heyerdahl was fascinated by the Maldives and its pre-Islamic culture. Although he spent many years trying to uncover the secrets of the past, many of his conclusions were later rejected.

THE 1988 COUP

In September 1988, 51-year-old Gayoom began a third term as president, having won an election where he was the only candidate, again. Only a month later a group of disaffected Maldivian businessmen attempted a coup, employing about 90 Sri Lankan Tamil mercenaries. Half of these soldiers infiltrated Male' as visitors, while the rest landed by boat. The mercenaries took several key installations, but failed to capture the National Security Service (NSS) headquarters.

More than 1600 Indian paratroopers, immediately dispatched by the Indian prime minister, Rajiv Gandhi, ended further gains by the invaders who then fled by boat towards Sri Lanka. They took 27 hostages and left 14 people dead and 40 wounded. No tourists were affected – many didn't even know that a coup had been attempted. The mercenaries were caught by an Indian frigate 100km from the Sri Lankan coast. Most were returned to the Maldives for trial: several were sentenced to death, but reprieved and returned to Sri Lanka.

The coup attempt saw standards of police and NSS behaviour decline. Many people in police captivity faced an increased use of torture and the NSS became a widely feared entity.

1972	1976
Kurumba Island, the Maldives' first holiday resort, opens	The British Naval Base at Gan closes

GROWTH & DEVELOPMENT

In 1993 Gayoom was nominated for a fourth five-year term, and confirmed with an overwhelming referendum vote (there were no free elections again, obviously). While on paper the country continued to grow economically, through the now massive tourism industry and the stable fishing industry, much of this wealth was concentrated in the hands of a small group of people, and almost none of it trickled down to the people of the atolls.

At the same time, the Maldives experienced many of the problems of developing countries, notably rapid growth in the main city, the environmental effects of growth, regional disparities, youth unemployment and income inequality.

The 1998 El Niño event, which caused coral bleaching throughout the atolls, was detrimental for tourism and it signalled that global warming might threaten the existence of the Maldives. When Gayoom began a fifth term as president in 1998, the environment and sea-level rises were priorities for him. For all his failings, Gayoom has certainly done a good job of promoting awareness of environmental change and rising sea levels, which are likely to see the country totally submerged by the end of the 21st century (see p44).

The 1990s saw the Maldives develop hugely – the whole country became linked up with a modern telecommunications system, and mobile phones and the Internet became widely available. By the end of the century 90% of Maldivians had electricity and basic hospitals and higher secondary schools centres had been established in outer atolls. With Japanese assistance Male' was surrounded by an ingenious sea wall, which was to prove very useful just a few years later when the tsunami struck. In 1997 work began on a new island, an extra metre or so above sea level, near the capital to accommodate a growing population. It's the only logical future the country has, given the total lack of action to prevent global warming by the international community.

Read about the human-rights situation in the Maldives in the Amnesty International reports 'Republic of Maldives: Repression of Peaceful Political Opposition' and 'Maldives: Human Rights Violations in the Context of Political Reforms', at http://web.amnesty.org /library/engindex

THE EVAN NASEEM KILLING

In September 2003 shots rang out in Maafushi Prison in South Male' Atoll, easily within earshot of tourists enjoying romantic evening walks on the beach of nearby Coco Island. Little were they to know that these were indiscriminate shootings of inmates protesting at the brutal murder of 19-year-old inmate Evan Naseem, a prisoner who was beaten to death by prison guards.

When Evan Naseem's family put their son's brutally tortured corpse on display there was a huge public outcry. Male' spontaneously erupted in rioting, the People's Majlis (Parliament), also known as the Citizen's Council, was stoned and police stations were burned by the mob. The NSS orchestrated mass reprisals and beatings against the rioters, making an ugly situation even worse. To fan the flames of popular anger, in the same month President Gayoom was renominated as the sole presidential candidate for the referendum by the Majlis, which is stacked full of Gayoom family members and other appointed flunkies. Realising that something was up, Gayoom did make an example of the torturers who killed Evan Naseem, but stopped short of punishing or removing any

1978	1982
President Gayoom comes to power	The Maldives rejoins the British Commonwealth

---

JENNIFER LATHEEF

A young journalist, human rights activist and member of the Maldivian Democratic Party (MDP), Jennifer Latheef was arrested during the Male' riots following the Evan Naseem murder in 2003, where she was protesting peacefully for an end to police brutality. She was eventually sentenced to 10 years' imprisonment for 'terrorism', was subjected to cruel and degrading treatment in jail and was declared a Prisoner of Conscience by Amnesty International. Jennifer was subsequently released after a presidential pardon she initially refused to accept, because it did not exonerate her of crimes. She continues to campaign for the release of political prisoners.

---

senior ministers or Adam Zahir, the NSS chief of staff. Gayoom's other measure was to hire the London office of PR giant Hill & Knowlton to whitewash his dictatorship, a job they continue to do today with sickening success. Meanwhile, the Maldivian Democratic Party (MDP) was founded in Colombo in nearby Sri Lanka.

BLACK FRIDAY

Under pressure from colleagues, and clearly trying to outsmart the reformists, Gayoom launched his own reform programme in 2004. His proposals were astonishingly all encompassing, including having more than one candidate in the presidential referendum, a two-term limit for the president and the legalisation of political parties.

However, just a month later Gayoom banned political meetings of prodemocracy activists in Male' as they are proving too popular. The darkest moment so far for the democracy movement, known to all now as Black Friday, took place on 13 August 2004. Reformist and prodemocracy campaigners all gathered in the capital's main square, encouraged by the apparent lack of obstruction from the NSS. Former political prisoners and well-known reformists all attended with the apparent blessing of Gayoom, and carried out a successful meeting calling for reform. Suddenly the NSS cleared the square, arresting and beating over a thousand people in the process. Women and children were savagely beaten, and many were taken into solitary confinement, where they remained for months.

'On the morning of 26 December 2004 the Indian Ocean tsunami devastated countries throughout the region.'

TSUNAMI

The stand-off between government and people continued without any obvious resolution throughout 2004, although international protests increased with human rights advocates Friends of Maldives attending the World Travel Market and handing out flyers to delegates to increase awareness of the country's domestic problems and the increased readership of anti-Gayoom Internet sites within the Maldives.

On the morning of 26 December 2004 the Indian Ocean tsunami devastated countries throughout the region. While it could have been much, much worse for the Maldives, whose vast, deep inter-atoll channels absorbed much of the strength of the wave, the result was still devastating. Eighty-three people were confirmed dead, with a further 25 feared dead, their bodies never having been discovered. Twenty-one islands were devastated, with over 11,000 people made homeless, many of whom continue

1988
A coup d'état attempt by Sri Lankan mercenaries in Male' is quickly foiled with Indian assistance

1998
The El Niño weather system causes coral bleaching in the Maldives

today to exist as IDPs (internally displaced persons). Large numbers of resorts were closed and although one was totally abandoned, the rest were rebuilt with incredible speed, nearly all being open again a year later.

In the aftermath of these terrible events, President Gayoom did at least drop charges against many of the Black Friday protestors and they were released, although at the time of writing the situation is still not very positive. While it's clear that torture has ceased being a major part of imprisonment in the Maldives, brutality both in and out of jail continues and basic freedom of expression is still not respected anywhere. The next few years will probably be key to the future of the country – Gayoom is under pressure and few expect him to last much longer. However, with no tradition of democracy, no independent print media and paper-thin civil society, there's little reason for optimism even if Gayoom does relinquish power any time soon.

The Culture

NATIONAL PSYCHE

The recent prodemocracy movement has revealed one deep truth about Maldivian people: their fierce independence, which runs true domestically as well as internationally. Tacitly accepting one-party state for years, until the alleged corruption and police brutality outstripped the benefits gained by the country through the vast-scale development of tourism, the Maldivians finally decided they had had enough in 2003 and the staunch and brave reform movement has made some huge gains over the past few years.

Maldivians are devout Muslims. In some countries this might be considered incidental, but the national faith is the cornerstone of Maldivian identity and it's defended passionately at all levels of society. Officially 100% of the population are practising Sunni Muslims. There's no scope for religious dissent, but there's also almost no desire *to* dissent. This deep religious faith breeds a generally high level of conservatism, but that does not preclude the arrival of hundreds of thousands of non-Muslim tourists to the islands every year, coming to bathe seminaked, drink lots of alcohol and engage in extra-marital sex. It's definitely an unusual contradiction. Arguably, were the tourist industry not so carefully engineered to separate the tourists and local population, there would be far more cultural clashes and tension between devout Islam and Western liberalism.

A deep island mentality (familiar to the British) also permeates the country. Not quite Asia, not quite Africa and not the Middle East despite the cultural similarities, the Maldives has been slow to join the international community (it joined the Commonwealth and the South Asian Association for Regional Co-operation only in the 1980s) and remains a nonaligned nation with no particular enemies or allies.

The hardship implicit in survival on these relatively barren islands so remote in the ocean has created a nation of hard workers. The work ethic runs throughout the country; historically a lazy Maldivian was a Maldivian who didn't eat.

Another much-ignored feature of the Maldivian people is their earthy humour and cheerfulness. Joking and laughter is a way of life and you'll notice this without even leaving your resort – take a few minutes to speak with the local staff and you'll see this for yourself.

> The annual rate of population growth is about 3%.

LIFESTYLE

The most obvious dichotomy in lifestyle in the Maldives is between people in the capital Male' and those 'in the atolls' – the term used by everyone to denote 'islanders' or anyone who lives outside the immediate area of bustling modernity that is Male'.

In Male' life is considerably easier and more comfortable than in the rest of the country on most fronts, with the obvious exception of space. Life in Male', one of the most densely populated places on earth, is only good for those who have decent-sized houses. With all the new developments on Hulhumale' island near to the capital, there should be a gradual decrease in population and thus a slight easing of the population crush there in the next few years. The Gayoom years have created a massive economy in Male', although many more intellectual residents of the city complain that while there are plenty of opportunities to earn and live well in the commercial and tourism sectors, there's a great lack of challenging,

> The Maldivian caste system has effectively disappeared today. Traditionally the very lowest caste was that of the palm-toddy tappers (*raa-veri*).

creative jobs if exporting fish and importing tourists is not your idea of fun. With limited education beyond high school and a lack of careers for the ambitious without good connections in the government, it's no surprise that many young people in Male' dream of going abroad, at least to complete their education and training.

In the islands things are far more simple and laid-back, but people's lives aren't always as easy as those in Male'. In the atolls most people live in the extended family homestead (it's unusual to live alone or just as a couple in a way that it wouldn't be in Male'), and both men and women assume fairly traditional roles. While men go out to work (in general either as fishermen or on jobs that keep them away from home for long stretches at a time in the tourist or shipping industry), women are the homemakers, looking after the children, cooking and maintaining the household. Fish is traded for other necessities at the nearest big island. Attending the mosque is the main religious activity, and on smaller islands it's probably the main social and cultural activity as well.

The most important ritual in a man's life comes when he is circumcised at the age of six or seven. These are big celebrations that last for a week and are far more significant than marriages (not a big deal) and birthdays (not celebrated). Marriage is of course important, but it's not a massive celebration like in most of the rest of Asia.

Rural life for the young can be fairly dull, although despite appearances even tiny fishing villages are surprisingly modern; most now have telephones, radio and TV. Nevertheless many teenagers effectively go to boarding school, as provision for education outside population centres is scant. There are a few preschools or kindergartens, where children start learning the Quran from about the age of three. There are government primary schools (madrasa) on every inhabited island, but some are very

> Life expectancy for a Maldivian is about 63 years for men and 65 years for women.

DOS & DON'TS

Maldivian resorts make it quite clear what guests should and shouldn't do. Guests must respect the environment (no damage to fish or coral) and they must respect Muslim sensibilities. Nudity is strictly forbidden and women must not go topless; bikinis and brief bathers are quite acceptable in resorts, though most prefer that you cover up in the bar, dining and reception areas. In Male' and on other inhabited islands, travellers should make an effort not to offend local standards. Men should never go bare-chested and women should avoid low-cut tops and tank tops. Long pants or long skirts are preferable, but shorts are OK if they cover the thighs.

It's best to dress neatly and conservatively when dealing with officials and businesspeople. Maldivian professional men always wear long trousers, clean shoes (often slip-ons), a shirt and usually a tie. Women usually wear dresses below the knee and covering the shoulders and arms.

Those who spend time outside the resorts should be aware of a few more points:

- Lose the shoes – people take their shoes off before going inside a house or mosque. Maldivians can slip off their footwear without breaking step, but visitors may find it inconvenient. Slip-on shoes are easier than lace-ups, and thongs (flip-flops) are easier than sandals.

- Keep your cool – be patient and polite, especially in government offices that can be painfully slow and frustrating.

- Payment etiquette – if you ask someone to lunch, that means you'll pay for it; and if someone else asks you, don't reach for the bill.

- Religion rules – Islam is the state religion, so be aware that prayer times take precedence over business and pleasure, and that Ramazan, a month of fasting, places great demands on local people. Visiting a mosque requires long pants or a long skirt and no shoes. Never consume alcohol or pork outside resorts.

small and do not go past fifth grade. For grades six and seven, children may have to go to a middle school on a larger island. Atoll capitals have an Atoll Education Centre (AEC) with adult education and secondary schooling to grade 10 (16 years old).

Officially, 90% of students finish primary school, and the adult literacy rate is 98%. English is taught as a second language from grade one and is the usual teaching language at higher secondary school – Maldivians with a secondary education speak excellent English.

The best students can continue to a free-of-charge higher secondary school, which teaches children to the age of 18 – there's one in Male', one in Hithadhoo, in the country's far south, and one in Kulhuduffushi, in the far north. Students coming to Male' to study generally take live-in domestic jobs, affecting their study time: girls are often expected to do a lot of housework.

The Maldives College of Higher Education, also in Male', has faculties of health, education, tourism-hospitality and engineering. For university studies, many young Maldivians go abroad, usually to Sri Lanka, India, Britain, Australia or Fiji.

There is a system of bonded labour under which people must work for the government at a meagre wage for a period that depends on the length of their education in government schools. For many this means a period in the National Security Service or in a government office. They may pursue another occupation part-time to establish their career or to make ends meet. Many people in Male' have a second job or a business interest on the side.

> You can address Maldivians by their first or last name. Since so many men are called Mohammed, Hassan or Ali, the surname is more appropriate. In some cases an honorary title like Maniku or Didi is used to show respect.

ECONOMY

Fish and ships just about sum up the Maldivian economy beyond the tourist industry. Despite this, the economy continues to experience large growth, even if it was inevitably curtailed by the tsunami in 2004. Despite a 5% contraction in GDP in 2005, the Maldives was already staging a strong recovery in 2006, with full capacity in most resorts, a great feat considering many had thought the tsunami spelled the end for the massive growth in travel to the Maldives.

Tourism is the country's biggest earner, accounting for around 20% of GDP. Fishing accounts for about 18% with skipjack tuna making the principal catch, followed by yellowfin tuna, little tuna and frigate mackerel.

Government policies have helped to mechanise the fishing fleet, introduce new packing techniques and develop new markets. Nevertheless, the fishing industry is vulnerable to international market fluctuations. Most adult males have some experience in fishing, and casual employment on fishing boats is something of an economic backstop. Men are unlikely to take on menial work for low pay when there is a prospect that they can get a few days or weeks of relatively well-paid work on a fishing dhoni (boat; see the boxed text, p29).

> Cars remain the ultimate status symbol here, even in a country with virtually no roads. Some atoll chiefs have cars simply to show off, on their entirely sand-covered islands. At least it's environmentally friendly…

Trade and shipping (nearly all based in Male') is the third biggest earner; nearly all food is imported and agriculture accounts for less than 3% of GDP. Manufacturing and construction make up 15% of GDP: small boat yards, fish packing, clothing and a plastic pipe plant are modern enterprises, but mostly it's cottage industries producing coconut oil, coir (coconut-husk fibre) and coir products such as rope and matting. Some of the new industrial activities are on islands near Male' while others, such as fish-packing plants, are being established in the outer atolls. There is no income tax.

POLITICS

The Maldivian parliament, the People's Majlis (Parliament; also known as the Citizens' Council), has 50 members. Male', the capital island, and each of the 20 administrative atolls have two representatives each, elected for five-year terms. All citizens over 21 years of age can vote. The president chooses the remaining eight parliamentary representatives, has the power to appoint or dismiss cabinet ministers, and appoints all judges.

Check out www .presidencymaldives.gov .mv for the latest infor- mation on what President Gayoom is up to.

The Majlis considers candidates for the presidency for each five-year term and makes a nomination, which is put to a national vote. Until recently only one candidate was put forward, so the vote is not so much an election as a national referendum. Since the nascent democratic movement became a big political player in 2003–4, President Gayoom has agreed to multiple candidates for the presidency as well as legalising political parties. However, at the time of writing the situation was looking bleak, with opposition leaders intimidated, in exile or imprisoned. The main opposition party, the Maldivian Democratic Party, was founded in Sri Lanka in 2003 and is most likely to succeed the Gayoom regime should free and fair elections be held and the results honoured.

In March 2006 President Gayoom launched his 'road map' for democracy, a hugely positive step that has nonetheless been greeted with great suspicion by reformists, coming as it does from the iron-fisted dictator himself. The road map foresees fully free presidential elections in mid-2008; although it's very possible pressure on the government will force them before that date. As they say, we'll believe it when it happens.

POPULATION

Roughly a quarter of the Maldives' estimated 359,000 population live on the tiny capital island of Male', where some 80,000 people are packed into a rectangle of land just a couple of kilometres across. The rest of the population is spread out on the atolls – there are hardly any other towns in the whole country. The second city is Hithadhoo on Addu Atoll, with a population of 13,000 and beyond that very few settlements with over 5,000 inhabitants. The annual growth rate is estimated at 2.8%, meaning the Maldives is a young country with a median age of 18 years. With no permanent migration, the Maldives is almost entirely ethnically homogenous.

Keep informed about the developments of Hulhumale' island, the reclaimed land that is to provide the future base for Male' and the government in the wake of rising sea levels, at www.hdc.com.mv.

The most recent census, in 2000, put the population at 270,101, with 74,000 in Male', however, the 2006 estimated population was 359,000, a big increase.

It is thought that the original settlers of the Maldives were Dravidian and Sinhalese people who came from south India and Sri Lanka. There has also been a great deal of intermarriage and mixing with people from the Middle East and Africa.

MEDIA

Nearly all print and TV media within the Maldives is strictly controlled, ensuring a pliant and largely ignored fourth estate, for the most part. However, there are some inspiring exceptions, mainly as a result of pressure on the Gayoom government after the prodemocracy protests in 2003 and 2004. Most notable is *Minivan Daily,* a Divehi newspaper that was granted a licence in 2005 and is an offshoot of the foreign-based radio station and Internet site of the same name, which makes an interesting case-in-point for how things work in the Maldives. Since being granted a licence as a sop to the international community, *Minivan* (meaning

'Independent') has been subject to harassment and intimidation. Rabidly anti-Gayoom (it's far less measured than the English-language website), its printing press was closed down, several of its journalists and editors were imprisoned and it was being printed using an office printer at the time of writing! The government is hoping to exploit a clause in the media law, which says a newspaper's licence can be revoked if it misses four successive editions. However, if the staff heroically keep it coming out regularly, it's such a popular paper that the government are likely to close it down at some point in the near future.

An interatoll ferry service, which was due to be inaugurated in 2004, has been put on hold indefinitely. If it ever makes a comeback, the scope for individual travel will increase massively.

The Internet is the medium of choice for people who want to write freely – any educated person with Internet access in Male' will start the day by reading the **Dhivehi Observer** (www.dhivehiobserver.com), a tabloid run from exile in the UK by modern-day folk hero Ahmed Moosa, known to one and all as Sappe'. Irreverent, hard-hitting and a self-declared anti-Gayoom site, the *Dhivehi Observer* is what anyone wanting to know the truth about the Maldives should read as a matter of urgency, written as it is by anonymous sources throughout the country. Other great Internet sites include the UK-based **Minivan News** (www.minivannews.com), which is also a radio station serving the Maldives when it's not jammed.

ALL-PURPOSE, ALL-MALDIVIAN DHONI

The truck and bus of the Maldives is the sturdy dhoni, a vessel so ubiquitous that the word dhoni will soon become part of your vocabulary. Built in numerous shapes and sizes, the dhoni has been adapted for use as an ocean freighter, inter-atoll cruiser, local ferry, family fishing boat, excursion boat, dive boat, live-aboard yacht, delivery truck and mini fuel tanker. The traditional dhoni is thought to derive from the Arab dhow, but the design has been used and refined for so long in the Maldives that it is truly a local product.

Traditionally, dhonis have a tall, curved prow that stands up like a scimitar cutting through the sea breezes. Most Maldivians say this distinctive prow is purely decorative, but in shallow water a man will stand at the front, spotting the reefs and channels, signalling to the skipper and holding the prow for balance. It can interfere with boarding or loading, so it's often dispensed with on modern utility craft, or there is the removable prow-piece that slots into the front of the boat to look good, but lifts out of the way for loading. If you want to stand at the front of a dhoni, be aware that a removable prow-piece can be a slightly wobbly balancing post!

The flat stern is purely functional – it's where the skipper stands and steers, casually holding the tiller with his foot or between his legs. The stern platform is also used for fishing, and for one other thing – when a small dhoni makes a long trip, the 'head' is at the back. If nature calls, go right to the stern of the boat, face forward or backwards as your need and gender dictate, and rely on the skipper, passengers and crew to keep facing the front.

The details on a dhoni are a mix of modern and traditional. The rudder is attached with neat rope lashing, but nowadays the rope is always plastic, not coir (coconut fibre). The dhoni design required very little adaptation to take a diesel engine, and a motorised *(ingeenu)* dhoni has the same shallow draft as a sail-powered *(riyalu)* dhoni. The propeller is protected so it won't snag on mooring lines or get damaged on a shallow reef. Despite modern materials (cotton caulking instead of coir; red oxide paint as well as shark oil), a modern dhoni will still leak, just like a traditional one, so there is a bilge pump just in front of the skipper – it's a simple but effective gadget made from plastic plumbing pipes.

Most inhabited islands have a dhoni or two under construction or repair and you may see them on an excursion from a resort. The best dhoni builders are said to come from Raa Atoll and teams of them can be contracted to come to an island to make a new boat. Twelve workers, six on each side of the boat, can make a 14m hull in about 45 days, if their hosts keep them well fed. The keel is made from imported hardwood, while the hull planks are traditionally from coconut trees. A lot of the work is now done with power tools, but no plans are used.

RELIGION

Islam is the religion of the Maldives, and officially there are no other religious groups present. All Maldivians are Sunni Muslims. No other religions or sects are permitted.

The Maldives observes a liberal form of Islam, like that practised in India and Indonesia. Maldivian women do not observe purdah, though many wear a headscarf. Children are taught the Arabic alphabet and learn to read and recite the Quran.

Most mosques are of simple, unadorned design, but some of the older mosques have intricate woodcarvings inside and elaborate carved gravestones outside. The Islamic Centre (p93) in Male' is especially imposing, with soaring ceilings and big carved wood panels and screens.

Officially only Muslims may become citizens of the Maldives. It is possible for foreigners to convert and later become Maldivian nationals, although this is extremely rare.

The Prophet Mohammed

Mohammed was born in Mecca (now in Saudi Arabia) in AD 570 and had his first revelation from Allah in 610. He began to preach against idolatry and proved to be a powerful and persuasive speaker. His teachings appealed to the poorer levels of society and angered the wealthy merchant class.

In 622 Mohammed and his followers were forced to migrate to Medina, 300km to the north. This migration, known as the Hejira, marks the start of the Islamic Calendar: AD 622 became year 1 AH. By AD 630 Mohammed had gained enough followers to return and take Mecca.

Within two decades of Mohammed's death, most of Arabia had converted to Islam. The Prophet's followers spread the word, and the influence of the Islamic state soon extended from the Atlantic to the Indian Ocean, south into Africa and east to the Pacific.

The Five Pillars of Islam

Islam is the Arabic word for submission and underlies the duty of all Muslims to submit themselves to Allah.

Shahada, the profession of faith that 'there is no God but Allah and Mohammed is his prophet', is the first of the Five Pillars of Islam: the tenets guiding Muslims in their daily life.

The second pillar, salath, is the call to prayer, and Islam decrees that Muslims must face Mecca and pray five times each day. In the Maldives, salath is also called namadh.

The third pillar is zakat, the act of giving alms to the needy. Some Islamic countries have turned this into an obligatory land tax that goes to help the poor.

IDOLATRY

Most countries prohibit the importation of things like narcotics and firearms, and most travellers understand such restrictions, but when you're forbidden to bring 'idols of worship' into the Maldives, what exactly does that mean? The Maldives is an Islamic nation, and it is sensitive about objects which may offend Muslim sensibilities. A small crucifix, worn as jewellery, is unlikely to be a problem, and many tourists arrive wearing one. A large crucifix with an obvious Christ figure nailed to it may well be prohibited. The same is true of images of Buddha – a small decorative one is probably OK, but a large and ostentatious one may not be.

Maldivian authorities are concerned about evangelists and the things they might use to spread their beliefs. Inspectors would not really be looking for a Bible in someone's baggage, but if they found two or more Bibles they would almost certainly not allow them to be imported. It would be unwise to test the limits of idolatrous imports – like customs people everywhere, the Maldivian authorities take themselves very seriously.

The fourth pillar is the fast during the day for the month of Ramazan, the ninth month of the Islamic calendar.

The fifth pillar is the hajj (pilgrimage) to Mecca, the holiest place in Islam. It is the duty of every able Muslim to make the hajj at least once in their life.

Prayer Times

The initial prayer session is in the first hour before sunrise, the second around noon, the third in midafternoon around 3.30pm, the fourth at sunset and the final session in the early evening.

The call to prayer is delivered by the *mudhim* (muezzin). In former days, he climbed to the top of the minaret and shouted it out. Now the call is relayed by loudspeakers on the minaret and the *mudhim* even appears on TV. All TV stations cut out at prayer time, although only MTV (the national channel) cuts out for the entire duration – satellite channels just have their broadcasts interrupted to remind Muslims to go to the mosque.

Shops and offices close for 15 minutes after each call. Some people go to the mosque, some kneel where they are and others do not visibly participate. Mosques are busiest for the sunset prayers and at noon on Fridays.

Ramadan

Called Ramazan in the Maldives, this is the month of fasting, which begins at the time of a particular new moon and ends with the sighting of the next new moon. The Ramazan month gets a little earlier every year because it is based on a lunar calendar of twelve 28-day months (see p176).

During Ramazan Muslims should not eat, drink, smoke or have sex between sunrise and sunset. Exceptions to the eating and drinking rule are granted to young children, pregnant or menstruating women, and those who are travelling. It can be a difficult time for travel outside the resorts, as teashops and cafés are closed during the day, offices have shorter hours and people may be preoccupied with religious observances or the rigours of fasting. Visitors should avoid eating, drinking or smoking in public, or in the presence of those who are fasting. After a week or so, most Muslims adjust to the Ramazan routine and many say they enjoy it. There are feasts and parties long into the night, big breakfasts before dawn and long rests in the afternoon. Kuda Eid, the end of Ramazan, is a major celebration.

Local Beliefs

On the islands, people still fear jinnis, the evil spirits that come from the sea, land and sky. They are blamed for everything that can't be explained by religion or education.

To combat jinnis there are *fandhita*, which are the spells and potions provided by a local hakeem (medicine man), who is often called upon when illness strikes, if a woman fails to conceive, or if the fishing catch is poor.

The hakeem might cast a curing spell by writing phrases from the Quran on strips of paper and sticking or tying them to the patient or writing the sayings in ink on a plate, filling the plate with water to dissolve the ink, and making the patient drink the potion. Other concoctions include *isitri*, a love potion used in matchmaking, and its antidote *varitoli*, which is used to break up marriages.

The mother-goddess cult of pre-Muslim Maldivian tradition has survived centuries of Islam and remains a key belief of islanders.

The Giravaaran people, who most believe were the first to settle in the Maldives, remain ethnically distinct from the rest of the population. However, they have left their native Giravaaru and now live in Male' since their number has decreased so dramatically. Their former home is now a resort.

SPORT

Soccer is the most popular sport and is played all year round. On most islands, the late-afternoon match among the young men is a daily ritual. There's a league competition in Male', played between club teams with names such as Valencia and Victory, and annual tournaments against teams from neighbouring countries. Matches are also held at the National Stadium (p102) in Male'.

Cricket is played in Male' for a few months, beginning in March. The president is a keen cricket fan and played for his school in Sri Lanka. Volleyball is played indoors, on the beach and in the waterfront parks. The two venues for indoor sport are the Centre for Social Education, on the

---

WOMEN IN SOCIETY *Aishath Velezinee*

In the 14th century, long before the call for equality took momentum, the Maldives were ruled by women. Three queens reigned; one, Sultana Khadija, held the throne for 33 years from 1347 to 1379. The shift from monarchy to a constitutional republic barred women from the post of President, and this fundamental clause is retained in the 1997 Constitution.

Traditional lifestyle, especially in the islands away from the capital, dictated gender-specific roles for women and men. Women tended to their children and the household duties during the day, and cooked fish in the evenings. Men spent the day fishing and then rested in the evenings. Modernisation and development changed the traditional way of life and conferred a double burden on many women – income generation plus domestic responsibilities. More opportunities and better education mean that more women are ready to join the workforce or take up income-generating activities at home. This has become a necessity rather than a choice for most women living in Male', as rising expenses and changing lifestyles demand a dual income to meet basic family expenses.

In Male' women work in all sectors, but mainly in teaching, nursing or administrative or secretarial positions. The government, which is the major employer of women, employs fewer than 5% women at policy level. Less stereotypical jobs such as the police force also recruit women and offer equal opportunities. With no childcare facilities available, and little help from husbands on the domestic side, working mothers depend heavily on the efforts of other women in the extended family – grandmothers, aunts, sisters etc. While the movement of women from domestic roles to paid employment has been rapid, there is very little progress in getting men to pour their own water, let alone share in domestic work.

On the outer islands, with little opportunity for formal employment, women tend to be self- employed, but with little financial gain. Markets are limited by geography, demography and the lack of regular and reliable interisland transport. Women on islands close to the tourism zones grow fruits and vegetables for sale to resorts. They also weave coconut-leaf matting *(cadjan)* and make rope and other products from coir. On remoter islands women make dried fish, a product that can withstand the long boat journey to the market. At least a few women on each island are experts at sewing and most women do home gardening for consumption. Some island girls get an education and train as teachers and health workers, but most prefer to stay on Male' where there are wider career choices, rather than return home. Recent appointments of a few women to the posts of *atolu verin* (atoll chief) and *kateeb* (island chief), till now the realm of men alone, opens new opportunities for educated women.

Marriage is seen as a must for all Maldivian women, and less than 1% of those over 30 have never married. Marriage and divorce have always been casual, giving a woman no security within a marriage. Until recently, she could be divorced on the whim of her husband, without reason or compensation. Divorce carries no stigma, and early marriage, divorce and serial marriages are the norm. A woman retains her own name after marriage – this is sensible as she could be Mrs X, Mrs Y and Mrs Z in the space of a single year.

west side of Male', and a new facility just east of the New Harbour, used for basketball (men and women), netball, volleyball and badminton.

Traditional games include *bai bala,* where one team attempts to tag members of the other team inside a circle, and a tug-of-war, known as *wadhemun. Bashi* is a girls' game, played on something like a tennis court, where a girl stands facing away from the net and serves a tennis ball backwards, over her head. There is a team of girls on the other side who then try to catch it.

Thin mugoali (meaning 'three circles') is a game similar to baseball and has been played in the atolls for more than 400 years. The *mugoali* (bases) are made by rotating on one foot in the sand through 360 degrees,

> The word 'atoll' in English is generally accepted to come from the Divehi word *atolu,* the only known example of a Maldivian word being used in English.

In an effort to strengthen family and bring down the high divorce rate (which was once the highest in the world), the first-ever codified Family Law came into force on 1 July 2001, raising the minimum age of marriage to 18 and making unilateral divorce illegal. Prenuptial contracts registered at the court can strengthen a woman's position within the marriage as she can stipulate her rights. Where once a man could divorce his wife merely by telling her that she was divorced, now both partners must go through the court to initiate divorce, and it is permitted only when all reconciliation attempts fail. While the divorce rate has gone down, questions remain as to whether fewer divorces mean a better life for women. Polygamy is legal, and men can have up to four wives at a time, although it is not common practice to have more than one wife.

Traditionally, a woman could choose a suitor and name a bride-price *(rhan).* The bride-price is paid by the husband to the wife, at the time of marriage or in instalments as mutually agreed, but must be paid in full if there's a divorce. Young women today quote higher bride-prices, reflecting higher expectations, and perhaps a scepticism about the fairytale happy-ever-after marriage. The wedding itself is a low-key affair, but is often followed by a large banquet for all family and friends, who can easily number in the hundreds.

Women in the Maldives can, and do, own land and property but, as in the rest of the world, women have a fraction of the property that men do. While inheritance generally follows Islamic Sharia'a law in the Maldives, land is divided according to civil law, whereby a daughter and son inherit equal shares of land.

There is little overt discrimination between the sexes. Though it's a fully Muslim society, women and men mingle freely and women enjoy personal liberty not experienced by women in most Muslim societies. However, Islam is used as a tool by some patriarchs to counter gender equality, even as they proclaim that Islam grants equality to women and men. Local discourse tends to say that the factors limiting gender equality are cultural rather than Islamic, and therefore it is possible to change them.

Movement of women is not officially restricted, but women's mobility is limited by factors such as domestic responsibilities and societal attitudes as to what is a woman's place. Home is where 'good girls' are. Although physical assaults against women are very unusual, women on streets and other public spaces can be harassed.

Most women in the Maldives go bareheaded though many are adopting a headscarf, a sign of growing commitment to Islam. The government has banned face coverings to limit the appearance of radical religious ideas. Gyms and fitness centres attract Maldivian women, as do hair and beauty salons. Formal functions require women to wear one of the officially sanctioned 'national dresses', which includes the traditional *libaas* (dress) and *dhiguhedhun* (traditional full-length dress with long sleeves and a wide collar) as well as a Malay-style skirt and blouse with *libaas*-style neck embroidery. For everyday wear, young women dress in T-shirts, tank tops, flimsy blouses, fashionable jeans, pants and short skirts. The more self-conscious choose Indian-style *shalwar kameez* (loose blouses and pants). Older women wear the traditional *dhiguhedhun* and *libaas.*

Aishath Velezinee is a Maldivian writer, researcher and women's rights advocate leaving a circle behind. You'll sometimes see *bashi* in Male' parks or on village islands in the late afternoon, but traditional games are becoming less popular as young people are opting for international sports.

ARTS

Though performances of traditional music and dance are not everyday events, contemporary Divehi culture is strong and adaptive, despite foreign influences, which range from martial arts and Hindi movies to Eminem and Muslim fundamentalism.

Western and Indian fashions, pop music and videos are highly visible, but on public occasions and festivals the celebrations always have a Maldivian style. Three daily newspapers and several magazines are published in the unique national language and rock bands sing Divehi lyrics. It's remarkable that such a tiny population maintains such a distinctive culture.

Rates of thalassaemia, a hereditary blood condition that makes regular blood transfusions necessary, is extremely high in the Maldives, with 18% of the population carrying the condition in some form.

Song & Dance

Bodu beru means 'big drum' and gives its name to the best-known form of traditional music and dance. It is what tourist resorts put on for a local culture night, and it can be quite sophisticated and compelling. Dancers begin with a slow, nonchalant swaying and swinging of the arms, and become more animated as the tempo increases, finishing in a rhythmic frenzy. In some versions the dancers enter a trance-like state. There are four to six drummers in an ensemble and the sound has strong African influences.

This is also the entertainment at private parties, where a few guys will play the drums and everyone else dances – more and more frenetically as the night goes on.

Local rock bands often perform at resorts, where they do credible covers of old favourites. They may incorporate elements of *bodu beru* in their music, with lots of percussion and extended drum solos when they're in front of a local audience. Two popular bands are Mezzo and Zero Degree Attol – CDs from these, and quite a few other bands, are sold in Male' music shops.

Literature

Despite the unique Maldivian script that dates from the 1600s, most Maldivian myths and stories are from an oral tradition and have only recently appeared in print. Many are stories of witchcraft and sorcery, while others are cautionary tales about the evils of vanity, lust and greed, and the sticky fates of those who transgressed. Some are decidedly weird and depressing, and don't make good bedtime reading for young children. Novelty Press has published a small book called Mysticism in the Maldives, which is still available. The Hammond Innes thriller *The Strode Venturer* is about the only well-known novel that is partly set in the Maldives.

To support the Society of Health Education (SHE), which works with victims of thalassaemia, visit www.she.org.mv.

Architecture

A traditional Maldivian village is notable for its neat and orderly layout, with wide streets in a regular, rectangular grid. Houses are made of concrete blocks or coral stone joined with mortar, and the walls line the sides of the streets. Many houses will have a shaded courtyard in front, enclosed by a chest-high wall fronting the street. This courtyard is an outdoor room, with *joli* and *undholi* seats (see the boxed text, opposite), where families sit in the heat of the day or the cool of the evening. A more private courtyard behind, the *gifili* has a well and serves as an open-air bathroom.

At intersections, the coral walls have rounded corners, which considerably soften the streetscape. These corners are seemingly designed to facilitate turning vehicles, but they are like this in small island villages that never see a vehicle. The same style is used in Male', where it does make turning easier for cars and trucks. On the upper floors of a modern building, the rounded corners are more for appearance than practicality, and seem to be a deliberate adaptation of a traditional feature.

The architecture of resorts is eclectic, imitative of anything from a Balinese *bale* to an African rondavel or an American motel. The most identifiably Maldivian feature is the open-air bathroom, a delightful feature popular with guests.

Visual Arts

There is no historical tradition of painting in the Maldives, but demand for local art (however fabricated) from the tourist industry has created a supply in the ultra-savvy Maldivian market, with more than a few locals selling paintings to visitors or creating beach scenes for hotel rooms.

Some islands were once famous for wood and stone carving – elaborate calligraphy and the intricate intertwining patterns are a feature of many old mosques and gravestones. A little of this woodcarving is still done, mainly to decorate mosques. The façade of the new Majlis building in Male' is decorated with intertwined carvings.

Coral stone was the main building material until relatively recently, and you can still see plenty of mosques and houses built with the unmistakable grey material. It's often engraved with beautiful designs and is a highlight of many villages.

Crafts

MATS

Natural-fibre mats are woven on many islands, but the most famous are the ones known as *tundu kunaa,* made on the island of Gadhdhoo in Gaaf Dhaal Atoll. This may have been an endangered art form, but renewed interest caused by the growing tourist industry has arguably saved it from disappearing. A Danish researcher in the 1970s documented the weaving techniques and the plants used for fibre and dyes, and noted that a number of traditional designs had not been woven for 20 years. Collecting the materials and weaving a mat can take weeks, and the money that can be made selling the work is not much by modern Maldivian standards. Some fine examples now decorate the reception areas of tourist resorts, and there's a growing appreciation of the work among local people and foreign collectors.

LACQUER WORK

Traditionally, lacquer work *(laajehun)* was for containers, bowls and trays used for gifts to the sultan – some fine examples can be seen in the National Museum (p93) in Male'. Different wood is used to make boxes, bowls, vases and other turned objects. Traditionally the lathe is hand-powered by a cord pulled round a spindle. Several layers of lacquer

---

SITTING IN THE MALDIVES

The Maldives has two unique pieces of furniture. One is the *undholi,* a wooden platform or a netting seat that's hung from a tree or triangular frame. Sometimes called a bed-boat, the *undholi* is a sofa, hammock and fan combination – swinging gently creates a cooling movement of air across the indolent occupant.

The *joli* is a static version – a net seat slung on a rectangular frame, usually made in sociable sets of three or four. They were once made of coir rope and wooden sticks, but steel pipes and plastic mesh are now almost universal – it's like sitting in a string shopping bag, but cool.

are applied in different colours. They then harden, and the design is incised with sharp tools, exposing the bright colours of the underlying layers. Designs are usually floral motifs in yellow with red trim on a black background (most likely based on designs of Chinese ceramics). Production of lacquer work is a viable cottage industry in Baa Atoll, particularly on the islands of Eydafushi and Thuladhoo.

JEWELLERY

Ribudhoo Island in Dhaalu (South Nilandhoo Atoll) is famous for making gold jewellery, and Huludeli, in the same atoll, for silver jewellery. According to local belief, a royal jeweller brought the goldsmithing skills to the island centuries ago, having been banished to Ribudhoo by a sultan. It's also said that the islanders plundered a shipwreck in the 1700s, and reworked the gold jewellery they found to disguise its origins.

Environment

'Our fate tomorrow,' Maldivian President Maumoon Abdul Gayoom has repeatedly warned the world, 'will be your fate the day after.' Hardly bestriding the international stage like a Colossus, the diminutive Maldivian leader has nevertheless done much to promote awareness of global warming and rising sea levels, the net results of which are likely to submerge this low-lying island nation almost completely by the end of the century. Kofi Annan has called him 'the godfather of environmental awareness' and the country's record at speaking up about and bringing attention to the grave realities of global warming make it one of the most ecologically aware in the world.

Along with Tuvalu, Bangladesh and parts of Holland, the Maldives has the misfortune to be one of the lowest lying countries in the world at a time in history when sea levels are rising. Its highest natural point – 2m – is the lowest in any country in the world. Realising that the political will to do anything about the upcoming disaster is extremely weak throughout both the developed and developing worlds, the Maldives are at least making a contingency plan by constructing an island near to Male' that's 2m above sea level, and will eventually be home to some 150,000 people, or about a half of the country's population. Several thousand people have already moved there in the first phase of development, and it's a compelling, if rather bleak look at the country's future to spend a few hours wandering around on a trip from Male'.

The tsunami, while still a national disaster, was actually far less damaging to the Maldives than it could have been. Scientists suggest the islands were saved by the deep channels running between the atolls, which absorbed much of the power of the waves.

THE LAND

Where is the Maldives? That's almost always the first question people ask when you tell them about going on holiday here. Confused with Mauritius, Martinique, Montserrat or Madagascar (there are indeed a strangely large number of tropical beach destinations beginning with M), or simply an unknown quantity, the Maldives is effectively a tiny country, whose land totals far less in area than the tiny European principality of Andorra, despite an overall area of 90,000 sq km, 99.9% of which is the Indian Ocean.

This 300 sq km of land is split up into an almost incalculable number of islands, spread out 'like a string of pearls' (copyright all guidebooks) due south of India and west of Sri Lanka, deep in the Indian Ocean. The number of islands is incalculable simply because the islands, or what we

---

RESPONSIBLE TRAVEL IN THE MALDIVES

- Drink water desalinated at your resort rather than imported mineral water.
- Take all batteries and plastic home with you for disposal.
- Offset your air travel by using companies such as www.climatecare.org.
- Minimise the use of air conditioning.
- Keep the use of running water in your room to a minimum – water is still expensive to desalinate, which uses fossil fuel to do so.
- When diving or snorkelling do not touch, feed or otherwise interfere with the fish and coral.
- Ask for your towels not to be rewashed every day.
- Don't purchase turtle-shell products.

define as islands, are so fluid. Some 'islands' exist at low tide and disappear at high tide, others are just sandbanks with no vegetation, potentially washed away by the next big storm.

Officially, it's a matter of vegetation – an island means a vegetated land area, but even this is not definitive. Some sandbanks sprout a small patch of scrub while others feature a single coconut palm, like the desert island of the comic-strip castaway.

The geological formation of the Maldives is fascinating and unique. The country is perched on the top of the enormous Laccadives–Chagos ridge, which cuts a swathe across the Indian Ocean from India to Madagascar. The ridge, a meeting point of two giant tectonic plates, is where basalt magma spews up through the earth's crust, creating new rock. These magma eruptions created the Deccan Plateau, on which the Maldives sit. Originally the magma production created huge volcanoes that towered above the sea. While these have subsequently sunk back into the sea as the ocean floor settled, the coral formations that grew up around these vast volcanoes became the Maldives, and this explains their idiosyncratic formation into vast round atolls.

Today then, the national territory officially comprises 1190 coral islands and innumerable reefs forming 26 atolls that are the natural geographic regions of the country – the English word 'atoll' actually derives from the Maldivian word *atolu*. The natural atolls are today divided up into 21 administrative districts, whose easy-to-pronounce code names are the ones we use to divide up the country by region in this book (see opposite).

Bodu raalhu (big wave) is a relatively regular event in the Maldives, when the sea sweeps over the islands, causing damage and sometimes loss of life.

WILDLIFE

The Maldives is notable for a concentration of several species that you'll see a lot of on the land and in the sky: compared to neighbouring countries, there's not a lot of variety. However, under water the variety is astonishing – hence the massive diving market here. The best thing about wildlife in the Maldives is that it's universally safe. You don't even get mosquitoes for the most part. Who said this wasn't paradise?

Animals

One of the most unforgettable sights in the Maldives is giant fruit bats flying over the islands to roost in trees at dusk. Their size and numbers can make it quite a spectacle. Colourful lizards and geckos are very common and there is the occasional rat, usually dismissed as a 'palm squirrel' or a 'Maldivian hamster' by resort staff keen to avoid cries of vermin.

The mosquito population varies from island to island but it's generally not a problem. There are ants, centipedes, scorpions and cockroaches, but they're not problematic at all.

AN ALTERNATIVE GEOGRAPHY

While the Maldives has appeared in the *Guinness Book of Records* as the world's flattest country, with no natural land higher than 2.3m above sea level, it's one of the most mountainous countries in the world. Its people live on peaks above a plateau that extends 2000km from the Lakshadweep Islands near India to the Chagos Islands, well south of the equator. The plateau is over 5000m high and rises steeply between the Arabian Basin in the northwest and the Cocos–Keeling Basin in the southeast. Mountain ranges rise above the plateau, and the upper slopes and valleys are incredibly fertile, beautiful and rich with plant and animal life. The entire plateau is submerged beneath the Indian Ocean and only scattered, flat-topped peaks are visible at the surface. These peaks are capped not with snow, but with coconut palms.

Local land birds include crows, the white-breasted water hen and the Indian mynah. The rose-ringed parakeet is introduced. There are migratory birds, such as harriers and falcons, but waders like plover, snipe, curlew and sandpiper are more common. Thirteen species of heron can be seen in the shallows and there are terns, seagulls and two species of noddy.

ENDANGERED SPECIES

Most turtle species are endangered worldwide. Four species are known to nest in the Maldives: green, olive ridley, hawksbill and loggerhead. Leatherback turtles visit Maldivian waters, but are not known to nest. Turtle numbers have declined in the Maldives, as elsewhere, but they can still be seen by divers at many sites. The catching of turtles and the sale or export of turtle-shell products is now totally prohibited.

Turtles are migratory and the population can be depleted by events many miles from their home beach, such as accidental capture in fishing nets, depletion of sea-grass areas and toxic pollutants. Widespread collection of eggs and the loss of nesting sites are problems that need to be addressed. The consequences do not show up in the adult turtle population for 10 to 20 years.

Turtle eggs are a traditional food and used in *velaa folhi*, a special Maldivian dish. Development of resorts has reduced the availability of

Maldivian turtles are protected, but they are still caught illegally. The charity Ecocare Maldives has almost single-handedly raised awareness of the turtles' plight.

THOSE UNPRONOUNCEABLE ATOLLS

Confusingly enough, the 26 atolls of the Maldives are divided for all official purposes into 21 administrative districts, which are named by the letters of the Thaana alphabet and as such are a lot easier to pronounce. Would you rather talk about South Miladhunmadulu Atoll or Noonu? Thought so. However, it's not that simple, as the traditional atoll names are still universally used for North and South Male' Atolls, North and South Ari Atoll and Addu Atoll in the far south, so we also use these instead of the more obscure names Kaafu, Alif and Seenu. The following table gives both traditional and administrative names for most parts of the country; those marked with an asterisk are the ones used in this book.

Administrative name	Atoll name
Haa Alif*	North Thiladhunmathee Atoll
Haa Dhaal*	South Thiladhunmathee Atoll & Maamakunudhoo Atoll
Shaviyani*	North Miladhunmadulu Atoll
Noonu*	South Miladhunmadulu Atoll
Raa*	North Maalhosmadulu Atoll
Baa*	South Maalhosmadulu Atoll
Lhaviyani*	Faadhippolhu Atoll
Kaafu	Male' Atoll*
Alif	Ari Atoll*
Vaavu*	Felidhe Atoll
Meemu*	Mulaku Atoll
Faafu*	North Nilandhe Atoll
Dhaalu*	South Nilandhe Atoll
Thaa*	Kolhumadulu Atoll
Laamu*	Hadhdunmathee Atoll
Gaaf Alif*	North Huvadhoo Atoll
Gaaf Dhaal*	South Huvadhoo Atoll
Gnaviyani*	Foammulah Atoll
Seenu	Addu Atoll*

nesting sites. Artificial lights confuse hatchling turtles, which are instinc-
tively guided into the water by the position of the moon. Beach chairs
and boats can also interfere with egg laying and with hatchlings. Some
attempts are being made to artificially improve the survival chances of
hatchlings by protecting them in hatching ponds.

Plants

Most islands have poor, sandy soil and vegetation ranges from thick to
sparse to none at all. The vegetated islands have mangroves, breadfruit
trees, banyans, bamboo, pandanus, banana, heliotrope, caltrop, hibiscus,
tropical vines and numerous coconut palms. Larger, wetter islands have
small areas of rainforest.

Maldives: Un mur contre l'océan is a French documentary by Patrick Fléouter. Investigating the construction of massive sea defences around Male', it raises questions about what will happen to the rest of the country's population as the waters rise.

Sweet potatoes, yams, taro, millet and watermelon are grown. The
most fertile island is Foammulah in the extreme south, which supports
a wider variety of crops, including mangoes and pineapples. Lemons and
limes once grew all over the islands, but a fungal disease killed them off,
and virtually all citrus fruit is now imported.

Marine Life

Seaweeds and hard coralline algae grow on the reefs, but are continuously
eaten by various herbivores. As well as the many types of coral, there are
various shells, starfish, crustaceans and worms inhabiting the reef. There
are more than 700 species of fish in the Indian Ocean, and these can be
divided into two types: reef fish, which live inside the atoll lagoons, on
and around coral-reef structures; and pelagics, which live in the open sea,
but may come close to the atolls or into channels for food. These include
some large animals, such as turtles and cetaceans, which are very popular
with divers.

CORAL

These are coelenterates, a class of animal that also includes sea anemones and jellyfish. A coral growth is made up of individual polyps – tiny
tube-like fleshy cylinders, which look very much like anemones. The top
of the cylinder is open and ringed by waving tentacles (nematocysts),
which sting and draw any passing prey inside. Coral polyps secrete a
calcium-carbonate deposit around their base, and this cup-shaped skeletal structure is what forms a coral reef – new coral grows on old dead
coral and the reef gradually builds up.

Most reef building is done by hermatypic corals, whose outer tissues
are infused with zooxanthellae algae, which photosynthesise to make
food from carbon dioxide and sunlight. The zooxanthellae is the main
food source for the coral, while the coral surface provides a safe home
for the zooxanthellae – they live in a symbiotic relationship, each dependent on the other. The zooxanthellae give coral its colour, so when
a piece of coral is removed from the water, the zooxanthellae soon die
and the coral becomes white. If the water temperature rises, the coral
expels the algae, and the coral loses its colour in a process called 'coral
bleaching'.

Polyps reproduce by splitting to form a colony of genetically identical polyps – each colony starts life as just a single polyp. Although
each polyp catches and digests its own food, the nutrition then passes
between the polyps to the whole colony. Most coral polyps only feed at
night; during the day they withdraw into their hard limestone skeleton,
so it is only after dark that a coral reef can be seen in its full, colourful glory.

HARD CORALS

These Acropora species take many forms. One of the most common and easiest to recognise is the staghorn coral, which grows by budding off new branches from the tips. Brain corals are huge and round with a surface looking very much like a human brain. They grow by adding new base levels of skeletal matter then expanding outwards. Flat or sheet corals, like plate coral or table coral, expand at their outer edges. Some corals take different shapes depending on their immediate environment.

SOFT CORALS

These are made up of individual polyps, but do not form a hard limestone skeleton. Lacking the skeleton that protects hard coral, it would seem likely that soft coral would fall prey to fish, but they seem to remain relatively immune either due to toxic substances in their tissues or to the presence of

RISE & RISE OF THE ATOLLS

A coral reef or garden is not, as many people believe, formed of multicoloured marine plants. It is a living colony of coral polyps – tiny, tentacled creatures that feed on plankton. Coral polyps are invertebrates with sac-like bodies and calcareous or horny skeletons. After extracting calcium deposits from the water around them, the polyps excrete tiny, cup-shaped, limestone skeletons. These little guys can make mountains.

A coral reef is the rock-like aggregation of millions of these polyp skeletons. Only the outer layer of coral is alive. As polyps reproduce and die, the new polyps attach themselves in successive layers to the skeletons already in place. Coral grows best in clear, shallow water, and especially where waves and currents from the open sea bring extra oxygen and nutrients.

Charles Darwin put forward the first scientific theory of atoll formation based on observations of atolls and islands in the Pacific. He envisaged a process where coral builds up around the shores of a volcanic island to produce a fringing reef. Then the island sinks slowly into the sea while the coral grows upwards at about the same rate. This forms a barrier reef, separated from the shore of the sinking island by a ring-shaped lagoon. By the time the island is completely submerged, the coral growth has become the base for an atoll, circling the place where the volcanic peak used to be.

This theory doesn't quite fit the Maldives though. Unlike the isolated Pacific atolls, Maldivian atolls all sit on top of the same long, underwater plateau, around 300m to 500m under the surface of the sea. This plateau is a layer of accumulated coral-stone over 2000m thick. Under this is the 'volcanic basement', a 2000km-long ridge of basalt that was formed over 50 million years ago.

The build-up of coral over this ridge is as much to do with sea-level changes as it is with the plateau subsiding. When sea levels rise the coral grows upwards to stay near the sea surface, as in the Darwin model, but there were at least two periods when the sea level actually dropped significantly – by as much as 120m. At these times much of the accumulated coral plateau would have been exposed, subjected to weathering, and 'karstified' – eroded into steep-sided, flat-topped columns. When sea levels rose again, new coral grew on the tops of the karst mountains and formed the bases of the individual Maldivian atolls.

Coral grows best on the edges of an atoll, where it is well supplied with nutrients from the open sea. A fringing reef forms around an enclosed lagoon, growing higher as the sea level rises. Rubble from broken coral accumulates in the lagoon, so the level of the lagoon floor also rises, and smaller reefs can rise within it. Sand and debris accumulate on the higher parts of the reef, creating sandbars on which vegetation can eventually take root. The classic atoll shape is oval, with the widest reefs and most of the islands around the outer edges.

Test drilling and seismic research has revealed the complex layers of coral growth that underlie the Maldives. The evidence shows that coral growth can match the fastest sea-level rises on record, some 125m in only 10,000 years – about 1.25cm per year. In geological terms, that's really fast.

sharp limestone needles. Soft corals can move around and will sometimes engulf and kill off a hard coral. Attractive varieties include fan corals and whips. Soft corals thrive on reef edges washed by strong currents.

REEF FISH

Hundreds of fish species can be spotted by anyone with a mask and snorkel. They're easy to see and enjoy, but people with a naturalist bent should buy one of the field guides to reef fish, or check the attractive posters, which are often displayed in dive schools. You're sure to see several types of butterflyfish, angelfish, parrotfish and rock cod, unicornfish, trumpetfish, bluestripe snapper, Moorish idol and oriental sweetlips. For more on fish see p72.

SHARKS

It's not a feat to see a shark in the Maldives, even if you don't get in the water; juvenile reef sharks love to swim about in the warm water of the shallow lagoon right next to the beach and eat fish all day long. They're tiny – most never grow beyond 50cm long – but are fully formed sharks, so can scare some people! They don't bite, although feeding or provoking them still isn't a good idea.

Get out into the deeper water and sharks are visible, but you'll have to go looking for them. The white-tip reef shark is a small, nonaggressive, territorial shark, rarely more than 1.5m long and often seen over areas of coral or off reef edges. Grey reef sharks are also timid, shallow-water dwellers and often grow to over 2m in length.

Other species are more open-sea dwellers, but do come into atolls and especially to channel entrances where food is plentiful. These include the strange-looking hammerhead shark and the whale shark, the world's largest fish species, which is a harmless plankton eater. Sharks do not pose any danger to divers in the Maldives – there's simply too much else for them to eat.

Maldivian sharks are rapidly decreasing in number, despite high ecological awareness. The small but active shark-meat trade still claims thousands of these incredible animals each year.

CORAL BLEACHING – DEATH ON THE REEF

In March 1998, the waters of the Maldives experienced a temporary rise in temperature associated with the El Niño effect. For a period of about two weeks, surface-water temperatures were above 32°C, resulting in the loss of the symbiotic algae that lives within the coral polyps. The loss of the zooxanthellae algae causes the coral to lose its colour ('coral bleaching'), and if this algae does not return, the coral polyps die. Coral bleaching has occurred, with varying degrees of severity, in shallow waters throughout the Maldives archipelago. When the coral dies, the underlying calcium carbonate is exposed and becomes more brittle, so many of the more delicate branch and table structures have been broken up by wave action. Mainly hard corals have been affected – soft corals and sea fans are less dependent on zooxanthellae algae, are less affected by the sea temperature changes and recover more quickly from damage.

Some corals, particularly in deeper water, recovered almost immediately as the symbiotic algae returned. In a few places the coral was not damaged at all. In most areas, however, virtually all the old hard corals died and it will take years, perhaps decades, for them to recover. Some of the biggest table corals may have been hundreds of years old. Marine biologists are watching this recolonisation process with interest (see p72).

The Maldives' dive industry has adapted to the changed environment, seeking places where the regrowth is fastest and where there are lots of attractive soft corals. There's still a vast number and variety of reef fish to see, and spotting pelagic species, especially mantas and whale sharks, is a major attraction. Some long-time divers have become more interested in the very small marine life, and in macrophotography.

WHALES & DOLPHINS

Whales dwell in the open sea, and so are not found in the atolls. Species seen in the Maldives include beaked, blue, Bryde's dwarf, false killer, melon-headed, sperm and pilot whales. You'll need to go on a specialised whale-watching trip to see them, however (see p53).

Dolphins are extremely common throughout the Maldives, and you're very likely to see them, albeit fleetingly. These fun-loving, curious creatures often swim alongside speedboats and dhonis, as well as swimming off the side of reefs looking for food. Most resorts offer dolphin cruises, which allow you to see large schools up close. Species known to swim in Maldivian waters include bottlenose, Fraser's, Risso's, spotted, striped and spinner dolphins.

STINGRAYS & MANTA RAYS

Some of the most dramatic creatures in the ocean, rays are cartilaginous fish – like flattened sharks. Ray feeding is a popular activity at many resorts and it's quite something to see these muscular, alienesque creatures jump out of the water and chow down on raw steak. Stingrays are sea-bottom feeders, and equipped with crushing teeth to grind the molluscs and crustaceans they sift out of the sand. They are occasionally found in the shallows, often lying motionless on the sandy bottom of lagoons. A barbed and poisonous spine on top of the tail can swing up and forward, and will deliver a very painful injury to anyone who stands on one.

Manta rays are among the largest fish found in the Maldives and a firm favourite of divers. They tend to swim along near the surface and pass overhead as a large shadow. They are quite harmless and, in some places, seem quite relaxed about divers approaching them closely. Manta rays are sometimes seen to leap completely out of the water, landing back with a tremendous splash. The eagle ray is closely related to the manta, and often seen by divers.

NATIONAL PARKS

There are 25 Protected Marine Areas in the Maldives, usually popular diving sights where fishing of any kind is banned. These are excellent, as they have created enclaves of huge marine life that's guaranteed a safe future. While there are no specially designated island reserves in the Maldives, there are a huge number of uninhabited islands and permission from the government is needed to develop or live there. With some of the tightest development restrictions in the world, the Maldives future as pristine wilderness in many parts is assured.

ENVIRONMENTAL ISSUES

As a small island nation in a big ocean, the Maldives had a way of life that was ecologically sustainable for centuries, but certainly not self-sufficient. The comparatively small population survived by harvesting the vast resources of the sea and obtaining the other necessities of life through trade. The impact on the limited resources of their islands was probably minimal.

Now the Maldives' interrelationship with the rest of the world is greater than ever, and it has a high rate of growth supported by two main industries: fishing and tourism. Both industries depend on the preservation of the environment, and there are strict regulations to ensure sustainability. To a great extent the Maldives avoids environmental problems by importing so many of its needs. It could be asked

'There are 25 Protected Marine Areas in the Maldives, usually popular diving sights where fishing of any kind is banned.'

whether this is environmentally friendly or whether it just moves the environmental problems offshore.

Bluepeace Maldives (www.bluepeacemaldives.org) is a fantastic organisation campaigning to save the turtles, rare birds and coral of the Maldives.

Global Warming

There are no prizes for guessing what the country's long-term environmental concern is. With waters rising faster than previously believed, low-lying islands are set to start disappearing in the next few decades.

WATER, WATER, EVERYWHERE

Ensuring a supply of fresh water has always been imperative for small island communities. Rainwater quickly soaks into the sandy island soil and usually forms an underground reservoir of fresh water, held in place by a circle of salt water from the surrounding sea. Wells can be dug to extract the fresh ground water, but if water is pumped out faster than rainfall replenishes the supply, then salty water infiltrates from around the island and the well water becomes brackish. Decaying organic matter and septic tanks can also contaminate the ground water, giving it an unpleasant sulphurous smell.

One way to increase the fresh-water supply is to catch and store rainwater from rooftops. This wasn't feasible on islands that had only small buildings with roofs of palm thatch, but economic development and the use of corrugated iron has changed all that. Nearly every inhabited island now has a government-supported primary school, which is often the biggest, newest building on the island. The other sizable building is likely to be the mosque, which is a focus of community pride. Along with education and spiritual sustenance, many Maldivians now also get their drinking water from the local school or the mosque.

Expanding tourist resorts required more water than was available from wells or rooftops and, as resorts grew larger, the tourists' showers became saltier. Also, the ground water became too salty to irrigate the exotic gardens that every tourist expects on a tropical island. The solution was the desalination of sea water using 'reverse osmosis' – a combination of membrane technology and brute force.

Now every resort has a desalination plant, with racks of metal cylinders, each containing an inner cylinder made of a polymer membrane. Sea water is pumped into the inner cylinder at high pressure and the membrane allows pure water to pass through into the outer cylinder from which it is piped away. Normally, when a membrane separates fresh water from salt water, both salt and water will pass through the membrane in opposite directions to equalise the saltiness on either side – this process is called osmosis. Under pressure, the special polymer membrane allows the natural process of osmosis to be reversed.

Small, reliable desalination plants have been a boon for the resorts, providing abundant fresh water for bathrooms, kitchens, gardens and, increasingly, for swimming pools. Of course it's expensive, as the plants use lots of diesel fuel for their powerful pumps and the polymer membranes need to be replaced regularly. Many resorts ask their guests to be moderate in their water use, while a few are finding ways to recycle bath and laundry water onto garden beds. Most have dual water supplies, so that brackish ground water is used to flush the toilet while desalinated sea water is provided in the shower and the hand basin.

Is desalinated water good enough to drink? If a desalination plant is working properly, it should produce, in effect, 100% pure distilled water. The island of Thulusdhoo, in North Male' Atoll, has the only factory in the world where Coca-Cola is made out of sea water. In most resorts, the water from the bathroom tap tastes just fine, but management advises guests not to drink it. One story is that the water is too pure and lacks the trace minerals essential for good health. Another is that the water is purified in the plant, but in the pipes it can pick up bacteria, which may cause diarrhoea. Usually, the resort and hotel management will suggest that guests buy mineral water from the bar, shop or restaurant, where it will cost between US$2 and US$4 for 1.5L. This water is bottled in the Maldives using purified, desalinated water.

In the long term it's simply not an option to protect low-lying islands with breakwaters, and if the sea continues to rise as predicted then there is no long-term future for much of the country. While a wait-and-see attitude appears to that adopted by most, there are clear efforts being made to support human life in the Maldives after the water has risen by 1m – most importantly the land reclamation project that has created 2m-high Hulhumale' island next to the airport, and one day will house around half the country's population.

If the day does indeed come when waters engulf the entire country, there are repeated rumours that Gayoom has struck a deal with Australia to take the people of the Maldives in return for signing over Maldivian fishing rights to them. This is denied strenuously by both sides, but may not be that fanciful – somebody, somewhere will have to agree to take the 300,000-plus people that global warming will one day leave homeless.

Tsunami

On 26 December 2004 the Indian Ocean tsunami caused devastation throughout southern Asia. Compared to Indonesia, Sri Lanka and Thailand, the Maldives escaped relatively lightly, although over 100 people were killed when the waves hit.

Despite fearing the worst, divers who took to the water to see the damage were heartened to discover that relatively little had been done. Many corals were destroyed by the power of the tidal wave, but the tsunami's effects have been negligible compared to the 1998 coral bleaching that occurred here.

Beaches on many islands were washed away or at least partially displaced. These were still being restored using sand pumps at the time of writing, but the chances are that during the lifetime of this book, the Maldives tourism industry will look just as good as it did before the tsunami, and perhaps even better.

Check out www
.bluepeacemaldives.org
for information on this
excellent Maldivian NGO's
work protecting the local
environment.

Fisheries

Net fishing and trawling is prohibited in Maldivian waters, which include an 'exclusive economic zone' extending for 320km beyond the atolls. All fishing is by pole and line, with over 75% of the catch being skipjack or yellowfin tuna. The no-nets policy helps to prevent over-fishing and protects other marine species, such as dolphins, from being inadvertently caught in nets.

The local tuna population appears to be holding up despite increased catches, and Maldivian fisheries are patrolled to prevent poaching. But the tuna are migratory, and can be caught without limit in international waters using drift nets and long-line techniques.

Tourism

Tourism development is strictly regulated and resorts are established only on uninhabited islands that the government makes available. Overwhelmingly, the regulations have been effective in minimising environmental costs – the World Tourism Organization has cited the Maldives as a model for sustainable tourism development.

Construction and operation of the resorts does use resources, but the vast majority of these are imported. Large amounts of diesel fuel are used to generate electricity and desalinate water. The demand for hot running water and air-conditioning has raised the overall energy cost per guest.

Sewage must be effectively treated on the resort island itself – it cannot be pumped out to sea. Efficient incinerators must be installed to dispose of garbage that can't be composted, but many resorts request that visitors take home plastic bottles, used batteries and other items that may present a disposal problem.

When the first resorts were developed, jetties and breakwaters were built and boat channels cut through reefs, without much understanding of the immediate environmental consequences. In some cases natural erosion and deposition patterns were disrupted, with unexpected results. More structures were built to limit the damage and sand was pumped up to restore the beach. This was expensive and it marred the natural appearance of the island, and now developers are more careful about altering coasts and reefs. Environmental studies are required before major works can be undertaken.

Choosing a Resort

Don't worry about being swayed by the judicious use of Photoshop in brochures – almost every resort in the Maldives will get you a superb beach, amazing weather and white sands overlooked by majestic palms. Indeed some visitors jokingly complain that any photograph they take just looks like one lifted from a promotional pamphlet, so uniform is the perfection.

It's what nestles among the trees beyond the beach that should most concern you, and we're not talking about creepy crawlies here. The standard of facilities and variety of accommodation in Maldivian resorts is enormous – from budget and extremely average accommodation to the best of everything if you can afford to pay through the nose for it. Therefore your choice of resort is absolutely key to getting the holiday you want. Take plenty of time and weigh up as many options as possible before settling for the resort or resorts you'll book into. This chapter will help you navigate the various factors to take into consideration when selecting a resort, as well as listing some of our favourites in the country.

George Corbin is credited with kick-starting the Maldives tourist industry. In 1971 he brought a small group of Europeans to the country despite there being no hotels.

ATMOSPHERE

What is surprising is that every resort has a fairly distinct atmosphere. Not totally unique in all cases – but it's surprising how quickly you can tell if you're visiting a honeymooners' paradise, a diving mecca or a family bucket-and-spade affair. This is the one thing that's totally impossible to judge from a website or brochure, so the most important decision to

---

FRIENDS OF MALDIVES RESORT BOYCOTT

In 2005 British-based campaign group **Friends of Maldives** (www.friendsofmaldives.org) unveiled a carefully targeted boycott of some of the Maldives' most popular resorts. Outraged at the torture in Maldivian prisons, the police brutality on the streets and the human rights abuses, the group unveiled its selective boycott to pressure the regime from within. The boycott targets any resort owned wholly or in part by a member of the government, the hope being that the loss of revenue will in turn cause associates of President Gayoom to put pressure on him to end human rights abuses, hold free and fair elections and rein in the police and National Security Services. Supporters of this boycott include **Tourism Concern** (www.touristconcern.org.uk), Amnesty International and *Ethical Consumer*.

We support this cleverly targeted campaign and suggest you do too; it fully supports tourism in the Maldives, conscious that it's the country's only major industry, but it tells adherents to avoid about one-fifth of the resorts, which bring ministers and other senior government figures significant revenue each year. The full list can be found at www.friendsofmaldives.org/fom-resortlist .htm – we do not publish it here as it could change; resorts often change hands and, also, some ministers have already responded to the boycott, resigning their positions in government in order not to be targeted, and thus sending a very clear message to the regime.

Friends of Maldives has been roundly discredited in the Maldives by a smear campaign calling them both Islamic terrorists and Christian missionaries. We can confirm that this is not the case, and that the Anglo-Maldivian staff who run the organisation have only the human rights and general welfare of the Maldivian people at heart. They have set up a separate charity, Maldives Aid (reachable through the Friends of Maldives website) that sends aid to the poorest regions of the country. Donations can be made here to projects that will help rural residents rebuild their lives and invest in their future.

make before choosing a resort is the type of holiday you want and the atmosphere most conducive to providing it. Honeymooners who find themselves surrounded by package tours and screaming children may quickly come to regret booking into the first resort whose website they looked at. Similarly divers and surfers may find the almost total social-life vacuum in a honeymoon resort a little dull after a week.

TOP FIVE BACK-TO-NATURE RESORTS

Nika Hotel (p144)

Makunudu (p112)

Soneva Fushi (p154)

Thulhaagiri (p110)

Vadoo (p131)

Back to Nature

If you've ever fancied the whole Robinson Crusoe experience, or the slightly less lonely Swiss Family Robinson get away, the Maldives is way ahead of you, having built much of its tourism industry on precisely this desert island ideal, albeit in many places also providing a butler, gourmet restaurant and a fleet of staff catering to your every whim, making it somewhat more fun than a Daniel Defoe novel. These resorts tend to be very well designed, use imported woods and natural fibres, have little or no air conditioning and often open-air rooms with no windowpanes. The simplicity (even at the top end) of such places, not to mention their peacefulness and relaxed feel, is what attracts people.

High Style

Maldives is surfing the current wave of the luxury and boutique-hotel craze without working up a sweat at all. Indeed, few countries in the world have such a wealth of choice in this market. All major luxury hotel brands have or are hoping to establish a presence here and at times things can look like a never-ending glossy *Condé Nast Traveller* editorial. As well as our personal favourites, at the time of writing there were a host of new properties opening by such brand names as W Resorts, Four Seasons and Shangri-La, and these are likely to be in the same league.

TOP FIVE HIGH-STYLE RESORTS

One & Only Reethi Rah (p125)

Dhoni Mighili (p145)

Island Hideaway (p148)

Hilton Maldives (p144)

Soneva Fushi (p154)

The pampering on offer here is almost legendary. You'll have your own *thakuru* (personal butler), who will look after you during your stay, you'll nearly always have a sumptuous architect-designed villa stuffed full of beautifully designed furniture and fabrics, a decadent bathroom (often open air) and a private open-air area (in a water villa this is usually a sun deck with a direct staircase into the sea). Some of our very favourite resorts in this category include private pools – OK, not big enough to swim in, but still a wonderful way to cool off or wash the salt off yourself after a dip in the sea. Food in these resorts is universally top notch. There will be a huge choice of cuisine, with European, Asian and Japanese specialist chefs employed to come up with an amazing array of dishes day and night. Social life will be quiet, and will usually revolve around one of the bars. Most of the market here are honeymooners, couples and families, but children will certainly not run riot (most resorts impose a limit on children numbers) and even if they do, there will be enough space to get away from them. Despite the general feel being romantic and stylish, activities will not be ignored – everything from diving to water sports and excursions will be well catered for. Essentially, if you can afford this level of accommodation, you are guaranteed an amazing time, whatever your interests.

TOP FIVE WATER VILLAS

Soneva Gili (p126)

One & Only Reethi Rah (p125)

Huvafen Fushi (p125)

Full Moon (p113)

Taj Exotica (p132)

Over-Water Villas

The over-water villa was introduced to the Maldives in the 1970s from Tahiti and has slowly become the ultimate status symbol and a feature at almost every resort – with the exception of the low budget. The variation in water villas is immense – at the cheaper end (Paradise, Summer Island) they are little more than cheap-looking modern structures that happen to be built on stilts over the water. However, where design has been considered they can be fabulous experiences, built with sunset watching, privacy and sea access direct from the bedroom in mind. The massive, almost entirely open-air villas at Soneva Gili are frankly impossible to beat, although the super sleek Lagoon and Ocean Villas at Huvafen Fushi run a very close second, largely as they all have their own infinity pools. Essentially you get what you pay for, so it's probably false economy to go for the very cheapest available. Prices have been driven down though, and midrange resorts nearly all have very high-quality water villas. Some good midrange options include Olhuveli, White Sands and Full Moon.

Romance

Romance is big business in the Maldives, where more than a few visitors are on their honeymoon, renewing their vows or just having an indulgent break with their significant other. Almost anywhere is romantic; although again, the more budget the resort, the more families and big charter groups you'll get – the intimacy of the romantic experience can be diminished if it's peace, quiet and candlelit dinners you are after. Romance does not necessarily mean huge cost. It's hard to think of anywhere more lovely than little Makunudu island for example, where there's no TV or loud music, just gorgeously simple and traditional houses dotted along the beach, and vegetation thick with trees planted by past honeymooners. However, the usual Maldivian maxim of getting what you pay for is still true here – the very most lovely, romantic resorts are certainly not cheap ones.

Be aware that you cannot actually get married in the Maldives; you'll have to do that elsewhere. However, if you really want to, you can organise non-legally binding services and effectively have your wedding here even if the legal formalities are completed elsewhere. Nearly all midrange and top-end resorts can organise such ceremonies, so check websites for details and special packages.

Diving

Every resort has its own diving school, and all are run to extremely professional standards as required by Maldivian law. Every resort has access to good diving, although nearly all diving is from boats – even if the house reef is excellent, any diver will tell you that variety is what they look for. It's very hard to say that one resort has better diving than another, when in fact all the sites are shared, but there are a few resorts that have obvious advantages, such as the Equator Village, where coral was not affected by the bleaching in 1998, or Helengeli, from where some 40 dive sites can be reached, giving a huge choice.

Ecotourism

Ecotourism can so often be a gimmick that it's important to sort the wheat from the chaff when selecting a place that claims to be approaching tourism in a unique way, both sustainable and educational. Despite the lip service paid by many resorts there are actually relatively few that have genuine ecotourism credentials. These include educational programmes, sustainable development, environmentally friendly building practices, minimal use of air conditioning and electricity in general and a resort ethos that fosters environmental awareness and care (ie not only offering you Evian when you ask for water – an accusation that can be laid at the door of many resorts – but water that has been desalinated on site as well). The resorts we recommend in this category are leading the way in the use of materials, their interaction with the local ecosystem and the activities they offer guests.

TOP FIVE ROMANTIC RESORTS

Makunudu (p112)

Meeru (p110)

Soneva Gili (p126)

Baros (p115)

Banyan Tree (p116)

TOP FIVE DIVING RESORTS

Helengeli (p111)

Bathala (p138)

Equator Village (p171)

Ellaidhoo (p139)

Machchafushi (p143)

TOP FIVE ECOTOURISM RESORTS

Banyan Tree (p116)

Angsana (p116)

Soneva Gili (p126)

Soneva Fushi (p154)

Nika Hotel (p144)

ACTIVITIES

Few people will want to spend an entire holiday sunbathing and swimming (although some do!), and so all resorts are careful to provide a programme of excursions and activities for guests. Bear in mind that this is the only way you'll be able to leave the island during your stay, public transport being nonexistent and opportunities for sightseeing almost as scarce. It's therefore important to give some thought to what you'd like to do other than sun-worship, and check that the resort you're interested in can cater sufficiently to your interest.

While all resorts have a diving centre, the uniformity ends there; you'll have to check and see if the resort you're planning to visit has a watersports centre or its own spa, organises guided snorkelling or yoga and does any number of other activities you're interested in. For example the only resort to offer a golf course is Kuredu in Lhaviyani, although there are plans to build a second golf course on one of the islands in the new wave of resort development.

Island Hideaway offers a nearby landing strip for those coming by private jet. The less fortunate must use IAS flights from Male'.

Day Trips

Day trips from your resort are one of the very few ways you'll be able to see something of the Maldives. Even if you are a fully independent traveller (FIT) this is still a good way to see otherwise inaccessible islands of the Maldives. Most commonly offered are day trips to the charming capital Male' from resorts in North and South Male' Atolls. These can be fun, but check that you're able to ditch the group and explore on your own if you want to. There's enough to see for a few hours plus plenty of shopping to merit this trip and it's a great way to get a feel for Maldivian people – you'll find the terrifyingly polite resort staff replaced by a friendly and funny city populace.

Another popular excursion is a trip to an inhabited island. These are a poor substitute for individual exploration of the country, but until that becomes possible this is as close as most people will be able to get to seeing a small island community, traditional housing, craftwork and lifestyle. The trip inevitably feels rather contrived, but can still be immensely enjoyable depending on how friendly the locals are and how many people are around (with children often in school or studying in Male', and menfolk away for work, some islands feel more like ghost towns than centres of population).

Banyan Tree and Angsana won huge acclaim when they helped neighbouring inhabited island Naalaafushi rebuild after the tsunami in partnership with the United Nations Development Programme.

Fishing

Just about any resort will do sunset, sunrise or night-fishing trips, but they are a more authentically Maldivian experience at small, locally run resorts like Asdu Sun Island and Thulhaagiri. Most resorts near Male' can arrange a big-game fishing trip, including Bandos, Baros, Club Med Faru, Full Moon, Kurumba, Laguna and Nakatchafushi. These work out more economically if there are several participants, as costs are high: from $400 for a half-day trip for up to four people. Large boats, fully equipped with radar technology, are used to catch dorado, tuna, marlin, barracuda, jackfish and sharks.

Snorkelling & Diving

The underwater world is definitely one of the best reasons to come to the Maldives. All resorts cater for divers and snorkellers, and organise twice- or thrice-daily diving excursions and usually at least one snorkelling trip a day. If you're keen on either, it'll always be cheaper to bring your own equipment, including snorkel, mask and fins, plus buoyancy control device (BCD) and dive computer, if you're a diver. Dive schools vary enormously in standard and helpfulness, but all are of an exceptionally high safety standard, as regulated by strict Maldivian laws. Resorts themselves are not so important for divers – it's their location and the ease of access to dive sights nearby. Most resorts have at least 10 sites nearby and visit them in rotation. If there's a particular dive site you want to visit, you should contact the dive school at the resort and check it'll be running a trip there during your stay. See p61 for more about snorkelling and diving.

Spa Treatments

As a destination for relaxation, the Maldives has also become well known for offering a huge array of treatments in purpose-built spas. These include all types of massage, beauty treatments, Ayurvedic medicine, acupuncture and traditional Maldivian treatments. Almost all midrange and top-end resorts have a spa and the best are sometimes booked up months in advance, so it can pay to plan ahead if you're interested in certain treatments. With staff often from Indonesia, India and Sri Lanka, you're in safe (if expensive) hands. You can check most resort websites for a full treatment list, but resorts well known for their spas include Full Moon, Banyan Tree, both One & Only resorts and both Soneva resorts. The underwater spa at Huvafen Fushi is the first of its kind in the world and is truly unique; you can be massaged while watching the fish swimming around the glass walls

---

QUALITY TOURISM STRATEGY

The first Maldivian resorts were basic beach huts made of local materials. Early visitors loved them, but the local economy didn't benefit much, environmental problems loomed, and the cultural impact was seen as a real threat, especially as the islands initially attracted pot-smoking, free-loving hippies rather than the smarter, more conservative crowd you'll find here today. In 1978 when President Gayoom came to power, the country adopted a strategy based on 'quality tourism', which is administered by tourism laws, all of which have proved prescient and extremely important in preventing overdevelopment in the Maldives.

Resorts can be established only on uninhabited islands when the government makes them available for commercial leases. Corporations bid for the lease with a development plan that must conform to strict standards. Resort buildings cannot cover more than 20% of an island's area or be higher than the tallest palm tree. Not a single tree can be cut down without explicit permission. The maximum number of rooms is limited according to the size of the island, and the resort developer must provide all the necessary infrastructure, from electricity and water supply to sewage treatment and garbage disposal.

When the lease on an island expires, the government can require a major renovation and upgrade as a condition of renewal, or it can make the island available for a new lease and call for bids and a redevelopment proposal. The bidding process is very competitive (not to mention frequently accused of being horrendously corrupt). Environmental impact and staff welfare are considerations in selecting the successful bid, but the main criterion is money – how much rent will the developer pay the government? This means that successful developers must earn the maximum return on each room, so new resorts are pushed towards the quality end of the market and old resorts are progressively upgraded. It also means that resorts need to fill their rooms, so prices are also competitive, especially during off-peak periods.

Because every resort is on its own island, a Maldives resort is an isolated and totally managed environment. Resorts can offer every modern convenience but still preserve that perfect tropical island ambience – the 'Robinson Crusoe' factor. There is minimal contact with the local people, and therefore little of the 'cultural pollution' that Maldivians saw as so undesirable in tourist destinations like Goa, Bali and the Thai coast. As resorts have a vested interest in preserving their immediate environment, there's no litter, no noise and no pollution.

RESORT BASICS

You'll be met at the airport by your resort representative, who will usually take your ticket and/or passport from you, something that is quite normal here despite feeling rather odd to the seasoned traveller.

Unless you're arriving after dark you'll soon be transferred to your resort – either by a waiting dhoni, speedboat or seaplane from the nearby lagoon airport. You may have to wait for other passengers to get through customs, but it shouldn't be too much of a wait. You can use US dollars or euros at the airport café, as well as change some cash into rufiya at the bank.

Travellers arriving after dark will have to spend a night at the airport hotel or at a hotel in Male', as neither boat nor seaplane transfers are carried out after sunset for obvious reasons.

On arrival at the resort you'll be given a drink, asked to fill out a registration form and taken to your room. Resort staff will bring your luggage separately.

Room Types

Some resorts have just one type of room, which confusingly may be called 'Superior', 'Deluxe', or 'Super Deluxe'. Most bigger, newer resorts have several types of room, ranging from the cheapest 'Superior Garden Villas' to the 'Deluxe Over-Water Suites'. A 'Garden Villa' will not have a beach frontage, and a 'Water Villa' will be on stilts over the lagoon – and twice the cost.

More expensive rooms tend to be bigger, newer, better finished, and can have a bathtub as well as a shower, a minibar instead of an empty fridge, tea- and coffee-making facilities (even an espresso machine), a CD sound system and/or a Jacuzzi. Smaller over-water accommodation is called a water bungalow, although the delineation of the terms water bungalow and water villa is fluid and largely interchangeable.

Single Supplements & Extra Beds

This book gives room rates for single/double occupancy, but most package-deal prices are quoted on a per-person basis, assuming double occupancy. Solo travellers have to pay a 'single-person supplement' for the privilege of having a room all to themselves.

Extra people can usually share a room, but there's a charge for the extra bed (at least US$15 for a child, US$30 for an adult) as well as additional costs for meals. In a package-tour price list, this appears as a supplement for children sharing the same room as parents, or for extra adults sharing a room.

For children two years and younger, usually just the US$6 bed tax is payable. From two to 12 years, the child supplement with full board will be from US$15 to US$30 in most budget to midrange resorts, but much more in expensive resorts. Transfers from the airport are charged at half the adult rate. A more expensive option is to get two adjacent rooms, ideally with a connecting door. You might get a discount on the second room.

Pricing Periods

Pricing patterns vary with the resort and the demands of its main market – some are incredibly detailed and complex with a different rate every week. The basic pattern is that Christmas–New Year is the peak season, with very high prices, minimum-stay requirements and surcharges for Christmas dinner and New Year's Eve. Early January to late March is high season, when many Europeans take a winter holiday. The weeks around Easter may attract even higher rates (but not as high as Christmas). From Easter to about mid-July is low season (and the wettest part of the year). July, August and September is another high season, for the European summer holidays. Mid-September to early December is low season again.

Specific markets can have their own times of high demand, such as the August holiday week for Italians, Chinese New Year in the Asian market or the end of Ramadan for some Middle Eastern guests.

of the room. Resorts well known for Ayurvedic therapy include Meedhup-paru, Vadoo, Hilton Maldives and Olhuveli Beach & Spa.

Surfing

The best resorts for surfing are Dhinveli Beach and Lohifushi, which are both great. The popularity of surfing is tangibly on the increase in the Maldives, with surfer arrivals going up massively in the past few years. However, it's really only these two resorts that are perfectly located near good breaks, although nearby resorts, such as Four Seasons Kuda Huraa and Club Med Kani, can organise boat trips. Truth be told, the best option for the serious surfer is to go on a 'surfari'. See p79 for details on surfing in the Maldives.

Kuredu is the only resort to offer a golf course – a real luxury in a country where land is at a premium!

Water Sports

Second only to diving schools, most resorts have a water-sports centre (but not all, so check before booking). These vary enormously – some offer the most basic array of canoes and windsurfing, while others run the gauntlet from water skiing to kite-boarding and the ever-popular banana boat. The best resorts for sailing and windsurfing have a wide lagoon that's not too shallow, and lots of equipment to choose from.

Resorts with particularly strong water-sports facilities include Kuredu, Lohifushi, Dhonveli Beach, Alimatha Aquatic, Bandos, Kuramathi, One & Only Kanuhura, Meeru, Summer Island, Club Faru, Club Med Kani, Vilu Reef, Olhuveli and Reethi Beach.

You'll find jet skis and other not-so-cheap thrills at Kuredu, One & Only Kanuhura, Dhonveli Beach, Ellaidhoo, Hilton Maldives, Reethi Beach, Fun Island, Holiday Island, Vilu Reef, Paradise Island and Royal Island, among others.

Wildlife Watching

Most resorts offer dolphin cruises, and although there's no guarantee you'll see anything, dolphins are a common sight in the Maldives and so you're always in with a good chance. Depending on favoured dolphin-feeding grounds near your resort the cruises can last from one to three hours and are usually by dhoni. These are often billed as 'champagne sunset dolphin cruises' – and it's often only one out of three on this score if the dolphins don't show, as the 'champagne' is Prosecco, even at top-end resorts.

Whale watching can be organised from a number of resorts. Be aware that the Whale Submarine (p95) in Male' is something of a misnomer; it's a submarine that visits a reef nearby – there are no whales to be seen here.

The twin-otter seaplanes used to transfer guests to resorts are all built in Canada and have to be flown around the world, a 16,700km journey that is still more economical than stripping the plane down and shipping it.

FOOD & DRINK

A miniature revolution in fine cuisine has occurred in the past few years in the Maldives. Once even the top-end hotels had decidedly average offerings at meal times, but now things are quite different, with luxury hotels offering a huge choice from an ever-growing number of eateries, allowing guests to eat somewhere different every day for several days.

The buffet, the standard lunch and dinner option is still in evidence, however, and extremely variable they can be too – the usual Maldivian maxim that you get what you pay for is true here. Some particularly good buffets we enjoyed while researching this book included those at Olhuveli, Banyan Tree and Soneva Gili.

Alcohol is also becoming more of a feature at resorts – many have spent years building up wine cellars to rival any French restaurant, and as you'd expect these are not cheap. Reethi Rah claims to have over 8,000 bottles of wine in its cellar, while Huvafen Fushi's wine cellar is a work of art itself, buried deep below the island and hired out for private dinners at great expense.

However, in all cases alcohol is expensive and with a few luxury exceptions, limited in range. Beers available will not thrill connoisseurs – although Kirin and Tiger are commonly seen amid the Heineken and Carling. All-inclusive packages include certain designated drinks, usually the cheapest non-brand-name beer going, a house red and white wine and non-brand-name spirits. People on these tours can usually be found drinking, perhaps to justify the price of the package.

MALDIVES RESORT RATINGS

Each resort is given a number out of three for how it scores on each front, three being the very highest standard in its field. A zero means that the resort has absolutely nothing worth mentioning on a subject; for example if it doesn't accept children, it gets a zero for children's activities.

A = Beach   F = Food
B = Romance   G = Design
C = Social Life   H = Diving
D = Pampering   I = Snorkelling
E = Children's Activities   J = Water Sports

Resort	A	B	C	D	E	F	G	H	I	J
Alimatha Aquatic	3	2	2	1	1	2	2	3	3	3
Angaga	3	2	2	1	2	2	2	3	3	2
Angsana	3	3	1	2	0	3	3	3	3	2
Bandos	2	1	3	1	3	2	1	2	3	3
Banyan Tree	3	3	1	3	1	3	3	3	3	2
Baros	3	3	1	3	1	3	3	3	2	2
Bathala	3	2	2	1	2	2	1	3	3	3
Bolifushi	2	2	2	1	2	1	1	3	3	3
Club Med Kani	3	1	3	1	3	2	2	3	3	3
Club Rannalhi	3	2	3	1	3	2	1	3	3	2
Cocoa Island	3	3	1	3	1	3	3	3	3	3
Dhiggiri	2	2	2	2	3	2	2	3	3	2
Dhoni Mighili	3	3	1	3	0	3	3	3	2	2
Dhonveli Beach	3	1	2	1	2	2	2	3	3	3
Ellaidhoo	3	1	2	1	2	2	2	3	3	3
Embudu Village	3	1	2	1	2	2	1	3	3	2
Equator Village	1	1	3	1	2	1	1	3	3	2
Eriyadu	3	2	2	1	1	2	1	3	3	2
Fihalhohi	3	2	2	1	2	2	1	3	3	2
Filitheyo	2	1	2	1	2	2	2	3	1	1
Full Moon	3	3	1	2	2	3	3	2	2	2
Hakuraa Club	3	3	2	1	2	2	2	3	1	1
Halaveli	3	2	2	2	2	2	2	3	2	2
Helengeli	3	2	2	1	1	1	2	3	3	0
Hilton Maldives	3	3	1	3	2	3	3	3	3	3
Holiday Island	3	1	2	1	2	1	1	3	1	2
Huvafen Fushi	3	3	1	3	1	3	3	3	3	3
Island Hideaway	3	3	1	1	3	3	3	3	3	2
Kihaadhuffaru	3	3	2	2	3	2	2	3	3	2
Komandoo	2	3	1	2	0	2	3	3	3	3

MEALS
Typically, breakfast will include a choice of cereals, fresh fruit, fruit juice from cans or concentrate, instant or real coffee, tea, bread rolls, toast, omelettes or fried eggs done as you like, sausages, bacon, baked beans, and often a curry and rice. At more upmarket resorts you could also have muesli, yoghurt, more fresh fruits, fresh-squeezed fruit juice, brewed coffee, better bread, croissants and real ham. You get what you pay for, remember.

For lunch, most resorts manage soup and a simple salad, pasta, rice, instant noodles, and at least one each of fish, beef and chicken dishes, often prepared as curry, casserole or stew, with fruit and dessert to

Resort	A	B	C	D	E	F	G	H	I	J
Kudarah	1	2	3	2	2	2	2	3	2	2
Kuramathi Blue Lagoon	3	2	1	2	1	2	3	3	3	3
Kuramathi Cottage & Spa	3	2	1	3	1	2	2	3	3	3
Kuramathi Village	3	1	3	1	1	2	1	3	3	3
Kuredu	3	2	3	2	2	2	1	3	3	3
Kurumba	3	2	1	2	3	3	2	3	3	3
Laguna Beach	3	2	2	2	3	2	1	3	2	2
Lily Beach	2	2	3	1	2	2	1	3	3	1
Lohifushi	2	1	2	1	1	2	1	3	2	3
Maayafushi	3	2	1	1	1	2	1	3	3	1
Machchafushi	2	2	2	1	2	2	1	3	3	1
Madoogali	3	3	1	2	1	2	2	3	3	2
Makunudu	2	3	1	2	1	2	2	3	3	1
Meedhupparu	3	2	2	2	2	2	1	3	2	3
Meeru	3	2	2	1	1	2	2	3	2	3
Mirihi	3	2	1	1	2	2	2	3	2	2
Moofushi	2	2	2	1	1	2	1	3	2	1
Nika Hotel	3	3	1	3	1	3	2	3	3	2
Olhuveli Beach	3	3	1	3	1	2	2	3	3	3
One & Only Kanuhura	3	3	2	3	3	3	3	3	3	3
One & Only Reethi Rah	3	3	1	3	1	3	3	3	3	3
Palm Beach	3	3	2	2	2	2	2	3	1	2
Paradise Island	3	1	2	1	2	1	1	3	3	3
Ranveli Village	3	2	2	2	2	3	2	3	3	2
Reethi Beach	3	2	1	1	1	2	2	3	3	3
Rihiveli Beach	3	3	1	2	1	3	2	3	1	3
Royal Island	3	2	1	2	1	2	2	3	3	3
Soneva Fushi	3	3	1	3	1	3	3	3	3	2
Soneva Gili	3	3	1	3	1	3	3	3	3	3
Summer Island Village	3	1	2	1	2	1	1	3	3	3
Sun Island	2	1	3	1	3	3	1	3	3	3
Taj Coral Reef	2	2	2	2	2	2	2	3	3	1
Taj Exotica	3	3	2	3	1	3	3	3	3	2
Thulhaagiri	3	2	2	1	1	2	1	3	3	2
Vadoo	3	3	1	2	1	2	1	3	3	2
Vakarufalhi	3	2	2	1	1	2	1	3	3	2
Velavaru	3	3	2	2	1	2	3	3	3	2
Velidhu	3	2	2	1	1	1	1	3	3	3
Veligandu	3	2	2	2	1	2	1	3	3	2
Vilamendhoo Island	2	2	2	1	2	2	2	3	3	2
Vilu Reef	3	3	2	3	1	2	2	3	3	3
White Sands	3	2	2	2	1	2	2	3	3	3

finish. Better resorts offer more varied salad vegetables, pasta freshly tossed with a choice of sauces, Hokkien noodles, freshly fried fish fillets and more creative chicken and beef dishes.

Dinner will usually have the biggest selection, and may be a 'theme night' specialising in regional cuisines such as Italian, Asian, Indian or Maldivian (usually meaning fanciful versions of local dishes, not authentic for the most part). Most resorts will have soup, salad and a dozen or so hot dishes, with at least two each of fish, beef and chicken. A few dishes will be vegetarian – ratatouille, vegetable curry, *pasta alla fungi* or potatoes Provençale. There'll be a pasta dish or three, possibly a lasagne, and stir-fried noodles, as well as plain rice, saffron rice, fried rice, and maybe risotto. There's a trend for 'live cooking stations' at one or more places along the buffet tables, where food is fried or barbecued to taste while you watch – great for fresh fish, prawns, pasta, steak and shish kebab. Whole fish and roast meats are carved and served as you like. Fancier resorts feature more and fresher seafood and it's less likely to be overcooked – the best places serve sashimi. Salad is another class marker – a budget resort will serve iceberg lettuce, coleslaw and cucumber with a basic bottled mayo, French or Thousand Island dressing. A better resort will have cos lettuce, rocket, radicchio, spinach leaves and three kinds of cabbage, with freshly made mayonnaise and your choice of vinegars and olive oils. Only the very best resorts have ripe, red, tasty tomatoes.

Desserts can be delicious, with pastries, fruit pies, tarts, tiramisu, mousse, blancmange, custard and cheesecake all on offer at the far end of the buffet. The best resorts might have crepes prepared at a live cooking station, and a choice of cheeses too.

Budget resorts might offer a set menu only for some meals – perhaps for lunch, or on alternate days for dinner. These are OK, and will give your waistline some respite. At the other end of the market, the best resorts serve some meals à la carte – the chef has a chance to do something special and creative, and the waiters enjoy giving full table service.

As well as the main buffet restaurant, big resorts usually have 'speciality restaurants' serving regional cuisine (Thai, Japanese, Italian, Indian etc) or grills and seafood. These can be expensive (main courses US$15 to US$50) but in better resorts are excellent,

Most resorts have a 'coffee shop' serving light meals, coffee and drinks, often 24 hours a day. They're good for people on half board who want a snack in the middle of the day.

Another alternative to the usual buffet is a 'speciality meal'. This might be a barbecue or a curry night, served on the beach, and open to anyone who pays the extra charge, perhaps US$25 (unlike a theme night

Always ask for desalinated water to drink; any good resort will provide this (preferably free) and not just a US$8 bottle of imported Evian, which is exorbitant in both cash and carbon.

A TASTE OF THE MALDIVES

It used to be rare to find Maldivian food in tourist resorts – the opinion was that Western stomachs couldn't cope with the spices. Now many resorts do a Maldivian barbecue once a week, which is very enjoyable if not totally authentic. These barbecues can be on the beach, by the pool or held in the restaurant. The main dishes are fresh reef fish, baked tuna, fish curries, rice and *roshi* (unleavened bread). The regular dinner buffet might also feature Maldivian fish curry. Less common is the Maldivian breakfast favourite *mas huni*, a healthy mixture of tuna, onion, coconut and chilli, eaten with *roshi*. If there's nothing Maldivian on the menu, you could ask the kitchen staff to make a fish curry or a tray of short eats – they may be making some for the staff anyway. Small resorts are usually amenable to special requests. Otherwise, do a trip to Male' or an island-hopping excursion to a fishing village, and try out a local teashop.

RESORT TIPS

It's always worth checking a resort website yourself and even contacting the resort for specific, up-to-date information, as things change regularly. Is there construction work happening on the island? Is the spa finished yet? Do they still offer kite-boarding? Also, be aware that many resort websites have never been updated since they were created. While there are exceptions, it's never a good idea to take the information there as fact – check when the page was last updated.

Check the dive-centre website. It might provide a discount if you book your dives before your arrival. Email them for any specific dive information.

If the trip is a honeymoon, or second honeymoon, or if you will be celebrating an anniversary or birthday, let your travel agent or tour company know – the resort might surprise you. Some rather tacky resorts on the other hand might require a wedding certificate before they do anything – the Maldives is notorious for couples claiming to be on their honeymoon just to get some freebies!

---

in the main restaurant, which is not charged as an extra). Or it can be a private dinner for two in romantic surroundings – on an inhabited island, on the beach, or on a sandbar in ankle-deep water. Most resorts will do special meals on request.

MEAL PLANS

Many guests are on full-board packages that include accommodation and all meals. Others take a half-board package, which includes breakfast and dinner, and pay extra for lunch. Some resorts offer a bed and breakfast plan, and guests pay separately for lunch and dinner. The advantage of not paying for all your meals in advance is that you permit yourself the freedom to vary where you eat (assuming your resort has more than one restaurant). However, at good resorts your full-board plan is usually transferable, meaning you can eat a certain amount at other restaurants, or at least get a big discount on the à la carte prices.

Room-only deals are also sometimes available, but they're rarely a great idea. Never underestimate the sheer expense of eating à la carte in the Maldives at any level, although at the top end it's positively outrageous – think US$100 per head without alcohol for a decent lunch. Self-catering is of course not possible and there's nothing worse than being unable to eat properly due to financial constraints. Unless you're very comfortable financially and want to eat in a variety of different places, we strongly encourage you to book full- or half-board meal plans.

All-inclusive plans are some of the best value of all, although in general they're associated with the core package-tourist market and tend to be available only in budget resorts. These typically include all drinks (non-brand-name alcohol, soft drinks and water) and some activities and water sports/diving thrown in for good measure. Always investigate carefully exactly what's on offer meal-wise before you make a decision – the meal plan can make an expensive package worthwhile or a cheap one a rip-off.

ENTERTAINMENT

Beware the animator! These lively people are forever trying to encourage group work-outs or karaoke competitions in Italian-dominated resorts even though they have been roundly rejected by the smarter resorts. Their days in the Maldives are numbered as the country's tourist industry increasingly tries to define the Maldives as a stylish and fashionable destination, but they're still determinedly hanging on in some places for the time being.

Look out for the barefoot pilots on Maldivian Air Taxi and Trans Maldivian. Not only do they go to work in shorts, many of them spend the nights in luxury resorts before flying back to Male' the next morning – not the world's worst job.

Be prepared to get on the weighing scales yourself if you are flying on Island Aviation Services, the domestic airline. The planes are small and everyone's weight needs to be taken into account.

The truth is that the Maldives is not a premium destination for entertainment. What little of it there is can be fairly naff and uninspiring, and the resorts that insist on a nightly disco often find them empty. Simply put, honeymooners, divers and families, the core demographic of Maldivian tourism, don't really come here for any kind of entertainment, preferring quiet romance and daily activities to night-time ones.

The biggest party and entertainment resort is Club Med Kani, with its tireless round of animator high jinks and nightly disco, and to a lesser extent Bandos, where visiting air crews can often be the life and soul of the party. The W Retreat & Spa, opening in late 2006, plans to be something of a party island with a 24-hour underground bar.

SAFARI CRUISES

Safaris are a superb option for anyone wanting the best possible combination of diving sites, the chance to travel outside the standard tourist zone and a sociable arena where both couples and noncouples will feel totally comfortable.

The massive expansion in the market for safari cruises has meant an increasingly sleek approach from the tour companies that run them; a typical, modern boat is air conditioned, spacious, and serves varied and appetising meals. It should have hot water, a sun deck, fishing and diving gear, mobile phone, full bar, DVD player and cosy, comfortable cabins.

Costs start at around US$90 per person per day, including the US$8 per day bed tax and all meals, plus roughly US$50 per day for diving trips. There's usually a minimum daily (or weekly) charge for the whole boat, and the cost per person is lower if there are enough passengers to fill the boat. You'll be charged extra for soft drinks and alcohol, which are priced as you'd expect to find in most resorts. You might splurge for the occasional meal at a resort, but generally there are few extras to spend money on.

The most basic boats are large dhonis with a small galley and communal dining area, two or three cramped cabins with two berths each, and a shared shower and toilet. Passengers often drag their mattresses out on deck for fresh air, and sleep under the stars. Food is prepared on board and varies from very ordinary to very good – it usually features lots of freshly caught fish. The bigger, better boats have air conditioning, more spacious accommodation, and a toilet and shower for each cabin. The best boats, like the best resorts, spare no effort in making their guests comfortable.

Most safari trips are for diving (see p63) or so-called 'surfaris' for surfing (see p82). A minority of safari trips are primarily for sightseeing, and usually offer a fair amount of fishing and snorkelling, stops at fishing villages and resorts, and picnics or a camp-out on an uninhabited island. Obviously it's important to make sure you're joining a trip that will cover what you want to do.

On a scheduled trip, a single passenger may have to share a cabin with another, or pay a premium rate. Compatibility isn't usually a problem on diving or surf trips, where everyone has a common interest, but it can be an issue on longer sightseeing cruises. If you arrange your own group of six or so people, you can charter a whole boat and tailor a trip to suit your interests.

Choosing a Safari Boat

More than 80 safari boats are operating in the Maldives. Some specific suggestions are given here, but you'll need to do some research yourself. When you're considering a safari-boat trip, ask the operator about the following.

- Boat size – Generally speaking, bigger boats will be more comfortable, and therefore more expensive, than small boats. Boats with more than 20 or so passengers may not have the camaraderie you'd get with a small group. Most boats have about 12 berths or less; few boats have more than 20.

Most resorts have some low-key entertainment a couple of evenings a week. Usually it's a fairly cringe-inducing covers band, although other more interesting performers such as traditional Maldivian *bodu beru* (big drum) players, Sri Lankan fire dancers or a jazz band are also common.

LUXURIES

You've come to the right place if this is your main interest – the Maldives' top-end resorts (and to a good extent even its midrange options) offer an eye-watering range of 'treatments', pampering, and a general level of luxury that you can find in few other places.

- Cabin arrangements – Can you get a two-berth cabin (if that's what you want)? How many cabins/people are sharing a bathroom?

- Comforts – Does the boat have air-con, hot water and desalinated water available 24 hours?

- Companions – Who else will be on the trip, what language do they speak, have they done a safari trip before? What are their interests – diving, sightseeing, fishing, surfing?

- Food and drink – Can you be catered for as a vegetarian or vegan? Is there a bar serving alcohol and, if so, how much is a beer/wine/scotch etc?

- Recreation – Does the boat have a video player, CD player, fishing tackle or sun deck? Does the boat have sails or is it propelled by motor only?

Safari Boat Operators

Safari boats often change ownership, or get refitted or acquire a new name or both. The skipper, cook and divemaster can change too, so it's hard to make firm recommendations. The following boats have a good reputation, but there are many others offering good facilities and services. The boats listed here all have a bar on board, oxygen for emergencies, and some diving equipment for rent. Universal's Atoll Explorer is like a mini-cruise ship with a swimming pool on deck, and the Four Seasons Island Explorer is the most luxurious and the most expensive of all. The websites are those of the boat operators. Many of these operators have other boats as well, which may also be very good. If the website does not give booking information (or it's not in your language), most of these boats can be booked through the bigger tour operators in Male' (see p91), or by overseas travel agents. The official **tourism website** (www.visitmaldives.com) has reasonably up-to-date details on almost every safari and cruise boat.

Adventurer I (☎ 3326734; www.maldivesdiving.com;) Boat 22m, six cabins, 12 berths, hot water.
Atoll Explorer (☎ 3314873; www.atollexplorer.com;) Boat 48m, 20 cabins, 40 berths, hot water.
Eagle Ray (☎ 3314841; www.maldivesboatclub.com.mv) Boat 26m, seven cabins, 14 berths, hot water.
Flying Fish (☎ 3310314; www.movinmaldives.com) Boat 26m, seven cabins, 14 berths, hot water.
Four Seasons Explorer (☎ 6644888; www.fourseasons.com/maldives;) Boat 39m, 11 cabins, 22 berths, hot water.
Gulfaam (☎ 3323617; www.voyagesmaldives.com;) Boat 20m; six cabins, 12 berths.
Haveyli (☎ 3320555; www.guraabu.com.mv) Boat 30m, 11 cabins, 22 berths, hot water.
Keema (☎ 3313539; www.interlinkmaldives.com;) Boat 27m; six cabins, 12 berths, hot water.
MV Carina (☎ 3316172 www.seamaldives.com.mv;) Boat 33m; 11 cabins, 33 berths, hot water.
Nautilus I (☎ 3315253; www.nautilus.at) Boat 30m, eight cabins, 16 berths, hot water.
Nooraanee Queen (☎ 3310314; www.movinmaldives.com;) Boat 43m, 19 cabins, 42 berths, hot water.
Soleil (☎ 3320555; www.guraabu.com.mv;) Boat 28m; nine cabins, 17 berths, hot water.
Sting Ray (☎ 3314841; www.maldivesboatclub.com.mv;) Boat 31m, nine cabins, 22 berths, hot water.
Sultan of Maldives (☎ 3310550; www.sultansoftheseas.com;) Boat 30m; eight cabins, 16 berths, hot water.

The current *sine qua non* of the luxury industry is the personal *thakuru*, otherwise known rather patronisingly as a 'man Friday' or the simply inaccurate description of butler. The *thakuru* is assigned to you throughout your stay. He's your point of contact for all small things (restocking the fridge, reconfirming your flight) and resembles a butler in no way at all really. Given that one *thakuru* will often be looking after up to ten rooms at a time, the term 'personal' is pushing it a bit.

The main centre of luxury at most resorts is the spa – until recently they were considered optional for resorts, whereas now they are usually at the very centre of the luxury experience. Expect to pay from about US$40 for a simple massage at a budget or midrange place to US$200 for a long session of pampering.

Resort spas in good resorts are often run by companies such as ESPA, Serena, Per Aquum and Six Senses. At this very highest level they offer a vast range of treatments from the sublime to the truly ridiculous. Some of our favourite names include Fit For Life Aromatic Moor Mud Wrap, Tamarind Fancy Wipe, Potato Purifier and Happy Man Relaxer (no jokes please). Perhaps it's because we can't afford to spend US$200 on a foot massage, but it all seems rather funny to us; there's a lot to be said for gorgeous relaxing treatments, but you'll meet your fair share of Bubbles Devere types here who go from treatment to treatment all day long.

'Believe it or not, there's almost no resort in the Maldives that does not have an amazing beach.'

BEACHES

Believe it or not, there's almost no resort in the Maldives that does not have an amazing beach. Throughout the course of researching this book, the only really mediocre beach we saw was at the Equator Village. It's still swimmable but narrow and strewn with seaweed, making swimming unpleasant. Beaches suffer a great deal from beach erosion and the tsunami did not help this at all, but resorts work very hard to redress erosion with sand pumps, which, while unsightly, are working day and night in many resorts to restore sand to its original place. Giravaru, near Male', suffers from litter washing up on its beaches regularly, but other than that the quality of beach is almost universally brilliant. However, for the record here's a few of our favourites: One & Only Kanuhura, Kuredu, Palm Beach, Soneva Fushi, Reethi Beach, Royal Island, Coco Palm, Meedhupparu, Eriyadu, Angsana, Bandos, Baros, Banyan Tree, Soneva Gili, Club Med Kani, Rihiveli, Club Rannalhi, Fihalhohi, Sun Island, Bathala, Thundufushi, Veligandu, Villu Reef, Vakarufalhi, Filitheyo, Fun Island and Hilton Maldives.

CHILDREN

If you're bringing children to the Maldives, it's very important to get your choice of resort right, as only a few resorts have kids clubs or baby-sitters available, and activities for older children can be limited at resorts more used to welcoming honeymooning couples. If you aren't looking for kids clubs and your kids are happy to spend the day on the beach, then almost every resort will be suitable. Note that Komandoo and Dhoni Mighili do not accept children aged under six and 12 respectively.

In general kids will love the Maldives, although for more than a week it might be pushing it unless you're staying in a big and friendly family resort where there are plenty of other children for them to play with and an endless parade of activities.

Some highly recommended resorts for children include: Kuredu, One & Only Kanuhura, Bandos, Kurumba, Medhufushi, Filitheyo, Club Med Kani, Paradise Island, Laguna Beach, Kuramathi Meeru, Lily Beach and Sun Island.

Snorkelling, Diving & Surfing

Unless you take some time to explore the magical world underneath the water in the Maldives, you're seeing just one tiny part of this incredibly diverse country. Yes, the flora and fauna on the tiny scraps of land poking their heads above the water are not the most spectacular or varied, but glance into the deep blue all around and you'll see marine life so incredible that you'll quickly understand why the Maldives is a favourite destination for divers around the world.

The visibility is incredible, the water so warm that many divers don't even wear a wetsuit and the sheer variety of life underwater is so fantastic that it's easy to understand why most people dive or snorkel during their travels here. Because of the thoroughly professional and safety-conscious approach from all resorts and excellent facilities it's common to learn to dive in the Maldives as well. Even if you don't do a full PADI or equivalent course, a brief scuba introduction is very cheap and lots of fun, while snorkelling can be done by anyone who can swim.

A further boon about the Maldives' submarine life is that as well as being plentiful, beautiful and accessible, it's also extremely unaggressive. Despite its being rich in sharks, there's not one type likely to attack a human, and the only possible reason it would attack in any case would be self-defence.

Diving in particular requires some planning; decide your level, what you want to see and how much diving you want to do before choosing a resort. Snorkelling is similar – some resorts have no good house reef and thus you have to go on a boat trip to see anything worthwhile. Surfing is the most seasonal of all – but it's an increasingly popular activity in the east of the country, with some great breaks coming off the Indian Ocean.

'Snorkelling is the first step into seeing a different world.'

SNORKELLING

Snorkelling is the first step into seeing a different world. Anyone who can swim can do it, it's very cheap (and often free at smarter resorts) to rent the equipment and the rewards make themselves known immediately. The colours of the fish and coral are far better at shallow depths, as water absorbs light, and so below 5m colours start to become less sharp (hence why so many divers carry torches to compensate). This means a visual feast awaits any snorkeller on any decent reef.

WHERE TO SNORKEL

Usually an island is surrounded firstly by a sand-bottomed lagoon, and then by the reef flat (*faru*), a belt of dead and living coral covered by shallow water. At the edge of the reef flat is a steep, coral-covered slope that drops away into deeper water. These reef slopes are the best areas for snorkelling – around a resort island this is called the house reef. The slope itself can have interesting features such as cliffs, terraces and caves, and there are clearly visible changes in the coral and marine flora as the water gets deeper. You can see both the smaller fish, which frequent the reef flats, and sometimes much larger animals that live in the deep water between the islands, but come close to the reefs to feed.

You can also take a boat from your resort to other snorkelling sites around the atoll. A giri (coral pinnacle) that rises to within 5m of the surface, is ideal for snorkelling, which is not difficult if it's in sheltered waters inside an atoll. A kandu (sea channel) will usually have excellent soft corals, schools of reef fish and large pelagic species.

The best resorts for snorkelling have an accessible house reef, where the deep water is not far offshore, at least around part of the island. There are usually channels you can swim through to the outer-reef slope. To avoid grazing yourself or damaging the coral, always use these channels rather than trying to find your own way across the reef flat. Another option is to walk out on a jetty to the reef edge – all resorts have at least one jetty, though sometimes they don't extend right to the edge of the reef.

Resorts with excellent house reefs tend to be popular with divers too. Some of the best are Ellaido, Bathala, Vadoo, Mirihi, Biyadhoo, Eriyadu, Machchafushi, Vilamendhoo, Filitheyo, Reethi Beach, Embudu Village, W Resort, Soneva Gili, Olhuveli Beach & Spa, Vakarufalhi and Kuredu.

Resorts that don't have an accessible house reef will usually provide a couple of boat trips per day to a good snorkelling site nearby, but this is a lot less convenient as you're limited in time and not usually alone. Many resorts offer island-hopping trips or snorkelling excursions that stop at really superb snorkelling sites, and these are a far better option. Full-day excursions usually cost from US$20 to US$30 or so, but are definitely worth it. Kuredu Island resort has the most comprehensive snorkelling programme, with guided snorkelling trips to many interesting sites, including a shipwreck. Sometimes snorkellers can go out with a dive boat, if the dive site is suitable and there's space on the boat.

The whale shark is the largest fish in the world – they regularly reach up to 12m in length and are one of the biggest diving attractions when they cruise the kandus in May.

TOP SNORKELLING SITES

If you stay in a resort with an interesting and accessible house reef, that will probably be your main snorkelling site. You can visit the same reef again and again, and get to know its nooks and crannies, its resident fish and its regular visitors.

A resort excursion can take you to the best snorkelling sites in your atoll, and if you're on a live-aboard safari boat you'll have an unlimited choice. The best snorkelling sites are also dive sites, with a lot of interest in the shallower water. Fit and experienced snorkellers can free-dive to 5m or more without too much trouble, and if the visibility is good they can appreciate any features down to about 10m. Many of the dive sites described in this book are also excellent for snorkelling.

PREPARATION

If you've never tried snorkelling before, you'll soon pick it up. Many resorts give brief snorkelling lessons free of charge in swimming pools or in shallow parts of the lagoon. Every resort will have snorkelling equipment that you can rent, but this will cost US$5 to US$10 per day (although less by the week and free at smarter resorts). It's definitely better to have your own. It's also cheaper in the long run and you can be sure that it suits you and fits properly. You can buy good-quality equipment at reasonable prices at the airport shop and in Male'. Most resort shops sell them too, but the range is smaller and the prices are higher. Ideally, you should bring your own set from home.

Mask

Human eyes won't normally focus in water, but a face mask keeps an air space in front of your eyes so that you can focus under water. Any mask, no matter how cheap, should have a shatterproof lens. Ensure that it fits you comfortably – press it gently onto your face, breathe in through your nose a little, and the suction should hold the mask on your face.

If you're short-sighted you can get the mask lens ground to your optical prescription, but this is expensive. Alternatively, get a stick-on optical lens to attach to the inside of the mask lens, or simply fold up an old pair of spectacles and wedge them inside the mask. There's no problem with contact lenses under the mask, although theoretically they can be lost if the mask is flooded.

Snorkel

The tube has to be long enough to reach above the surface of the water, but should not be either too long or too wide. If it is too big then you have more water to expel when you come to the surface. Also, each breath out leaves a snorkel full of used air, and if the snorkel is too big, you will rebreathe a larger proportion of carbon dioxide.

Fins

These are not absolutely necessary, but they make swimming easier and let you dive deeper, and they give a margin of safety in currents. Fins either fit completely over your foot or have an open back with an adjustable strap around your heel, designed for use with wetsuit boots.

Shirt

A Lycra swim shirt or thin wetsuit top will protect against sunburn and minor scratches from the coral or rocks. Even a T-shirt will give some sun protection – sunburn is a real hazard – but don't use a favourite as the sea water won't do the fabric any favours, unless you're going for that distressed look.

SNORKELLING SAFELY

Don't snorkel alone, and always let someone else know where and when you'll be snorkelling. Colourful equipment or clothing will make you more visible. Beware of strong currents or rough conditions – wind chop and large swells can make snorkelling uncomfortable, or even dangerous. In open waters, carry a safety balloon and whistle to alert boats to your presence.

'For keen divers, a safari trip is a great way to get in a lot of dives at a variety of sites, and it will probably work out cheaper than a resort-based dive trip.'

DIVING

Taking the proper plunge into the deep blue is the most exciting thing imaginable and the rewards massive, especially in the Maldives, which is rightly known as a world-class scuba diving destination. The enormous variety of fish life is amazing, and there's a good chance you'll see some of the biggest marine creatures – a close encounter with a giant manta or a 2m Napoleon wrasse is unforgettable, and the friendly sharks of the Maldives are legendary.

Combine this with warm water, visibility reliably over 25m and professional dive centres, and you'll know why divers come back again and again.

DIVING SAFARIS

On a diving safari, a dozen or so divers cruise the atolls in a live-aboard boat fitted out for the purpose. You can stop at your pick of the dive sites, visit uninhabited islands and local villages, find secluded anchorages and sleep in a compact cabin. If you've had enough diving, you can fish, snorkel or swim off the boat.

Generally, bigger boats are more comfortable, more fully equipped and more expensive. For keen divers, a safari trip is a great way to get in a lot of dives at a variety of sites, and it will probably work out cheaper than a resort-based dive trip. See p58 for general information about cruises and choosing a safari boat.

Everyone on a diving safari should be a qualified diver. If you need to do a diving course, contact the boat operator in advance (you may need a minimum of two to four people for a course). Dive clubs can often get together enough members to fill a safari boat and design a programme and itinerary that suits their needs. Ideally, everyone on board should be of a similar diving standard.

A diving safari should have a separate dhoni that has the compressor and most of the equipment on board. This means that compressor noise doesn't disturb passengers at night, and the smaller boat can be used for excursions near shallow reefs. All dive safari boats will have tanks and weights, and they'll be included in the cost of dives. Regulators, buoyancy control devices (BCDs), depth gauges, tank pressure gauges and dive computers are available on most boats for an additional charge. It's best to bring your own mask, snorkel, fins and wetsuit. Ask about the availability of specialised equipment such as cameras, lights and nitrox. A video player is good for entertainment and playing back dive videos. Facilities for recharging camera batteries are handy. Check www.visitmaldives.com for reasonably up-to-date details on what each boat provides.

For safety, every dive-safari boat should have oxygen equipment, a first-aid kit and good radio and telephone communications with Male'. The divemasters should give thorough predive briefings and emergency plans, have a check list of every diver and do a roll call after each dive. It's good to have descent lines and drift lines available for use in strong currents, and to be able to hang a safety tank at 5m for deeper dives. Night diving requires powerful lights, including a strobe light.

WHERE TO DIVE

There are hundreds of recognised and named dive sites, and dozens accessible from nearly every resort. Many of the best dives are described in detail in Lonely Planet's *Diving & Snorkeling Maldives*. In general there are four types of dive sites in the Maldives.

Reef Dives

The edges of a reef, where it slopes into deep water, are the most interesting part of a reef to dive. Inner-reef slopes, in the sheltered waters inside an atoll, are generally easier dives and feature numerous smaller reef fish. Hard corals on inner-reef slopes were badly damaged by bleaching, but are growing back at various rates. The reef around a resort island is known as its 'house reef', and only the guests of that resort are allowed to dive or snorkel on it.

At some resorts qualified divers can do unguided dives on the house reef. This is cheaper and more convenient than a boat dive, and gives divers a chance to get really well acquainted with the reef. House reefs

The whale shark is an evolutionary oddity, skipping almost the whole food chain to ensure its survival: despite being the biggest fish in the water, it feeds solely on plankton.

can be terrific for night dives too. See p49 for more on the resorts with the best house reefs.

Reef	Atoll	Reef type
Banana Reef	North Male'	reef & kandu
Devana Kandu	Vaavu	kandu & thila
Embudhoo Express	South Male'	kandu
Fotteyo	Vaavu	kandu
Fushifaru Thila	Lhaviyani	thila kandu
Kuda Giri	South Male'	giri & wreck
Kuda Kandu	Addu	kandu
Kuredhoo Express	Lhaviyani	kandu
Lion's Head	North Male'	outer-reef slope
Maa Kandu	Addu	kandu & reef
Macro Spot	Dhaal	giri
Manta Reef	Ari	reef & kandu
Milaidhoo Reef	Baa	kandu
Orimas Thila	Ari	thila
Panetone	Ari	kandu
Rakeedhoo Kandu	Vaavu	kandu
Rasdhoo Madivar	Ari	outer-reef slope
Two Brothers	Faafu	giri
Vaadhoo Caves	South Male'	kandu

Outer-reef slopes, where the atoll meets the open sea, often have interesting terraces, overhangs and caves, and are visited by pelagics. Visibility is usually good, but surf and currents can make for a demanding dive.

Kandus

These are channels between islands, reefs or atolls. Obviously, kandus are subject to currents and this provides an environment in which attractive soft corals thrive. Water inside an atoll is a breeding ground for plankton, and where this water flows out through a kandu into the open sea, the rich supply of plankton attracts large animals such as manta rays and whale sharks. During the southwest monsoon (May to November), currents will generally flow out of an atoll through kandus on the eastern side, while in the northeast monsoon (December to March), the outward flow is on the western side.

Thilas & Giris

A thila is a coral formation that rises steeply from the atoll floor and reaches to between 5m and 15m of the water surface – often it's a spectacular underwater mountain that divers fly around like birds. The top of a thila can be rich in reef fish and coral, while the steep sides have crannies, caves and overhangs, which provide shelter for many small fish, and larger fish come, in turn, to feed on the smaller fish.

A giri is a coral formation that rises to just below the water surface. It has many of the same features as a thila, but the top surface may be too shallow to dive.

Thilas and giris are found inside kandus, where the nutrient-rich currents promote soft-coral growth. They also stand in the sheltered waters inside an atoll, where the sea is warmer and slower moving. Hard-coral structures on sheltered thilas and giris suffered most from the 1998 coral bleaching, and have been the slowest to recover.

Wrecks

While many ships have foundered on Maldivian reefs over the centuries, there are few accessible wrecks with any historical interest. Most were on outer-reef slopes and broke up in the surf long ago, leaving remnants to be dispersed and covered in coral. Any wreck sites of historical significance will require special permission to dive. The wrecks you can dive at are mostly inside the atolls and not very old. They are interesting for the coral and other marine life that colonises the hulk within just a few years. Quite a few of the wrecks have been sunk deliberately, to provide an attraction for divers.

TOP DIVING SITES

Some of the better-known dive sites are described in the chapters covering each atoll and marked on the maps. For examples of the different types of dive sites, look up the following.

'If you're at all serious about diving, you should do an open-water course.'

Dive	Atoll	Dive type	Page
British Loyalty	Addu	wreck	168
Dhidhdhoo Beyru	Ari	outer reef	138
Embudhoo Express	South Male'	kandu	128
Fish Head	Ari	thila & giri	137
Guraidhoo Kandu	South Male'	kandu	128
Halaveli Wreck	Ari	wreck	137
Helengeli Thila	North Male'	thila & giri	107
HP Reef	North Male'	thila & giri	107
Kakani Thila	North Male'	thila	153
Maa Kandu & Kuda Kandu	Addu	kandu	168
Maayafushi Thila	Ari	thila & giri	137
Bodu Hithi Thila	North Male'	thila	107
Shark Point	Addu	outer reef	168

DIVING SEASONS

January to April are generally considered the best months for diving, and should have fine weather and good visibility. May and June can have unstable weather – storms and cloudy days are common until September. October and November tend to have calmer, clearer weather, but visibility can be slightly reduced because of abundant plankton in the water. Some divers like this period because many large fish, such as whale sharks and mantas, come into the channels to feed on the plankton. December can have rough, windy weather and rain.

LEARNING TO DIVE

Diving is not difficult, but it requires knowledge and care, and a lot of experience before you can safely dive independently. It doesn't require great strength or fitness although if you can do things with minimum expenditure of energy, your tank of air will last longer. An experienced diver will use much less air than a beginner. Women often have an advantage because they don't breathe as much air as men.

There's a range of courses, from an introductory dive in a pool or lagoon, to an open-water course that gives an internationally recognised qualification (usually PADI). Beyond that, there are advanced and speciality courses, and courses that lead to divemaster and instructor qualifications. Courses in the Maldives are not a bargain, but they're no more expensive than learning at home and this way you are assured of high standards, good equipment and extremely pleasant conditions. On the other hand, if you do a course at home you'll have more time for diving when you get to the Maldives.

We recommend all learner divers do an open-water referral course in their home country (ie all the theory and basics in the pool), allowing you to complete the course in the Maldives in just two days rather than the four or five needed for the full course. After all, you didn't fly half way around the world to sit in a room watching a PADI CD-ROM, did you? If you do this, ensure you have all your certification from the referral course with you, otherwise you'll have to start from scratch.

An introductory dive, including equipment, will cost about US$30, which is sometimes credited towards a proper course if you decide to do so. Some resorts offer a free introductory dive to get you in.

If you're at all serious about diving, you should do an open-water course. This requires nine dives, usually five in sheltered water and four in open water, as well as classroom training and completion of a multiple-choice test. The cost in the Maldives is from US$450 to US$650. Sometimes the price is all-inclusive, but there are often a few extra charges – US$12 for each boat trip, US$50 for equipment hire, US$80 for logbooks, certificates, dive tables, course materials, 10% service charge etc. These can really add up. You could do the course in as little as five days, or take your time and spread it over a week or two. Don't try it on a one-week package – transfers and jet lag will take a day or so, and you shouldn't dive less than 24 hours before a plane flight. Besides, you'll want to do some recreational dives to try out your new skills.

The next stage is an advanced open-water course, which will involve five dives (including one night dive), and will cost from US$280 to US$400, depending on the dive school. Then there are the speciality courses in night diving, rescue diving, wreck diving, nitrox diving and so on.

Dive Schools & Operators

Every resort has a professional diving operation and can run courses for beginners, as well as dive trips and courses that will challenge even the most experienced diver. The government requires that all dive operations maintain high standards, and all of them are affiliated with one or more of the international diving accreditation organisations – most are with diving behemoth PADI.

Certificates

When you complete an open-water course, you receive a certificate that is recognised by diving operators all over the world. Certificates in the Maldives are generally issued by the Professional Association of Diving Instructors (PADI), the largest and the best-known organisation, but certificates from Confédération Mondiale des Activités Subaquatiques (CMAS; World Underwater Federation), Scuba Schools International (SSI) and a number of other organisations are quite acceptable.

EQUIPMENT

Dive schools in the Maldives can rent out all diving gear, but most divers prefer to have at least some of their own equipment. It's best to have your own mask, snorkel and fins, which you can also use for snorkelling. The tank and weight belt are always included in the cost of a dive, so you don't need to bring them – sealed tanks are prohibited on aircraft anyway, and

'It's best to have your own mask, snorkel and fins, which you can also use for snorkelling.'

you'd be crazy to carry lead weights. The main pieces of diving equipment to bring with you are described in the following sections.

Wetsuit

The water may be warm (27°C to 30°C) but a wetsuit is often preferable for comfortable diving. A 3mm suit should be adequate, but 5mm is preferable if you want to go deep or dive more than once per day. Some resorts don't have a good selection of wetsuits for rental, so this is a good item to bring if you can. When dive centres say 'full equipment rental', that doesn't usually include a wetsuit. Renting a suit will cost about US$5 per day. It's possible to dive in a T-shirt if you don't feel the cold too much.

Regulator

Many divers have their own regulator, with which they are familiar and therefore confident about using, and a 'reg' is not cumbersome to carry. Rental will cost from US$3 to US$7 per dive.

> 'The cost of diving varies between resorts, and depends on whether you need to rent equipment.'

Buoyancy Control Device

These are readily available for hire, costing US$3 to US$7 per dive, but bring your own if possible.

Depth Gauge, Tank Pressure Gauge & Timer

These are usually available too, but if you have them, bring them.

Dive Computer

Universally used over dive tables, these are now compulsory in the Maldives. They're available for rent, for US$4 to US$7 per dive.

Logbook

You'll need this to indicate to divemasters your level of experience, and to record your latest dives. You can usually buy them for around US$10 at dive schools.

Other items you might need are an underwater torch (especially for cave and night dives), waterproof camera, compass and safety buoy or balloon, most of which are available for rental. Some things you won't need are a spear gun, which is prohibited, and diving gloves, which are discouraged since you're not supposed to touch anything anyway.

DIVING COSTS

The cost of diving varies between resorts, and depends on whether you need to rent equipment. A single dive, with only tank and weights supplied, runs from US$30 to US$70, but is generally around US$35 or US$40 (night dives cost more). If you need to rent a regulator and a BCD as well, a dive will cost from US$40 to US$80. Sometimes the full equipment price includes mask, snorkel, fins, dive computer and pressure gauge, but they can cost extra. A package of 10 dives will cost roughly from US$250 to US$350, or US$350 to US$450 with equipment rental. Other possibilities are five-, 12- and 15-dive packages, and packages that allow you as many dives as you want within a certain number of consecutive days. In addition to the dive cost, there is a charge for using a boat – about US$12 for half a day, US$20 for a full day. There may also be a service charge of 10% if diving is billed to your room.

If you plan to do 10 dives in a week, budget around US$600, perhaps US$100 or US$150 less if you bring all your own equipment.

DIVING HEALTH & SAFETY
Health Requirements
Officially, a doctor should check you over before you do a course, and fill out a form full of diving health questions (see p187). In practice, most dive schools will let you dive or do a course if you're under 50 years old and complete a medical questionnaire, but the checkup is still a good idea. This is especially so if you have any problem at all with your breathing, ears or sinuses. If you are an asthmatic, have any other chronic breathing difficulties, or any inner-ear problems you shouldn't do any scuba diving.

Diving Safely
In the Maldives the dive base will ensure you are aware of the following points to ensure a safe and enjoyable experience, whether scuba diving, skin diving or snorkelling:

- If you are scuba diving, you must possess a current diving certification card from a recognised scuba diving instructional agency. The resort dive base will check your card and provide training if you need it. A check dive is often required.
- Be sure you are healthy and feel comfortable diving.
- Obtain reliable information about physical and environmental conditions at the dive site. The dive base will always provide this.
- Be aware of local laws, regulations and etiquette about marine life and the environment.
- Dive only at sites within your experience level.

Be aware that underwater conditions vary significantly from one site to another. Seasonal changes can significantly alter any site and dive conditions. These differences influence the way divers dress for a dive and what diving techniques they use.

'Be aware that underwater conditions vary significantly from one site to another.'

The following laws apply to recreational diving in the Maldives, and divemasters should enforce them:

- Maximum depth is 30m – this is the law in the Maldives.
- Maximum time is 60 minutes.
- No decompression dives.
- Each diver must carry a dive computer.
- Obligatory three-minute safety stop at 5m.
- Last dive no later than 12 hours before a flight.

Decompression Sickness
This is a very serious condition – usually, though not always, associated with diver error. The most common symptoms are unusual fatigue or weakness; skin itch; pain in the arms, legs (joints or mid-limb) or torso; dizziness and vertigo; local numbness, tingling or paralysis; and shortness of breath. Signs may also include a blotchy skin rash, a tendency to favour an arm or a leg, staggering, coughing spasms, collapse or unconsciousness. These symptoms and signs can occur individually, or a number of them can appear at one time.

The most common causes of decompression sickness (or 'the bends' as it is commonly known) are diving too deep, staying at depth for too long, or ascending too quickly. This results in nitrogen coming out of solution in the blood and forming bubbles, most commonly in the bones and particularly in the joints or in weak spots such as healed fracture sites.

Other factors contributing to decompression sickness include excess body fat; heavy exertion prior to, during and after diving; injuries and illness; dehydration; alcohol; cold water, hot showers or baths after diving; carbon dioxide increase (eg through smoking); and age.

Avoid flying after diving, as it causes nitrogen to come out of the blood even faster than it would at sea level. No resort in the Maldives will allow you to dive less than 24 hours before a flight. Low-altitude flights, like a seaplane transfer to the airport, may be just as dangerous because the aircraft are not pressurised. There are various opinions about the risks and the time required to minimise them – a lot depends on the frequency, depth and duration of dives over several days before the flight. Seek the advice of an instructor when planning the dives during the final few days of your stay, and try to finish up with shallow dives.

Even if you take all the necessary precautions, there is no guarantee that you will not be hit by the bends. It's a diver's responsibility to be aware of their own condition, and that of their diving buddy, after a dive.

The only treatment for decompression sickness is to put the patient into a recompression chamber. That puts a person back under pressure similar to that of the depth at which they were diving so nitrogen bubbles can be reabsorbed. The time required in the chamber is usually three to eight hours. The treatment is usually effective, with the main problem being caused by delay in getting the patient to the chamber. If you think that you, or anyone else you are diving with, are suffering from the bends, get to a recompression chamber as soon as possible; there are two in the Maldives, at Bandos and Kuramathi resorts.

'Visitors must do their best to ensure that their activities don't spoil the experience of those who will come in the future.'

Ear Problems
Many divers experience pain in the ears after diving, which is commonly caused by failure of the ears to compensate properly for changes in pressure. The problem will usually fix itself, but injuries are often caused when people try to treat themselves by poking cotton buds or other objects into the ear.

Emergencies
The **Divers Alert Network** (DAN; in USA ☎ 919-684-8111; www.diversalertnetwork.org) operates a 24-hour diving emergency hotline in the USA. **DAN Maldives** (☎ 6640088) is based at Bandos resort, on North Male' Atoll, where there's a recompression chamber and a complete divers health service. There's also a new recompression facility and fully staffed diving clinic at **Kuramathi** (☎ 6660527), in Rasdhoo Atoll at the far north of Ari Atoll. They are both commercial facilities.

Insurance
In addition to normal travel insurance, it's a very good idea to take out specific diving cover, which will pay for evacuation to a recompression facility and the cost of hyperbaric treatment in a chamber. Evacuation would normally be by chartered speedboat or seaplane (both very expensive). Recompression treatment can cost thousands of dollars, especially since time required in the chamber could reach eight hours.

Some dive operations insist on diving insurance, or will provide it for about US$10 for three weeks. Others may include the coverage in their rates.

DAN (www.diveralertnetwork.org) can be contacted through most dive shops and clubs, and it offers a DAN TravelAssist policy that provides evacuation and recompression coverage.

MARINE ENVIRONMENT PROTECTION

The waters of the Maldives may seem pristine but, like everywhere, development and commercial activities can have adverse effects on the marine environment. The Maldivian government recognises that the underwater world is a major attraction, and has imposed many restrictions and controls on fishing, coral mining and tourism operations. Twenty-five Protected Marine Areas have been established, and these are subject to special controls.

You'll find dive operators throughout the country are overwhelmingly conservation-minded too, which is a fantastic development. Diving techniques have been modified to protect the environment, and operators now use drift diving or tie mooring ropes by hand rather than drop anchors. The practice of feeding fish has been abandoned, and most operators are careful to ensure that unskilled divers are not taken on dives where they may accidentally damage coral.

Visitors must do their best to ensure that their activities don't spoil the experience of those who will come in the future. The following rules are generally accepted as necessary for conservation, and most of them apply equally to snorkellers and divers.

- Do not use anchors on the reef, and take care not to ground boats on coral. Encourage dive operators and regulatory bodies to establish permanent moorings at popular dive sites.
- Avoid touching living marine organisms with your body or dragging equipment across the reef. Polyps can be damaged by even the gentlest contact. Handling fish can remove the slimy coating that protects the animal's skin.
- Never stand on corals, even if they look solid and robust. If you must hold on, to prevent being swept away in a current, hold on to dead coral.
- Be conscious of your fins. Even without contact the surge from heavy fin strokes near the reef can damage delicate organisms. When treading water in shallow reef areas, take care not to kick up clouds of sand. Settling sand can easily smother the delicate organisms of the reef.
- Collecting lobster or shellfish is prohibited, as is spearfishing. Removing any coral or shells, living or dead, is against the law. All shipwreck sites are protected by law.
- Take home all your rubbish and any litter you may find as well. Plastics in particular are a serious threat to marine life. Turtles can mistake plastic for jellyfish and eat it. Don't throw cigarette butts overboard.
- Resist the temptation to feed fish. You may disturb their normal eating habits, encourage aggressive behaviour or feed them food that is detrimental to their health.
- Minimise your disturbance of marine animals. Chasing, grabbing or attempting to ride on turtles, mantas or any large marine animal can frighten them and deter them from visiting a dive site.
- Practise and maintain proper buoyancy control. Major damage can be done by divers descending too fast and colliding with the reef. Make sure you are correctly weighted and that your weight belt is positioned so that you stay horizontal. If you have not dived for a while, have a practice dive in a pool or lagoon before taking to the reef.
- Take great care in underwater caves. Spend as little time within them as possible as your air bubbles may be caught within the roof and thereby leave previously submerged organisms high and dry. Taking turns to inspect the interior of a small cave will lessen the chances of damaging contact.

'It's true that coral bleaching killed nearly all of the hard coral in the Maldives, but that's not the end of the story.'

BACK FROM THE BLEACHING

It's true that coral bleaching killed nearly all of the hard coral in the Maldives, but that's not the end of the story. In a few places old coral has unaccountably survived, and you can occasionally be surprised by a big-table coral or a long-branching staghorn. Soft corals and sea fans were less affected by coral bleaching and have regrown more quickly. Magnificent soft-coral gardens thrive at many dive sites, especially around channels that are rich with water-borne nutrients, and a few fine specimens can be seen at snorkelling depths on many house reefs.

The underlying hard-coral structure is still there of course – new coral grows on the skeletons of its predecessors. The healthiest living coral has many metres, perhaps kilometres, of dead coral underneath. New coral is growing on reefs all over the Maldives, though the large and elaborately shaped formations will take many years to build. It's fascinating to observe the new coral growth – the distinctly coloured patches with the finely textured surface of a living, growing organism. The first regrowth often occurs in crevices on old coral blocks, where it's protected from munching parrotfish. The massive Porites-type corals seem to come first, but they grow slowly – look for blobs of yellow, blue or purple that will eventually cover the whole block in a crust or a cushion or a brainlike dome. The branching corals (Acropora) appear as little purplish trees on a coral block, like a pale piece of broccoli. Growing a few centimetres per year (15cm in ideal conditions), they will eventually become big, extended staghorn corals or wide, flat-topped tables.

The recovery for coral is not uniform. Some parts of a reef can be doing very well, with 80% or 90% of the old surfaces covered with new and growing coral, while 100m along the same reef, new coral growth cover is less than 20%. Reef formation is a very complex natural process, but surprisingly the marine ecosystem as a whole seems to be undamaged by the coral bleaching. Fish life is as abundant and diverse as ever.

The sea snake is an air-breathing reptile with venom 20 times stronger than any snake on land. Basically, don't touch them if you're lucky enough to see any!

FISH-SPOTTER'S GUIDE

You don't have to be a hardcore diver to enjoy the rich marine life of the Maldives. You'll see an amazing variety just snorkelling, walking in the shallows, peering off the end of a jetty. This guide will help you identify a few of the most colourful and conspicuous varieties; see the colour pictures from p74. A point to remember is that even within the same species, colour and patterning can vary greatly over a fish's life cycle, as well as according to gender.

For a comprehensive online guide to the fish of the Maldives, visit www.popweb.com/maldive.

Angelfish

Of the many species, there are 14 in the Maldives, mostly seen in shallow water, though some inhabit reef slopes down to 20m. They can be seen individually or in small groups. Small species are around 10cm, the largest around 35cm. They feed on sponges and algae. Regal (or empress) angelfish have bright yellow bodies with vertical dark blue and white stripes. The emperor, or imperial, angelfish (p75) are larger (to 35cm) and live in deeper water, with almost horizontal blue-and-yellow lines and a dark blue mask and gill markings; juveniles are quite different in shape and markings. The shy blue-faced angelfish (p75) also change colour dramatically as they age.

(Continued on page 77)

Clown triggerfish (p79)

Black-footed anemonefish (p77)

Blue-striped snapper (p78)

Moorish idol (p77)

Vermillion rock cod (p78)

Bicolour parrotfish (p77)

Grey reef shark (p78)

Previous page: Searching for waves on a surfing safari (p82)

MICHAEL AW

Black-spotted stingray (p78)

PHOTOLIBRARY

Flutemouth (p77)

CASEY & ASTRID WITTE MAHANEY

Powder-blue surgeonfish (p78)

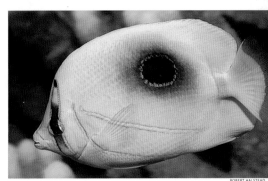
ROBERT HALSTEAD

Bennett's butterflyfish (p77)

CASEY & ASTRID WITTE MAHANEY

Emperor angelfish (p72)

MICHAEL AW

Oriental sweetlips (p77)

CASEY & ASTRID WITTE MAHANEY

Blue-faced angelfish (p72)

CASEY & ASTRID WITTE MAHANEY

Bignose unicornfish (p79)

CASEY & ASTRID WITTE MAHANEY

Napoleonfish (p79)

MICHAEL AW

The pelagic hawksbill turtle (p39) swims in the channels for food

CASEY & ASTRID WITTE MAHANEY

Both hard and soft corals (p40) live in the Maldivian atolls

Swim with a whale shark (p42), the world's largest fish species

CASEY & ASTRID WITTE MAHANEY

(Continued from page 72)

Butterflyfish

There are over 30 species in the Maldives; they are common in shallow waters and reef slopes, singly, in pairs or small schools. Species vary in size from 12cm to 30cm, when mature, with a flattened body shape and elaborate markings. Various species of this carnivorous fish have specialised food sources, including anemones, coral polyps, algae and assorted invertebrate prey. Bennett's butterflyfish (p75), bright yellow and 18cm long, is one of several species with a 'false eye' near the tail to make predators think it's a larger fish facing the other way. Spotted butterflyfish, which grow to 10cm long, are camouflaged with dark polka dots and a dark band across its real eye.

Anemonefish

Maldives anemonefish (p74) are indigenous to the Maldives. They are around 11cm, orange, dusky orange or yellow, with differences in face colour and the shape and thickness of the head bar marking. Their mucous coating protects them from the venomous tips of sea anemone tentacles, allowing them to hide from predators among the anemones' tentacles. In return for this protection, they warn the anemones of the approach of fish such as butterflyfish, which feed on the tentacle tips. Juveniles are lighter in colour than adults, and have greyish or blackish pelvic fins.

> Anemonefish are so called as they cover themselves in a special mucous from the anemone, which protects them from its sting.

Flutemouth

One species of flutemouth (or cornetfish; p75) is very common in shallow waters in the Maldives, often occurring in small schools. They are very slender, elongated fish, usually around 60cm in length, but deep-sea specimens grow up to 1.5m. Flutemouths eat small fish, often stalking prey by swimming behind a harmless herbivore. The silver colouring seems almost transparent in the water, and it can be hard to spot flutemouths even in shallow sandy lagoons.

Moorish Idol

One species of moorish idol (p74) is commonly seen on reef flats and reef slopes in the Maldives, often in pairs. Usually 15cm to 20cm long, the moorish idol is herbivorous, feeding primarily on algae. They are attractive, with broad vertical yellow-and-black bands, pointed snouts, and long, streamer-like extensions to the upper dorsal fin.

Sweetlips

Only a few of the many species are found in the Maldives, where they inhabit outer-reef slopes. Some species grow up to 1m, but most are between 50cm and 75cm; juveniles are largely herbivorous, feeding on algae, plankton and other small organisms; older fish hunt and eat smaller fish. Oriental sweetlips (p75), which grow to 50cm, are superb-looking with horizontal dark and light stripes, dark spots on fins and tail, and large, lugubrious lips. Brown sweetlips are generally bigger, duller and more active at night.

> Young male anemonefish living within the anemone are under the control of a single dominant female. When she dies the largest male fish changes sex and replaces her as the dominant female.

Parrotfish

More than 20 of the many parrotfish species are found in the Maldives – they include some of the most conspicuous and commonly seen reef fish. The largest species grow to more than a metre, but those around 50cm long are more typical. Most parrotfish feed on algae and other organisms growing on and around a hard-coral structure. With strong, beaklike

mouths they scrape and bite the coral surface, then grind up the coral
chunks, swallowing and filtering to extract nutrients. Snorkellers often
hear the scraping, grinding sound of parrotfish eating coral, and notice
the clouds of coral-sand faeces that parrotfish regularly discharge. Colour,
pattern and even sex can change as parrotfish mature – juveniles and females are often drab, while mature males can have brilliant blue-green designs. Bicolour parrotfish (p74) start life white with a broad orange stripe,
but the mature males (up to 90cm) are a beautiful blue with hot-pink
highlights on the scale edges, head, fins and tail. Green-face parrotfish
grow to 60cm, with the adult male identified by its blue-green body, bright
green 'face' and white marks on fins and tail. Heavybeak (or steephead)
parrotfish can be 70cm long, and have a distinctive rounded head.

Snapper

There are 28 species of snapper that have been documented in the Maldives, mostly in deep water. Small species are around 20cm and the largest
grow to 1m (snapper, themselves carnivorous, are popular with anglers
as a fighting fish, and are excellent to eat). Blue-striped snapper (p74),
commonly seen in schools near inshore reefs, are an attractive yellow
with blue-white horizontal stripes. Red snapper (or red bass) are often
seen in lagoons.

Rock Cod

Hundreds of species are currently classified as Serranidae, including rock
cod and groper which are common around reefs. Smaller species reach
20cm; many larger species grow to 50cm and some to over a metre. Rock
cod are carnivorous, feeding on smaller fish and invertebrates. Vermillion rock cod (or coral groper; p74) are often seen in shallow waters and
near the coral formations in which they hide; they are a brilliant crimson
colour covered with blue spots, up to 40cm long.

Male sharks show their
interest in females by
biting them on the sides,
often causing wounds,
even though the female
shark skin has evolved to
be thicker than the male
equivalent!

Stingray

Several species, such as the black-spotted stingray (p75) are often seen
in very shallow water on the sandy bed of a lagoon where they are often
well camouflaged. Most rays seen inshore are juveniles, up to about
50cm across; mature rays can be over a metre across, and maybe 2m
long including the whiplike tail. A barbed and venomous spine on top
of the tail can swing up and forward, and will deliver a painful injury to
anyone who stands on it.

Reef shark

Several smaller shark species frequent reef flats and reef edges inside Maldivian atolls, often in schools, while larger pelagic species congregate around
channels in the atoll rim at certain times of the year. Most reef species are
small, typically 1m to 2m. Reef sharks hunt small fish (attacks on swim-
mers and divers are almost unknown). White-tips grow from 1m to 2m
long and have white tips on dorsal fins. They are often seen in schools of
10 or more in the sandy shallows of a lagoon. Black-tips, distinguished by
tips on dorsal fins and tail, grow to 2m. Grey reef sharks (p74) are thicker
in the midsection and have a white trailing edge on the dorsal fin.

Surgeonfish

The surgeonfish are so named for the tiny scalpel-sharp blades that are
found on the sides of their bodies, near their tails. When they are threatened they will swim beside the intruder swinging their tails to inflict

cuts, and can cause nasty injuries. Over 20 species of surgeon, including the powder-blue surgeon (p75), are found in the Maldives, often in large schools. The adults range from 20cm to 60cm. All species graze for algae on the sea bottom or on coral surfaces.

Triggerfish

There are over a dozen species in the Maldives, on outer-reef slopes and also in shallower reef environments. Small species grow to around 25cm and the largest species to over 75cm. Triggerfish are carnivorous. Orange-striped triggerfish (30cm) are common in shallow reef waters. Titan triggerfish have yellow and dark-brown crisscross patterning, grow up to 75cm and can be aggressive, especially when defending eggs, and will charge at divers. The clown triggerfish (up to 40cm; p74) is easily recognised by its conspicuous colour pattern with large, round, white blotches on the lower half of the body.

Male and female shark populations live in same-sex groups and rarely meet, save for mating.

Unicornfish

From the same family as the surgeonfish, unicornfish grow from 40cm to 75cm long (only males of some species have the horn for which the species is named), and are herbivores. Spotted unicornfish are very common blue-grey or olive-brown fish with narrow dotted vertical markings (males can change their colours for display, and exhibit a broad white vertical band); their prominent horns get longer with age. Bignose unicornfish (or Vlaming's unicorn; p75) have only a nose bump for a horn.

Wrasse

Some 60 species of this large and very diverse family can be found, some on reefs, others on sandy lagoon floors, others in open water. The smallest wrasse species are only 10cm; the largest over 2m. Most wrasse are carnivores; larger wrasse will hunt and eat small fish. Napoleonfish (also called Napoleon wrasse and humphead wrasse; p75) are the largest wrasse species, often seen around wrecks and outer-reef slopes; they are generally green with fine vertical patterning. Large males have a humped head.

Moon wrasse, about 25cm, live in shallow waters and reef slopes, where adult males are beautifully coloured in green with pink patterning and a yellow marking on the tail. Cleaner wrasse have a symbiotic relationship with larger fish, which allows the wrasse to eat the small parasites and food scraps from their mouths, gills and skin surface. At certain times, large numbers of pelagic species congregate at 'cleaning stations' where cleaner wrasse abound – a great sight for divers.

SURFING

Surfing has been slow to take off in the Maldives, but its popularity is on the increase, especially since the O'Neil Deep Blue Contest was held at Lohifushi in 2005. There's some great surf throughout the country although only a few breaks are in the tourism zone, and they are only surfable from March to November. Surfers have a choice of basing themselves at a resort and taking a boat to nearby breaks, or arranging a liveaboard safari cruise. In either case, make arrangements in advance with a reputable surf travel operator who knows the area well. The Maldives is definitely not the sort of place where a surfer can just turn up and head for the waves.

The period of the southwest monsoon (May to November) generates the best waves, but March and April are also good and have the best weather. June can have bad weather and storms, and is not great for boat trips, but it is also a time for big swells. The best breaks occur on the outer reefs on the southeast sides of the atolls, but only where a gap in the reef allows the waves to wrap around.

Surfing in the Maldives was pioneered by Tony Hussein (also known as Tony Hinde), a Sydney surfer who was shipwrecked in the Maldives in the early 1970s. Before the first tourist resorts were opened, he discovered, surfed and named all the main breaks, and had them all to himself for many years. Surfing has caught on with many young Maldivians – check the local surf scene at www.maldivesurf.org.mv.

Guided seaplane surfaris around the Maldives are offered year round by Tropicsurf (www .tropicsurf.net) in Australia. Spot the best surf from the sky, land and you're surfing in minutes.

NORTH MALE' ATOLL

This is where the best-known breaks are, and they can get a bit crowded, especially if there are several safari boats in the vicinity. The following breaks are listed from north to south.

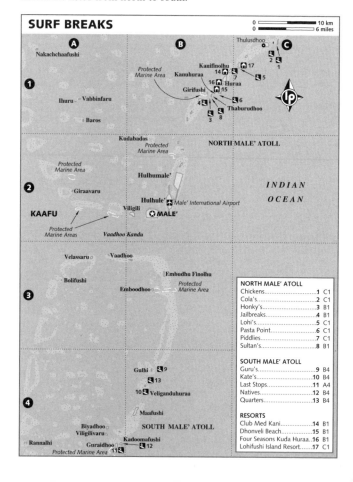

SURF BREAKS

NORTH MALE' ATOLL
Chickens..............................1 C1
Cola's.................................2 C1
Honky's...............................3 B1
Jailbreaks............................4 B1
Lohi's..................................5 C1
Pasta Point..........................6 C1
Piddlies...............................7 C1
Sultan's...............................8 B1

SOUTH MALE' ATOLL
Guru's.................................9 B4
Kate's.................................10 B4
Last Stops...........................11 A4
Natives...............................12 B4
Quarters..............................13 B4

RESORTS
Club Med Kani.....................14 B1
Dhonveli Beach....................15 B1
Four Seasons Kuda Huraa....16 B1
Lohifushi Island Resort.......17 C1

Chickens A left-hander that sections when small, but on a bigger swell and a higher tide it all comes together to make a long and satisfying wave. It's named for the old poultry farm onshore, not because of any reaction to the conditions here.

Cola's A heavy, hollow, shallow right-hander; when it's big, it's one of the best breaks in the area. This is a very thick wave breaking hard over a shallow reef, so it's definitely for experienced, gutsy surfers only. Named for the Coca-Cola factory nearby on the island of Thulusdhoo, it's also called Cokes.

Lohi's A solid left-hander that usually breaks in two sections, but with a big enough swell and a high enough tide the sections link up. You can paddle out there from the resort island of Lohifushi, and guests of that resort have exclusive access to the break.

Piddlies A slow, mellow, mushy right-hander, a good Malibu wave. It's also called Ninja's because of its appeal to Japanese surfers. It's off the island of Kanifinolhu, home of the Club Med Kani resort, but it's very difficult to reach from the shore, and the wave is available to any boat-based surfer, not just Club Med guests.

Pasta Point A perfect left that works like clockwork on all tides. There's a long outside wall at the take-off point, jacking into a bowling section called the 'macaroni bowl'. On big days the break continues to another section called 'lock jaws', which grinds into very shallow water over the reef. It's easily reached from the shore at Dhonveli Beach resort, whose guests have exclusive use of this break. This used to be an all-Italian resort (hence the name of the break), but now it also attracts surfers from all over.

Sultan's This is a classic right-hand break, and the bigger the swell, the better it works. A steep outside peak leads to a super-fast wall and then an inside section that throws right out, and tubes on every wave.

Honky's During its season, this is the best wave in the Maldives. It's a super long, wally left-hander that wraps nearly 90 degrees and can nearly double in size by the end section.

Jailbreaks A right-hander that works best with a big swell, when the three sections combine to make a single, long, perfect wave. There used to be a prison on the island and the surrounding waters were off-limits, but now it's open to surfers.

SOUTH MALE' ATOLL

The breaks in South Male' Atoll are smaller than those in North Male' Atoll and generally more fickle. It will be harder here to find a boatman who really knows the surf scene.

Guru's A nice little left off the island of Gulhi; it can get good sometimes.

Quarters Another small right-hander, rarely more than a metre.

Kate's A small left-hander, rarely more than a metre.

Natives A small right-hander, rarely more than a metre.

Last Stops This is a bowly right-hander breaking over a channel reef. It's a Protected Marine Area, and can get very strong currents when the tides are running.

OUTER ATOLLS

Only a few areas have the right combination of reef topography and orientation to swell and wind direction. Laamu and Addu both have surfable waves on occasions, but they're not reliable enough to be worth a special trip.

Gaaf Dhaal has a series of reliable breaks that are accessed by safari boats in the season. From west to east, the named breaks are Beacons, Castaways, Blue Bowls, Five Islands, Two Ways (also called Twin Peaks; left and right), Love Charms, Antiques and Tiger. They're all outside the tourism zone and can only be visited with permits from Atolls Administration.

RESORT-BASED SURFING

The most accessible surf breaks are in the southeastern part of North Male' Atoll. Half a dozen resorts are within a short boat ride, but only a couple of them cater for surfers by providing regular boat service to the waves.

'The most accessible surf breaks are in the southeastern part of North Male' Atoll.'

Dhonveli Beach (p112) is the resort that's best set up for surfers – the reliable waves of the 'house break', Pasta Point, are just out the back door, while Sultan's and Honky's are close by. A surfside bar provides a great view of the action. Surfing packages at Dhonveli Beach include unlimited boat trips to the other local breaks with surf guides who know the conditions well, leaving and returning on demand. The surf programme is run by Atoll Adventures under the direction of Maldives surf pioneer Tony Hussein and can be booked only through a limited number of surf travel agents.

Lohifushi (p109), a few kilometres northeast of Dhonveli, is a bigger, more expensive resort with more facilities and it also has its own, exclusive surf break at the southern tip of the island. A bar and a viewing terrace overlook the wave, which has hosted international surfing competitions. Most of the rooms are quite a long walk from the surf. Boats to other surf breaks go for three hour sessions, one leaving at about 9am, the other at about 2pm (US$10 per person for three hours, extra hours US$2 per person). Boat trips must be booked by 8pm the day before. Many agents and tour companies sell rooms in Lohifushi.

Club Med Kani (p114) is the other resort island with an adjacent surf break, but you need a boat to reach it from the resort. There's no surfing programme, no surf guides and no boats available for surfers. When Four Seasons Kuda Huraa reopens, it will probably run boat trips to the surf for guests, but surfers should confirm this with the resort.

> 'A one-week inner-atoll surf trip will start at around US$850 per person.'

SURFING SAFARIS

Most of the safari boats in the Maldives claim to do surfing trips, but very few of them have a specialised knowledge of surfing or any experience cruising to the outer atolls. Ideally, a surfing safari boat should have an experienced surf guide, and a second, smaller boat to accompany it, for accessing breaks in shallower water and getting in close to the waves. A surfing safari ('surfari') boat should also be equipped with fishing and snorkelling gear, for when the surf isn't working or you need a rest.

An inner-atolls surfari will just cruise around North Male' Atoll, visiting breaks that are also accessible from resorts in the area. If the swell is big and the surf guide is knowledgeable, the boat may venture down to South Male' Atoll to take advantage of the conditions. A one-week inner-atoll surf trip will start at around US$850 per person. This might be cheaper than resort-based surfing, but it won't be as comfortable, and it won't give access to a handy and uncrowded house break.

An outer-atolls surfari is the only feasible way to surf the remote waves of Gaaf Dhaal – an experienced outer-atoll guide is essential. Ideally, the safari boat should be based in Gaaf Dhaal, and the surfers take an Island Aviation flight to the domestic airport on the island of Kaadedhoo where the boat crew meets them. This requires good coordination and management, but the experienced surfing tour operators have the procedure well organised. They should also have a good relationship with Atolls Administration, so that they can get the necessary permits before you arrive.

You need at least six people to make a safari boat affordable; the surfing specialists should be able to put together the necessary numbers. Don't book into a safari trip that is primarily for diving or cruising. Allow at least two weeks for the trip or you'll spend too much of your time getting to the waves and back. A 10-night surfari will cost from about US$2000 per person, including domestic airfares.

SURF TRAVEL OPERATORS

The following agents specialise in surf travel and book tours and safaris to the Maldives.

Atoll Travel (☎ 1800-622310, 03-5682 1088; www.atolltravel.com; PO Box 205, Foster, Vic 3960, Australia) Australian and international agent for Atoll Adventures. It offers surfing packages to Dhonveli Beach resort, premium surfing safari tours in Male' Atoll and to the outer atolls.

Maldives Scuba Tours (☎ 01449-780220; www.scubascuba.com; Walsham Rd, Finningham, Suffolk, IP14 4JGPH, UK) Maldives dive travel agency and UK agent for Atoll Adventures.

Surf Travel Company (☎ 02-9527 4722; www.surftravel.com.au; PO Box 446, Cronulla, NSW 2230, Australia) Venerable surf travel operator; it books surfers into Lohifushi resort and does boat-based tours in North and South Male' Atolls.

Turquoise Surf Travel (☎ 04 72 44 29 10; www.turquoise-voyages.fr; 8 rue Neuve St Martin, Marseille, France) This agent offers surfing holidays at Lohifushi Island Resort and boat-based surfari trips in Male' Atoll.

World Surfaris (☎ 1800-611163, 07-5444 4011; www.worldsurfaris.com; PO Box 180, Ste 8, 47 Brisbane Rd, Mooloolaba, Qld 4557, Australia) Offering tours to various surfing destinations, it books surfers into Lohifushi Island Resort and also does boat-based trips in the inner atolls.

Food & Drink

Your culinary experience in the Maldives could be, depending on your resort, anything from *haute cuisine* ordered from a menu you've discussed with the chef in advance, to bangers and mash at the all-you-can-eat buffet in the communal dining room. What it's unlikely to be in either case is particularly Maldivian, given the dislocation from local life experienced in resorts. However, anyone staying in Male' or visiting inhabited islands should take advantage of this opportunity to try real Maldivian food (rather than the somewhat fanciful fare produced on Maldivian cuisine nights in resorts, which often owes more to Indian and Sri Lankan cooking than anything local). Maldivian cuisine is unsurprisingly simple and testament to a nation's historic survival on a relatively small, but bountiful, amount of locally occurring ingredients.

Don't be fooled by beer in Male' – it's all nonalcoholic, even if it doesn't look it!

STAPLES & SPECIALITIES

All that grows in the Maldives are coconuts, mangoes, papayas and pineapples; the only other locally occurring product is fish, which explains the simplicity of Maldivian cuisine historically.

However, as trade with the Indian subcontinent, Africa, Arabia and the Far East have always brought influences of a more exciting nature, the result is far less bland than it could be. That said, don't expect to see a Maldivian takeaway open up on a street near you any time soon.

Kavaabu are small deep-fried dough balls with tuna, mashed potato, pepper and lime – a very popular 'short eat'.

The Indian influence is clear in local cuisine above all; Maldivian food is often hot and spicy. If you're going to eat local food, prepare your palate for spicy fish curry, fish soup, fish patties and variations thereof. A favourite Maldivian breakfast is *mas huni*, a healthy mixture of tuna, onion, coconut and chilli, eaten cold with *roshi* (unleavened bread, like an Indian chapati) and tea.

For snacks and light meals, Maldivians like *hedhikaa*, a selection of little finger foods. In homes the *hedhikaa* are placed on the table, and everyone helps themselves. In teashops this is called short eats – a choice of things like *fihunu mas* (fish pieces with chilli coating), *gulha* (fried dough balls filled with fish and spices), *keemia* (fried fish rolls in batter) and *kuli boakiba* (spicy fish cakes). There are also samosa-like triangles of curried vegetables, and even small pizza squares are appearing in teashops now. Sweets include little bowls of *bondi bai* (rice pudding), tiny bananas and *zileybee* (coloured coils of sugared, fried batter). Generally, anything small and brown will be savoury and contain fish, and anything light or brightly coloured will be sweet.

A main meal will include rice or *roshi* or both, plus soups, curries, vegetables, pickles and spicy sauces. In a teashop, a substantial meal with rice and *roshi* is called long eats. The most typical dish is *garudia*, a

---

DOS & DON'TS

■ Always eat with your right hand; your left hand is considered unclean

■ Do ask for a spoon if you aren't comfortable eating with your bare hands Maldivian style; this won't offend.

■ Remember that during Ramazan it's not acceptable to eat in public during daylight hours outside of resorts.

TRAVEL YOUR TASTEBUDS

If you are feeling like trying something both exotic and dear to the Maldivian people, go for *miruhulee boava* (octopus tentacles). This is not commonly found, but is often prepared in the atolls as a speciality, should you be lucky enough to visit an inhabited island as a guest. The tentacles are stripped and cleaned and braised in a sauce of curry leaves, cloves, garlic, chilli, onion, pepper and coconut oil – delicious.

---

soup made from dried and smoked fish, often eaten with rice, lime and chilli. The soup is poured over rice, mixed up by hand and eaten with the fingers. Another common meal is *mas riha*, a fish curry eaten with rice or *roshi* – the *roshi* is torn into strips, mixed on the plate with the curry and condiments, and eaten with the fingers. A cup of tea accompanies the meal, and is usually drunk black and sweet.

The Maldivian equivalent of the after-dinner mint is the areca nut, chewed after a meal or snack. The little oval nuts are sliced into thin sections, some cloves and lime paste are added, the whole lot is wrapped in an areca leaf, and the wad is chewed whole. It's definitely an acquired taste.

DRINKS

The only naturally occurring fresh water in the Maldives is rainwater, which is stored in natural underground aquifers beneath each island. This is quite a feat, and water conservation has always been extremely important in Maldivian culture, to the extent that the Maldives Tourism Law states that no water resources may be diverted from an inhabited island to supply a resort. All resorts have their own desalinating plants to keep visitors supplied with their (by local standards incredibly wasteful) water needs.

In resorts, consider the sheer carbon costs of only drinking imported Evian – even if you can afford to at $5 a bottle – and go for desalinated water, which is perfectly good to drink, if perhaps something of an acquired taste initially.

The main drinks other than rainwater are imported tea and toddy tapped from the crown of the palm trunk at the point where the coconuts grow. Every village has its toddy man *(raa veri)*. The *raa* is sweet and delicious if you can get over the pungent smell. It can be drunk immediately after it is tapped from the tree, or left to become a little alcoholic as the sugar ferments.

Fermented *raa* is of course the closest most Maldivians ever get to alcohol; the Maldives is strictly dry outside of resorts (and Maldivian staff cannot drink alcohol even there). Despite this, nonalcoholic beer is very popular in Male'. Soft drinks, including the world's only Coca-Cola made from salt water anywhere in the world, are available in Male' and in villages, at prices much lower than in resorts. The range of drinks is very limited. Teashops will always serve *bor feng* (drinking water), and of course *sai* (tea). Unless you ask otherwise, tea comes black, with *hakuru* (sugar). *Kiru* (milk) isn't a common drink, and is usually made up from powder.

WHERE TO EAT & DRINK

In most cases you won't have much choice – all resorts have at least one restaurant, typically two or more affording some choice. Buffets (always for breakfast, often for lunch and dinner too) allow for lots of different cuisines and plenty of choice to feature everywhere. In Male', where there's a much broader choice, the most obvious place for authentic Maldivian short eats is in any teashop in the town (see p100). Small

Bis hulavuu is a popular snack – a pastry made from eggs, sugar and ghee and served cold. You may well be invited to try some if you visit an inhabited island.

towns and villages elsewhere will also have teashops and are a great way to sample real Maldivian food.

VEGETARIANS & VEGANS

Vegetarians will have no problem in resorts (although if there's only a set meal rather than a buffet spread, veggies will often be stuck with an unimaginative pasta dish or ratatouille at cheaper resorts). In general, resorts are well prepared for all types of diet, and in better resorts the chef may cook you a dish by request, if what's on offer isn't appealing. Vegans, again, should fare reasonably well – soya milk is on offer in most resorts and the buffet allows each diner to pick and mix. Outside resorts and Male' things won't be so easy – fish dominates menus in the islands, but people will make an enormous effort to accommodate your wishes and *something* will always be found.

Maldivians love their coffee and you can get very good quality espresso, latte or cappuccino anywhere in Male'.

EATING WITH KIDS

There are very often kids' sections to menus and buffets in resorts, giving youngsters a choice of slightly less-refined foods ranging from spaghetti to fish fingers and chicken nuggets. Even if there's nothing dedicated to the kids' tastes, resort buffets are usually diverse enough to cater to even the fussiest eaters. Baby-food products are not on sale in resorts, so bring whatever junior will need for the trip.

HABITS & CUSTOMS

There's not a huge amount of etiquette to worry about if you eat in Male' or resorts. If you're lucky enough to be entertained in a local house, you should obey some basic rules, but again, the Maldivians are very relaxed and as long as you show respect and enjoyment, they'll be very glad to have you eating with them.

When going to eat, wait to be shown where to sit and wait for the *kateeb* (island chief) or the male head of the household to sit down before you do. Take a little of everything offered and do so only with your right hand, as the left hand is considered unclean by Muslims. Do ask for cutlery if you find it hard to roll your food into little balls like the Maldivians do; this is quite normal for foreigners. Thanks should not be overdone, as this can suggest a person was not happy to do whatever it was in the first place, although expressing gratitude to the head of the household, the *kateeb* and the cook will always be welcome.

Wine is available in resorts, but only in the better ones. Expect to pay extraordinary mark-ups; you'll do well to find anything OK for under US$50.

EAT YOUR WORDS

Most people you meet will speak at least rudimentary English, although if you are lucky enough to visit an inhabited island and to be a guest in a local's house then it's likely they won't speak a word.

I'm a vegetarian	*aharen ehves baavatheh ge maheh nukan*
What is the local speciality?	*dhivehi aanmu keumakee kobaa?*
What is this?	*mee ko-on cheh?*
The meal was delicious	*keun varah meeru*
Thank you for your hospitality	*be-heh-ti gaai kamah shukuriyya*

Food Glossary

Any substantial meal, with rice and *roshi,* is called long eats, and might include the following:

bai	rice
bis	egg

garudia	the staple diet of fish soup, often taken with rice, lime and chilli
kandukukulhu	a special tuna curry
mas	fried fish; usually refers to skipjack tuna or bonito
mas huni & hana kuri mas	dried, tinned, fried or cold fish mixed with coconut, onion, chilli and spices
mas riha	fish curry
modunu	a simple salad
paan	bread
rihakuru	garudia boiled down to a salty sauce or paste
roshi	flat, unleavened bread
valo mas	smoked fish
hiki mas	sundried fish

Short eats *(hedhikaa)* is the selection of little sweet and savoury items displayed on the counter of a local teashop:

gulas	fish ball; deep-fried in flour and rice batter
kuli boakiba	spicy fish cake
bondi bai	rice pudding; sometimes with currants
kastad	sweet custard
foni boakiba	gelatin cakes and puddings

Most fruit is imported, but the following are grown locally:

kurumba	coconut, especially a young or new coconut
donkeo	little bananas
bambukeyo	breadfruit
bambukeyo hiti	breadfruit used in curries
bambukeyo bondibai	breadfruit used in desserts

Male'

A tiny island, densely crowded with motorbikes, bustling business people, stern-faced police-men, hawkers and crisply uniformed school children, Male' (*mar*-lay) is the modern, mercantile face of the Maldives that few people take the time to see. Overlooked by brightly coloured tall thin buildings and surrounded by incongruously turquoise water all around, this is the centre of the Maldives, the engine driving its economic progress and the forum for the country's (stifled) political debate.

Far smaller than the neighbouring airport island of Hulhumale' – where long-haul flights land on a runway that dwarfs the main avenues of the capital – Male' nevertheless feels like an important place, where the economic, political and cultural leaders of the republic congregate, where nearly all the country's massive number of exports arrive and where more than a few expats and travellers find themselves from time to time. That said, Male' is interesting to visit mainly for a taste of Maldivian life more than for its inherent wealth of things to see and do. Independent travellers (or FITs as they are known locally) will find that this is a place they see a lot of – it's also one of the few places where palm trees and sandy beaches aren't on the menu.

Male' is pleasant and pleasingly quirky – its alcohol-free bars and restaurants jostle with its incredible array of shops and lively markets (imagine that in this tiny space all imports into the country are administered and sold) and the general hubbub of a capital is very much present. This is a chance to get a real feel for the Maldives, what makes its people tick and to meet Maldivians on an equal footing.

HIGHLIGHTS

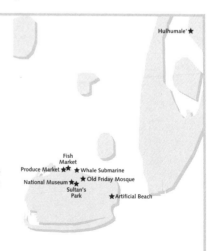

- Get a taste of everyday Maldivian life at the fish and produce **markets** (p95)

- See the interesting collection in the **National Museum** (p93) and enjoy the shade in **Sultan's Park** (p93)

- Admire and explore the fascinating coral stone **Old Friday Mosque** (p95)

- If you're not a diver, see a reef up close and personal on the **Whale Submarine** (p95)

- Check out the fascinating tetrapods and the quirky tetrapod monument on the southern side of the island at **Artificial Beach** (p96)

- Take a ferry trip to **Hulhumale'** (p104) and see the Maldivian Brave New World under construction

| AREA: 1.77 SQ KM | ELEVATION: 2M | POPULATION: 80,000 |

HISTORY

Male' has been the seat of the Maldives' ruling dynasties since before the 12th century,
though none left any grand palaces. Some
trading houses appeared in the 17th century,
along with a ring of defensive bastions, but
Male' did not acquire the trappings of a city
and had a very limited range of economic
and cultural activities. Visitors in the 1920s
estimated the population at only 5000.

Growth began with the 1930s modernisation, and the first banks, hospitals, high
schools and government offices appeared in
the following decades. Only since the 1970s,
with wealth from tourism and an expanding
economy, hast the city really burgeoned and
growth emerged as a problem.

But a problem it has very definitely become; despite extending the area of the city
through land reclamation over the island's
reef, Male' is unable to extend any further and so the government is looking to
projects such as nearby Hulhumale' to accommodate the future overspill of the city.

ORIENTATION

Male' is a roughly rectangular shape, its centre being spread out along the north side of
the island – where all the main jetties and
harbours are. The main street is the waterfront Boduthakurufaanu Magu, which now
goes all the way around the island. Many central government institutions are on this street
and it opens up half-way down to include
the city's main square, Jumhooree Maidan.
Male' is divided into four administrative districts, from west to east: Maafannu, covering
most of the western end of the island; Mach-
angolhi, running north–south across the
middle; Galolhu, a crowded residential maze
in south-central Male'; and Henveiru, covering the east and northeast. These districts
are indiscernible to visitors, but taxi drivers
understand the addresses. Street numbers are
rarely used – the building name will do.

Maps

Given Male's size the two maps in this book
should be sufficient. The Maldives Tourism Promotion Board's *Resort/Hotel Guide*
brochure has an adequate map of Male';
it's given out free at the airport and at the
MTPB office (p91) in town. There are town
plans pointing out the major sights of the
island along Boduthakurufaanu Magu.

INFORMATION

Bookshops

Asrafee Bookshop (Map p94; ☎ 3323424; Chandanee
Magu) Has a good selection of English paperbacks upstairs.

Asters Bookshop (Map p94; ☎ 3335505; www.asters
.com.mv; Majeedee Magu) Has one of the best selections
of English-language books in town, including Lonely Planet
guides, a good history section and more highbrow fiction
than the usual offerings.

Novelty Bookshop (Map p94; ☎ 3318899; Fareedhee
Magu) This outlet for Novelty Publishing, the country's
main publisher, has a great range of books about the
Maldives, as well as some imported titles.

Emergency

Ambulance ☎ 102

Fire ☎ 118

Police ☎ 119

Police station (Boduthakurufaanu Magu) On the corner
of Jumhooree Maidan.

Internet Access

There is no shortage of Internet cafés in
Male'. You will see plenty throughout the
town, but the following are the best located.

Bistro Jade (Map p94; Boduthakurufaanu Magu;
⊗ 8am-11pm Sat-Thu, 3-11pm Fri) A hub for expats,
this great café is a wi-fi hotspot so if you have your own
laptop come here for a fast connection and good coffee.

Cyber Café (Map p94; Ameer Ahmed Magu; per hr Rf15;
⊗ 9am-midnight Sat-Thu, 2pm-midnight Fri) Connections can be slow here, but the booths offer privacy.

Dhiraagu Cyber Café (Map p94; Chandanee Magu;
⊗ 9am-1am Sat-Thu, 4pm-1am Fri & religious holidays)
Dhiraagu, the country's main mobile-phone provider, has
free wi-fi in this, their central outlet. Assuming you have a
laptop you can come in and go online for free.

Laundry

Any hotel will take care of your laundry for
a few dollars per item. Guesthouses will do
it more cheaply. Allow a couple of days if
the weather is rainy. There are no laundro-
mats, and only a couple of dedicated laundry services.

Baansaree Laundry (Map pp90-1; ☎ 3327134; shirts
& shorts Rf4; ⊗ closed Fri) It's out of the way, a few
blocks northeast of the New Harbour, but is reliable and
extremely cheap.

Left Luggage

There are no dedicated left-luggage facilities
in Male' itself. The only option is taking a
day room at a hotel, or asking nicely at reception if you can leave your bags. There is

MALE'

a left-luggage service at the airport that costs US$3 per item, per 24 hours.

Libraries

National Library (Map p94; Majeedee Magu; ☿ closed Fri) In a big, newly renovated building, and has quite a few English books. Nonresidents can't borrow books, but are welcome to sit and read in the library.

Medical Services

Both the following will make arrangements with travel insurance companies, and both have doctors trained to do a diving medical check.

ADK Private Hospital (Map p94; ☎ 3313553; Sosun Magu) Private facility with Western-trained doctors and dentists, excellent standards of care, and quite high prices.

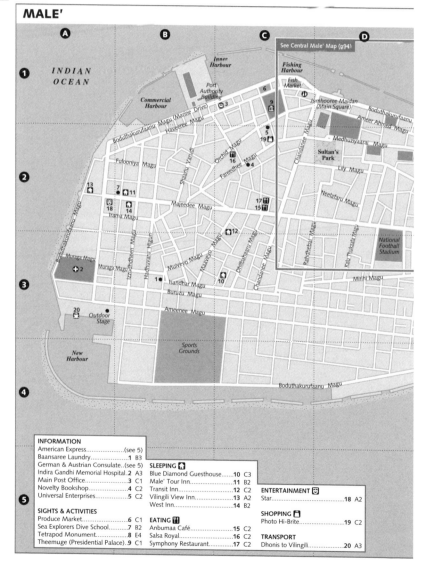

MALE'

INDIAN OCEAN

INFORMATION
American Express..................(see 5)
Baansaree Laundry....................1 B3
German & Austrian Consulate..(see 5)
Indira Gandhi Memorial Hospital.2 A3
Main Post Office......................3 C1
Novelty Bookshop.....................4 C2
Universal Enterprises...............5 C2

SIGHTS & ACTIVITIES
Produce Market......................6 C1
Sea Explorers Dive School........7 B2
Tetrapod Monument.................8 E4
Theemuge (Presidential Palace).9 C1

SLEEPING 🏠
Blue Diamond Guesthouse.......10 C3
Male' Tour Inn.......................11 B2
Transit Inn...........................12 C2
Vilingili View Inn....................13 A2
West Inn..............................14 B2

EATING 🍴
Anbumaa Café......................15 C2
Salsa Royal.........................16 C2
Symphony Restaurant.............17 C2

ENTERTAINMENT 🎭
Star...................................18 A2

SHOPPING 🛍
Photo Hi-Brite......................19 C2

TRANSPORT
Dhonis to Vilingili..................20 A3

Indira Gandhi Memorial Hospital (Map pp90-1; ☎ 3316647; Buruzu Magu) Modern public facility, well equipped and staffed with English-speaking doctors .

Money

For reliable service, try the State Bank of India, Bank of Maldives, Bank of Ceylon or HSBC Bank, all near each other on Bodu-

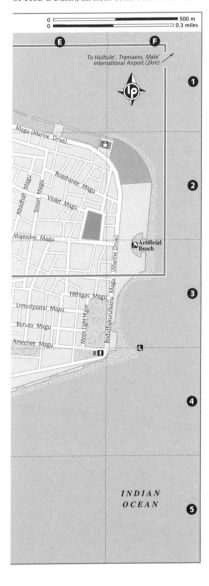

thakurufaanu Magu (Map p94). All have ATMs that accept international cards.

More local banks are clustered near the harbour end of Chandanee Magu and east along Boduthakurufaanu Magu. They all change travellers cheques, usually for a small transaction fee. Bank of Maldives doesn't charge a fee if you change travellers cheques for Maldivian rufiya, but does charge if you want US dollars.

Universal Enterprises Ltd (Map pp90-1; ☎ 3322971; www.unisurf.com; 39 Orchid Magu) The Amex agent in the Maldives.

Post

Main post office (Map pp90-1; ☎ 3315555; www .maldivespost.com; Boduthakurufaanu Magu; ☷ 8.15am-9pm Sun-Thu, 3-9pm Fri, 9.15am-9pm Sat) Brand new and efficiently run, just opposite the Maldives Port Authority building. Go to the 1st floor to post a parcel. There's a post office at the airport too.

Telephone & Fax

Although they seem to go largely unused, there are Dhiraagu telephone booths around the town. Lots of shops offer discounted calls abroad and phone cards. Anyone in the Maldives for long might profit from getting a local SIM card for their mobile phone (see p180).

Toilets

The most conveniently located public toilet (Rf2) is on the back street between Jade Bistro and the small Mosque on Ameer Ahmed Magu. However, you're equally able to pop in and use the toilets of most cafés or restaurants; the owners are almost universally polite and don't seem to mind.

Tourist Information

Metropolitan Tourism Promotion Board (MTPB; Map p94; ☎ 3323228; www.visitmaldives.com; 12 Boduthaku-rufaanu Magu; ☷ 7.30am-2.30pm Sun-Thu) The MTPB has an information counter on the 3rd floor of an office building on the seafront. It gives away free booklets and maps and can answer specific inquiries. The information desk at the airport is supposedly open when international flights arrive, but sometimes this isn't the case. Even when it's not staffed, look on the shelf out the front for some useful booklets.

Travel Agencies

There's a plethora of travel agents in Male'. Most of the smaller ones do nothing but try to sell an allocation of rooms at a resort or two. If you're an independent traveller looking for a resort or a safari tour, see p14, and be prepared to do some shopping around – ask in town, or call one or more of those listed below. A full list of Male' travel agents can be found at www.visitmaldives.com.

Crown Tours (Map p94; ☎ 3329889; www.crowntours maldives.com; Fasmeeru Bldg, 5th fl, Boduthakurufaanu Magu)

Inner Maldives (Map p94; ☎ 3315499; www.inner maldives.com.mv; Ameer Ahmed Magu)

Sultans of the Sea (Map p94; ☎ 3320330; www.sultansoftheseas.com; Fasmeeru Bldg, ground fl, Boduthakurufaanu Magu)

Sun Travel & Tours (Map p94; ☎ 3325977; www.sunholidays.com; Meheli Goalhi)

Sunland Travel (Map p94; ☎ 3324658; www.sunland.com.mv; STO Trade Centre, Orchid Magu)

Sunny Maldives (Map p94; ☎ 3338527; www.sunny maldives.com; Ameer Ahmed Magu)

Villa Travels (Map p94; ☎ 3332555; www.villatravels.com; 1/12 Boduthakurufaanu Magu)

Voyages Maldives (Map pp90–1; ☎ 3323617; www.voyagesmaldives.com; Chandhanee Magu)

DANGERS & ANNOYANCES

The main danger in Male' is posed by the mopeds that seem to appear from nowhere at great speeds. Keep your wits about you and look around before crossing the road. Crime against travellers is not unknown, but it is quite rare. Pickpocketing is probably the biggest threat, particularly in crowded shopping areas and around the markets; but again, it is not common. The

main annoyance in Male' is the lack of alcohol. If you really want a drink, take the ferry from Jetty No 1 to the Hulhule' Island Hotel (p100) near the airport.

SIGHTS

Male' is more of an experience than a succession of astonishing must-sees. The best thing to do is enjoy a stroll and absorb the atmosphere of this oddest of capitals. That said, there are a few genuine sights well worth a day's exploration.

Old Friday Mosque

Hukuru Miskiiy (Map p94; Medhuziyaarai Magu) is the oldest mosque in the country, dating from 1656. It's a beautiful structure made from coral stone into which intricate decoration and Quranic script have been carved. Even though an ugly corrugated-iron cover is protecting the roof and some of the walls, this is still a fascinating place. The interior is superb and famed for its fine lacquer work and elaborate woodcarvings. One long panel, carved in the 13th century, commemorates the introduction of Islam to the Maldives. Visitors wishing to see inside are supposed to get permission from an official of the **Ministry of Islamic Affairs** (☎ 3322266). However, most of the staff are officials of the ministry and, if you are respectful and well dressed, they will usually give you permission to enter the mosque on the spot – just hang around outside and try to get the attention of someone, although don't bother if you're underdressed.

MALE' IN ONE DAY

Take a stroll down Boduthakurufaanu Magu, the main street running along the waterfront, and enjoy a relaxed breakfast at **Bistro Jade** (p89). Carry on down the waterfront, see the President's Office and the main square, turning left to visit the **Grand Friday Mosque** (opposite), if you're dressed respectfully enough. Next door, drop in to see the small but interesting collection at the **National Museum** (opposite) and enjoy the lovely gardens of the **Sultan's Park** (opposite) before some shopping around Fareedhee Magu. For lunch the open-air **Seagull Cafe** (p101) or **Salsa Café** (p101) are great options, after which you can explore the **market** (p95), where you'll see the morning catch being brought in and gutted (you'll be glad you ate beforehand) and everything else imaginable on sale. Carry on to the president's jetty where you can take the boat to the **Whale Submarine** (p95) for a fascinating trip to the reef nearby, and if you still have some energy head over to the artificial beach on the east of the island where you can cool off, or just chill out with the locals after work and watch the impromptu soccer matches. As night falls, the city comes alive with promenading couples and teenagers clogging the streets on their motorpeds. Round the day off with a delicious meal at **Thai Wok** (p101) and join the crowds walking along the seafront – the closest Male' has to a nightlife scene.

HOUSE NAMES

Street numbers are rarely used in Male', so most houses and buildings have a distinctive name, typically written in picturesque English as well as in the local Thaana script. Some Maldivians prefer rustic titles like Crabtree, Forest, Oasis View and Banana Cabin. Others are specifically floral, like Sweet Rose and Luxury Garden, or even vegetable, like Carrot, or the perplexing Leaf Mess. There are also exotic names like Paris Villa and River Nile, while some sound like toilet disinfectants – Ozone, Green Zest, Dawn Fresh.

Some of our quirkier favourite house names include Hot Lips, Subtle Laughter, Remind House, Pardon Villa, Frenzy and Mary Lightning and Aston Villa.

Shop names and businesses, on the other hand, often have an overt advertising message – People's Choice Supermarket, Bless Trade, Fair Price, and Neat Store. Premier Chambers is not a pretentious house name – it's where you'll find Male's first barrister.

The mosque was built on the foundations of an old temple that faced west to the setting sun, not northwest towards Mecca. Consequently, the worshippers have to face the corner of the mosque when they pray – the striped carpet, laid at an angle, shows the correct direction.

Overlooking the mosque is the solid, round, blue-and-white tower of the *munnaaru* – the squat minaret. Though it doesn't look that old, it dates from 1675. West of the mosque is a graveyard, with many elaborately carved tombstones. Stones with rounded tops are for females, those with pointy tops are for males and those featuring gold-plated lettering are the graves of former sultans. The small buildings are family mausoleums and their stone walls are intricately carved. Respectably dressed non-Muslims are welcome to walk around the graveyard; you don't require permission for this.

National Museum & Sultan's Park

The small **National Museum** (Map p94; ☎ 3322254; Medhuziyaarai Magu; adult/child under 12 US$3/1; ☼ 8am-6pm Sun-Thu, closed Fri & holidays) is well worth a visit. Housed in a small, three-storey building in one corner of the Sultan's Park, it is the only remaining part of the original sultan's palace – the rest was demolished in 1968 at the beginning of the second republic.

The museum has a small collection that is displayed over three floors and well labelled in English. You'll be accompanied throughout by one of the staff. A useful, illustrated guide to the museum, sold at the entrance for Rf50, has colour pictures and more detailed descriptions of the exhibits. Many of the exhibits are things once owned

by the sultans – clothing, utensils, weapons and a throne. Some of the fabrics are beautiful, especially the rich brocades. Excellent, traditional lacquer work is displayed on large bowls and trays used to bring gifts to the sultan. Weapons include *bonthi* sticks, which were used in martial arts, and a *silvan bonthi*, used by a husband to punish an unfaithful wife.

Especially interesting are the museum's pre-Islamic stone carvings collected by Thor Heyerdahl, and other examples from sites all over the country. They include a fine Buddha's head and various phallic images. Most of them are labelled, but little is really known about the significance or historical context of these fascinating finds. Quirky additions to the historic collection include a tiny Maldivian flag taken on one of the Apollo missions and some moon rock, both gifts from Richard Nixon.

The **park** (☼ 8am-6pm Sun-Thu, 4-6pm Fri) surrounding the museum was once part of the grounds of the sultan's palace. It's a beautifully planted park full of flowers and trees and one of the best public spaces in Male'.

Grand Friday Mosque & Islamic Centre

The golden dome of this impressive **mosque** (Map p94) dominates the skyline of Male' and has become something of a symbol for the city. Set back off the main square, Jumhooree Maidan, and opposite the sinister National Security Service Headquarters, this is the biggest mosque in the country.

Opened in 1984, and built with help from the Gulf States, Pakistan, Brunei and Malaysia, the Grand Friday Mosque is striking in its plainness, built in white

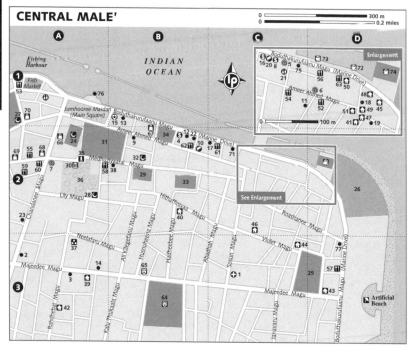

marble and virtually free from decoration. From a boat coming into Male's harbour, you can still see the gold dome glinting in the sun, although the gold is actually anodised aluminium. The *munnaaru*, with its space-age shape and distinctive zigzag decoration, was supposed to be the tallest structure in Male', but that title now goes to the telecommunications towers.

Visits to see the Grand Friday Mosque must be between 9am and 5pm, but not during prayer times. It closes to all non-Muslims 15 minutes before prayers and for the following hour. Before noon and between 2pm and 3pm are the best times to visit. Invading bands of casual sightseers are not encouraged, but if you are genuinely interested and suitably dressed, you'll be welcomed by one of the staff members who hangs out by the entrance. Men must wear long pants and women a long skirt or dress.

The main prayer hall inside the mosque can accommodate up to 5000 worshippers and has beautifully carved wooden side panels and doors, a specially woven carpet

and impressive chandeliers. The **Islamic Centre** also includes a conference hall, library and classrooms.

Muleeaage & Medhu Ziyaarath

Across the road from the Old Friday Mosque is a blue-and-white building with colourful gateposts. This is the **Muleeaage** (Map p94), built as a palace in the early 20th century. The sultan was deposed before he could move in and the building was used for government offices for about 40 years. It became the president's residence in 1953 when the first republic was proclaimed, but President Gayoom moved to a new official residence in 1994. At the eastern end of the building's compound, behind an elaborate blue-and-white gatehouse, the **Medhu Ziyaarath** (Map p94) is the tomb of Abu Al Barakaath, who brought Islam to Male' in 1153.

Tomb of Mohammed Thakurufaanu

In the back streets in the middle of town, in the grounds of a small mosque, is the **tomb** (Map above) of the Maldives' greatest hero,

INFORMATION		SIGHTS & ACTIVITIES		KPS Mart	54 C1
ADK Private Hospital	1 C3	Grand Friday Mosque	24 A2	Olive Garden	55 A2
Asrafee Bookshop	2 A3	Henvairu Stadium	25 D3	Queen of the Night	56 D1
Asters Bookshop	3 A3	Islamic Centre	(see 24)	Red Zanzibar	57 D3
Bank of Ceylon	(see 12)	Majeediyya Carnival	26 D2	Royal Garden Café	58 A2
Bank of Maldives	4 B2	Mosque	27 A1	Salsa Café	59 A2
Bistro Jade	5 C1	Mosque	28 A2	Seagull Café	60 A2
Crown Tours	(see 17)	Muleeaage & Medhu Ziyaarath	29 B2	Shell Beans	61 C2
Cyber Café	6 D1	National Museum	30 A2	Supermarket	(see 70)
Denmark Embassy	(see 20)	National Security Service	31 A2	Thai Wok	62 B2
Dhiraagu Cyber Café	7 A2	Old Friday Mosque	32 B2	Trends	63 D1
Dutch Consular Agent	(see 60)	People's Majlis	33 B2		
Finland Embassy	(see 20)	President's Office	34 B2	ENTERTAINMENT 🕃	
HSBC Bank	8 C1	Republican monument	35 A2	National Football Stadium	64 B3
Immigration Office	9 B2	Sultan's Park	36 A2	Olympus	65 B3
Indian High Commission	10 B2	Tomb of Mohammed			
Inner Maldives	11 C1	Thakurufaanu	37 A3	SHOPPING 🛈	
Italian Consular Agent	(see 17)	Whale Submarine Office	38 B2	Antique & Style	66 A2
Maldives Travel Promotion				Atoll Surf	67 B2
Board	12 B2	SLEEPING 🛈		Dive Shop	68 A2
Ministry of Atolls		Athama Palace Hotel	39 A3	FDI Station	69 A2
Administration	13 B1	Buruneege Residence	40 B2	Gloria Maris	(see 66)
National Library	14 A3	Candies	41 D1	STO Trade Centre	70 A1
Norway Embassy	(see 20)	Central Hotel	42 A3	Villa Photo	(see 70)
NZ Consulate	(see 17)	City Palace	43 D3	Water World	(see 68)
Police Station	15 B1	Extra Haven Guesthouse	44 C3		
State Bank of India	16 C1	Fariva Inn	45 D1	TRANSPORT	
Sultans of the Sea	17 C2	Kai Lodge	46 C2	Air India	71 C2
Sun Travel & Tours	18 D1	Kam Hotel	47 D1	Airport Ferry Arrival Jetty	72 D1
Sunland Travel	(see 70)	Maagiri Lodge	48 D1	Airport Ferry Departure Jetty	73 D1
Sunny Maldives	19 D1	Mookai Hotel	49 D1	Cosmos	(see 71)
Sweden Embassy	20 C1	Nasandhura Palace Hotel	50 D1	Huhulmale' Ferry Terminal	74 D1
Toilet	21 C1	Relax Inn	51 D1	Island Aviation	75 C1
UK Consular Agent	(see 7)			Malaysian Airlines	(see 22)
Villa Travels	22 B2	EATING 🍴		President's Jetty	76 A1
Voyages Maldives	23 A2	Buruzu Hotaa	52 D1	Qatar Airways	(see 75)
Western Union	(see 22)	City Snacks	(see 12)	Singapore Airlines	(see 75)
		Dawn Cafe	53 A1	Sri Lankan Airlines	77 D3

the man who liberated the country from Portuguese rule and was then the sultan from 1573 to 1585. Thakurufaanu is also commemorated in the name Boduthakurufaanu Magu (bodu means 'big' or 'great').

Mosques

There are over 20 miskiiys (mosques) in Male'; some are simple coral buildings with an iron roof and others are quite stylish with elegant minarets. Outside there is always a well or an outdoor bathroom, because Muslims must always wash before they pray. Visitors usually can't go inside, but there's no need – the doors are always wide open, and you can clearly see that the interior is nearly always devoid of furniture or decoration.

Markets

The busy **produce market** (Map pp90–1) gives a real flavour of the Maldives – its people at turns friendly and surly as they pack out all available space selling home-grown and im-

ported vegetables. Coconuts and bananas are the most plentiful produce, but look inside for the stacks of betel leaf, for wrapping up a 'chew'. This is the heart and soul of the capital and just wandering around, watching the hawkers and the shoppers and seeing the vast array of products on display is fascinating.

Nearby is the **fish market** (Map p94), which is not to be missed, although the squeamish may well object to the buckets of entrails or the very public gutting of fish going on all around. This is the soul of Male' – and there's little more authentically Maldivian than watching the day's catch being brought in to the market from the adjacent fishing harbour. Fishing and marketing are men's work here, and Maldivian women don't usually venture into these areas.

Whale Submarine

The **Whale Submarine** (Map p94; ☎ 3333939; www.submarinesmaldives.com.mv; Medhuzuyaarai Magu; adult/child/family US$75/38/170) can hardly be described as a sight of Male', but it's a popular excursion and departs from a submarine dock just off the western side of Male'. First things first, this is not a submarine for whale watching – its name is slightly misleading. It is, in fact, a submarine for looking at life on a reef. It's hard to recommend for divers, as the trip can't really compare to a real dive, but for kids and those who don't dive, this is a great (if pricey) little excursion. As the submarine departs from off the coast you have to get a boat either from the airport or Jetty No 1 (the jetty in front of Jumhooree Maidan, also known as the President's Jetty) – one boat picks up from both about 30 minutes before the scheduled departure of the submarine. You should ring ahead and book a place (there are several departures daily) so the boat can pick you up. At the submarine dock (the 'Whale House') you pay your money, have a cool drink and board the sub.

The sub takes a few minutes to get to its dive spot, and then descends to about 35m while passengers gaze out through large, lenslike windows. A variety of fish come very close to the windows, attracted partly by the food that the sub dispenses – surgeonfish, blue-striped snapper, and unicornfish are among the most commonly seen, but you have an excellent view of smaller creatures too, such as lionfish and anemonefish. The sub goes very close to a reef wall, and its lights illuminate crevices and show up colours that wouldn't be visible in natural light.

Underwater time is about 45 minutes, but allow 1½ hours for the whole trip. Quite a few people fit in a submarine trip if they have a few hours to spare at the airport before their departure flight. The sub maintains normal surface pressure inside, so it's quite safe to fly straight afterwards.

Artificial Beach

The western seafront of Male' is its recreational centre. Here, a sweet little **beach** has been crafted from the breakwater tetrapods and there's a whole range of fast food cafés next to it as well as open fields for ad hoc games of soccer and cricket. Further up towards the airport ferry there are fairground attractions at the **Majeediyya Carnival** (Map p94) including a bowling alley and more eateries. The other way you'll see the charming **tetrapod monument** (Map pp90–1), a local salute to the mini concrete structures that together form a life-saving breakwater for the city (see below).

WALKING TOUR

Male' is best seen on foot – you can circumnavigate the entire island in a couple of hours; but to get a proper feel for the place, try to get into the crowded, chaotic backstreets in the island's centre.

THE MAGNIFICENT TETRAPOD

The installation of tetrapod walls around much of Male' saved it from the huge potential devastation of the Indian Ocean tsunami in 2004. Tetrapods are concrete blocks with four fat legs, each approximately 1m long, sticking out like the four corners of a tetrahedron. These blocks can be stacked together in rows and layers so they interlock together to form a wall several metres high, looking like a giant version of a child's construction toy. A tetrapod breakwater has gaps that allow sea water to pass through, but collectively the structure is so massive and its surface so irregular that it absorbs and dissipates the force of the waves and protects the shoreline from the physical impact of a storm. As Male' has expanded through land reclamation to cover its entire natural coral reef, its natural buffer from the force of strong waves has disappeared.

A severe storm in 1988 flooded Male's streets, but the worst damage was on the southern and eastern edges of the island. Huge waves broke up tons of landfill that was part of a land-reclamation scheme, and much of this land was re-claimed by the sea.

The solution was to protect the whole island with a rim of tetrapod breakwaters, constructed as part of a Japanese foreign-aid project. In some places the tetrapod walls are used to retain landfill, and have a path on top forming an attractive seaside promenade. In other places, tetrapod walls enclose an artificial harbour that provides a sheltered anchorage for small boats, and a safe spot for kids to swim.

MALE'

Start from the waterfront near **Jumhooree Maidan (1)**, the main square, conspicuous for the huge Maldivian flag flying on its eastern side. It seems a pleasant and relaxed place, with friends and families relaxing around the square, but this was the setting for previously unthinkable antigovernment demonstrations in August 2004, and you'll notice that it remains a well-guarded place, with the police station on one side and the sinister white **National Security Services Headquarters (2)** to the south, strewn with orders not to take photographs.

To the right of the NSS is the **Grand Friday Mosque (3**; p93), walk down the sandy street past its main entrance and you'll arrive at the **Republican Monument (4)**, a modern-style centrepiece to a roundabout unveiled in 1999 to commemorate 30 years of Maldivian independence. Avoiding the traffic, cross over to the **Sultan's Park (5**; p93) and walk through its well-laid-out flowerbeds and plantings to Lily Magu. Exit the park and turn left, where you'll see a charming coral stone **mosque (6)** in the corner of the park, typical of the intricate 17th-century Maldivian design. Continue south from here through streets far more typical of the crowded capital until you reach the **Tomb of Mohammed Thakurufaanu (7)**, a much-loved shrine honouring the man who liberated the Maldives from the Portuguese in the 16th century. Cut down to Majeedee Magu, the city's main thoroughfare and absorb the shops, noise and bustle of the town's commercial heart as you walk west. Cut up through the good shopping streets of Fareedhee Magu and Orchid Magu, passing the striking **Theemuge** (Presidential Palace; **8**), official residence of Maumoon Abdul Gayoom. The charming **mosque (9)** next door is also worth a peek at from the street.

From here head north towards the seafront and turn left for the wonderful **produce**

WALK FACTS

Start Jumhooree Maidan
Finish Bistro Jade
Distance 3km
Duration One hour

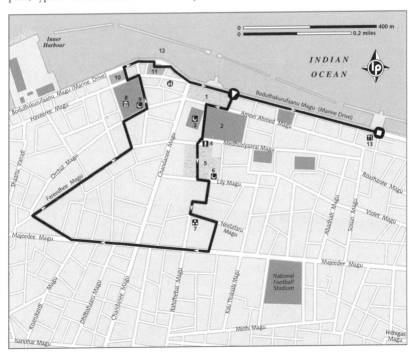

MALE'

market (10; p95). Continue for a few more blocks along the waterfront, a bustling area with hardware shops and hangouts for sailors and fishermen. Go back along the seafront to the **fish market (11)**, which, along with the adjacent **fishing harbour (12)**, is a must-see for anyone in Male'. Wander along the seafront, which is always fascinating as people crowd on and off boats, and you can see more and more obscure cargo being brought ashore. Finish up at **Bistro Jade (13**; p89) for a drink out of the heat.

MALE' FOR CHILDREN

The Whale Submarine (p95) will appeal to kids of all ages, while the Artificial Beach (p96) and the recreational areas nearby is also a great place for them to swim, and older kids can join in an ad hoc football or cricket game with local children. The nearby Majeediyya Carnival has some fun activities for kids as well, including the Slam Bowling Alley.

SLEEPING

Space being at a premium on the overcrowded island, hotels are not cheap here, and even top-end rooms are not large by any standard. Despite that, hotel prices are so low compared to the expensive resorts that Male' remains the cheapest place in the country to stay. There's not an enormous choice and no real top end – even the more expensive hotels are not world class, and there are no international hotel groups represented.

Budget

West Inn (Map pp90-1; ☎ 3317152; Majeedee Magu; s/d with fan US$27/35) A new place with small, clean, dark rooms, the West Inn is off a narrow balcony at the far end Majeedee Magu. Rooms have quite good bathrooms, but no other comforts. Room rates do not include breakfast.

Male' Tour Inn (Map pp90-1; ☎ 3326220; Shaheed Ali Higun; s/d US$28/40; 🞸) Small, unattractive rooms come with cleanish bathrooms. Also at the west end of the island, it's mainly used by visiting workers. Upgraded rooms including breakfast come for an extra US$10.

Blue Diamond Guesthouse (Map pp90-1; ☎ 3326125; fax 3316404; Badifasgandu Magu; s/d with fan US$30/40) On a small street south of Majeedee Magu, the Blue Diamond has small, simple en-suite rooms that were undergoing renovation when we visited. Breakfast and drinking water are included in the price. It's in a residential part of town, interesting for its authentic local ambience, but not very convenient for shops, restaurants or transport. The Maldivian family management is friendly and quite efficient, and the place is popular with Voluntary Service Overseas (VSO) workers and various visitors on limited budgets.

Fariva Inn (Map p94; ☎ 3337611; amsha@dhivehinet .net.mv; Boduthakurufaanu Magu; s/d US$35/45; 🞸) The rooms without air-con here are clean with TV, phone and a basic bathroom. All rooms come with fans and a slight smell of damp. Excellently located.

Midrange

This type of accommodation in Male' starts at around US$50 for singles or doubles including breakfast, and offers much better standards than the budget places. Most rooms will have air-con, a phone and hot water in the bathroom, and the better ones will have a TV. You might get a discount at some of these places if you stay more than a few days.

Extra Haven Guesthouse (Map p94; ☎ 3327453; fax 3325362; s/d with fan US$30/40, with air-con US$40/50; 🞸) In the back streets at the east end of town, Extra Haven attracts a mixed clientele of visiting workers and budget travellers. The rooms with air-con are small and nothing fancy, and the fan-cooled rooms are even smaller and plainer, but they're all clean and have bathrooms. Some have an outlook over the town. There's satellite TV in the lobby and fresh water is available.

Athama Palace Hotel (Map p94; ☎ 3313118; athamapalace@yahoo.com; Majeedee Magu; s/d US$40/55; 🞸) It's hard to imagine anything less palatial, but the rooms are surprisingly spacious and the location is perfectly fine. There is a whiff of charm created by the Maldivian art and the fish chart–strewn walls throughout.

Maagiri Lodge (Map p94; ☎ 3322576; www .maagirilodge.com.mv; Boduthakurufaanu Magu; s/d US$46/56; 🞸) This charming little place quickly grows on you. Functional rooms with an en suite and TV are perfectly OK, but it's the staff that make you feel welcome. The breakfast is one of the best in town and the excellent location makes this a great option. At the time of research the owners were planning to expand from five to 17 rooms.

Transit Inn (Map pp90-1; ☎ 3320420; transit@dhivehinet.net.mv; Maaveyo Magu; s/d/t US$48/58/68; ✹) The Transit Inn is a pleasant, relaxed, slightly chaotic place with a friendly little coffee shop downstairs through which you enter from the street. All rooms include a fridge and TV; bathrooms are tatty but spacious. It's a well-run establishment, and quite often full.

Buruneege Residence (Map p94; ☎ 3330011; www.frontline.com.mv; Hithaffinivaa Magu; s/d US$48/60; ✹) There is a smattering of old-world charm about this place, which is hidden away on a side street not far from the Majlis. It's set around a courtyard and has a slightly colonial feel. However, the rooms are devoid of character and are completely functional, and the receptionist did not speak a word of English on our last visit. It's not far from the airport ferries, and handy to the centre of town, so you could do much worse.

Kai Lodge (Map p94; ☎ 3328742; kailodge@dhivehinet.net.mv; Violet Magu; s/d/t US$52/70/89; ✹) A few blocks inland from the airport ferry landing, the relatively atmospheric Kai Lodge has clean, comfortable rooms with bathroom, hot water, phone, satellite TV and air-con; some have a balcony. A couple of two-room apartments accommodate four people. Day rooms for transit passengers start at US$39.

City Palace (Map p94; ☎ 3333990; citymale@dhivehinet.net.mv; Filigas Higun; s/d/tr US$60/75/100; ✹ ⌨) There are some very nice touches at this midrange hotel that overlooks the football field: free Internet is available for guests and two bottles of fresh water a day suggest more than the usual thought for the guests. Rooms are basic but comfortable, and this area of town is lovely and relaxed, a short stroll from the artificial beach.

Vilingili View Inn (Map pp90-1; ☎ 3318696; villiview@dhivehinet.net.mv; Majeedee Magu; standard s/d US$65/75, deluxe US$60/75; ✹ ⌨) At the far west end of Majeedee Magu, this inn has only a couple of rooms with views over the water to Viligili island – most have no outlook at all, but they are extremely pleasant and well designed, including some interesting split-floor rooms. It's not convenient for access to the town centre, but it has wi-fi throughout and is quirkily attractive.

Top End

Five of Male's top-end hotels are on the northeast corner of the island, handy to the airport dhonis, and a fifth one is in the middle of town – all are comfortable, but none outstanding. Note that alcohol is not served at any of the Male' hotels – for that you have to either stay at or drop by the Hulhule' Island Hotel (p100).

Central Hotel (Map p94; ☎ 3317766; www.centralmaldives.com; Rahdhebai Magu; s/d from US$64/80; ✹) While the big pink tower of the Central Hotel is literally in the centre of the island, this is no great shakes, given that the centre of town is the northern shore. It's actually just a little too far from everything else for comfort here, and even though the management runs a free shuttle to the airport ferry jetty, this isn't a great choice. The rooms are oddly shaped and a little cramped. Avoid the balcony-less junior suites in favour of the standard rooms, all of which have balconies and some great views.

Relax Inn (Map p94; ☎ 3314531; www.relaxmaldives.com; Ameer Ahmed Magu; standard s/d from US$68/83; ✹) No Frankie Goes to Hollywood theme here at the one-time main business hotel of Male', now somewhat eclipsed by the Mookai and the Kam. The rooms are fine but a bit tired (we heard a UN functionary complaining about his at reception) and the furniture distinctly garish, but this remains a popular choice with the NGO sector.

Kam Hotel (Map p94; ☎ 3320611; Ameer Ahmed Magu; s/d from US$75/90; ✹) One of three high-rise top-end hotels near the Male' waterfront, the Kam has smart and comfortable rooms, a notch better than its rivals. It's well located, with helpful staff, and is very popular with businesspeople.

Nasandhura Palace Hotel (Map p94; ☎ 3323380; www.nasandhurapalace.com; Boduthakurufaanu Magu; s/d US$82/97; ✹) This superbly located hotel, which is opposite the airport ferry jetty, has the advantage of feeling like a social hub – people pack out its popular garden restaurant, Trends, day and night, and the staff are very welcoming. The rooms are comfortable, if a little dated, and each has a minibar, a phone and a bathtub. Some of the upstairs rooms have a view of the sea (if you stand on tiptoes).

Mookai Hotel (Map p94; ☎ 3338811; mookai@dhivehinet.net.mv; Meheli Goalhi; s/d US$92/109; ✹ ⌨) One of the top hotels in town, the Mookai

MALE'

has a great location just seconds from the waterfront, rooms with great views on the higher floors. And, up on the roof, there is a small but effective swimming pool to cool down in. Rooms are small but clean and well furnished. Breakfast is served over at the sister Kam Hotel opposite. It's recommended.

Hulhule' Island Hotel (Map p105; ☎ 3330888; www.hih.com.mv; Hulhule' island; s & d US$254, ste US$400; ☒ ☐ ☒) Certainly the priciest hotel in the area, the Hulhule' Island is on the airport island, a 10-minute dhoni ride from Male'. Very convenient for air crews, business people travelling all over the Maldives and those in transit, it's a well-run business hotel with clean and spacious rooms (most of which have great sea views), and the only hotel in Male' serving alcohol, for which expats and visitors alike frequently make the pilgrimage across the lagoon. The pool is another great attraction – it's by far the nicest in Male'. Many transit passengers take a room on a 'day use' basis (until 11pm) for US$155.

THE AUTHOR'S CHOICE

Candies (Map p94; ☎ 3310220; candies@dhivehinet.net.mv; Dheefuram Gholhi; s/d US$65/75; ☒ ☒) Once part of the Kam Hotel next door, this now-independent venture is a great little place – the bar is popular with locals and the swimming pool just next to reception is a great touch. Rooms are smallish but comfortable and the whole place feels much more like a big house than a hotel. Superb location and the possibility of a morning swim make this our hotel of choice in Male'.

EATING

Rather like the accommodation scene, eating in Male' is perfectly decent without being excellent, but it's blessedly less expensive than eating à la carte at most resorts. There's plenty of choice from local cuisine to various Asian cuisines, Italian and American.

Teashops

Local teashops are frequented by Maldivian men; it's not the done thing for local women to be in one, but there is no law against it. Foreign women use them some-

times, generally with a male companion, and there's no problem. Some traditional teashops have broadened the menus, installed air-conditioning and improved service – you should feel quite comfortable in these places. Teashops are a great place to meet local people, and they're very cheap. A bigger and slightly better teashop might be called a café or 'hotel'.

Teashops have their goodies displayed on a counter behind a glass screen, and customers line up and choose, cafeteria style – if you don't know what to ask for, just point. Tea costs around Rf2 and the *hedhikaa* ('short eats'; finger food snacks) from Rf1 to Rf3. You can fill yourself for under Rf10. At meal times they also serve 'long eats', such as soups, curried fish and *roshi* (unleavened bread). A good meal costs from Rf12 to Rf25.

Teashops open as early as 5am and close as late as 1am, particularly around the port area where they cater to fishermen. During Ramazan they're open till 2am or even later, but closed during the day.

Queen of the Night (Map p94; Boduthakurufaanu Magu) A very popular spot facing the waterfront near the airport ferry, the Queen has tables next to the street where men play *carrom* (a snooker-like board game) and chess until all hours. The tables in the back and upstairs are always busy with guys grabbing some *hedhikaa*.

Buruzu Hotaa (Map p94; Ameer Ahmed Magu) An extremely friendly place packed with locals throughout the day. Pick from a big selection of curries and Maldivian dishes and you'll soon find yourself being befriended.

Dawn Cafe (Map p94; Haveeree Higun) One of the bigger teashops in the area, and it's around the fish market. You can get a brilliant meal here. Try it on Friday afternoon when people come in after going to the mosque.

Anbumaa Café (Map p94; Sayyidhukilegefaanu Magu) This two-floor, extremely chilled-out budget snack bar, off Majeedee Magu, will rustle up chicken and rice, fish and chips or a bowl of noodles for R20.

Cafés

Royal Garden Café (Map p94; Medhuziyaarai Magu; mains from Rf40) Despite its location opposite the southern wall of the creepy NSS Headquarters, this is a fantastic little place, with a charming garden and an air-conditioned, stylish dark-wood interior. The menu is a typical combination of Italian, Indonesian, American and Indian cuisines.

Shell Beans (Map p94; ☎ 3333686; Boduthakurufaanu Magu; sandwiches Rf30) More a coffee bar than a restaurant, Shell Beans serves a good range of tasty pastries, sandwiches and snacks as well good coffee. The fresh bread and cakes come daily from the Bandos resort bakery. This is a fixture among travellers and expats and a good place to meet them.

Seagull Cafe (Map p94; ☎ 3323792; cnr Chandanee Magu & Fareedhee Magu; mains Rf50) One of the most pleasant and popular places, the Seagull boasts a delightfully shaded outdoor eating area and a delicious American-style menu with a kicking club sandwich. There's also a rightly popular gelataria attached, serving up the city's best ice cream.

City Snacks (Map p94; ☎ 3349302; Boduthakurufaanu Magu; sandwiches Rf25) This convivial waterfront place is a popular meeting place after work and its few tables are always busy with coffee-drinking locals and people picking up sandwiches on the go.

Salsa Café (Map p94; ☎ 3310319; Keneree Magu; mains Rf40) The Salsa is similar in style to the Seagull – it has an open-air dining area with a garden setting and cooling fans. Situated on a back street near the shopping area, it's a long-standing favourite with expats. The menu features Maldivian, Asian and European dishes, all well prepared and presented.

Restaurants

Typically restaurants in Male' have several different cuisines on offer – most popular are Thai, Indonesian, Indian, Italian and American-style grills. Nearly everything is imported, including the prawns and the lobsters, which will be the most expensive items. The customers are mostly businesspeople, young Maldivian couples, sundry expats and day-trippers from nearby resorts. Some places have a starchy ambience, with stiff tablecloths and chilly air-con, but more casual outdoor eating is becoming popular.

None of the Male' restaurants serve alcohol, but some serve nonalcoholic beer for about Rf10 to Rf20 per can. Nearly every restaurant has now acquired an espresso

THE AUTHOR'S CHOICE

Red Zanzibar (Map p94; ☎ 3340951; Boduthakurufaanu Magu; mains Rf60) This relative newcomer to the city's dining scene is about as hip as Male' restaurants get and it's highly recommended. The very funky two-floor open-air restaurant and bar offers great views towards the open-air beach and the opulent traditional wooden furnishings have a distinctly boutique feel to them. The menu is by far the most interesting in the city, taking in a variety of delicious devilled fish, excellent salads and sublime desserts. There's free Internet in the bar downstairs and a cool crowd there throughout the day.

machine, and you can get a good cup of coffee, a cappuccino or a café latte almost anywhere.

Thai Wok (Map p94; ☎ 3310007; Ameer Ahmed Magu; mains Rf35-50; 🔀) Quite formal by local standards – bow-tied waiters fall over themselves to assist you, often outnumbering the diners – Thai Wok has some of the best food in town, serving from a huge menu of authentic Thai dishes.

Salsa Royal (Map pp90-1; ☎ 3327830; Orchid Magu; mains Rf70; 🔀) Formerly the Twin Peaks Restaurant, this airy, high-ceilinged hall now serves up Italian and Thai food from two separate menus. The restaurant is non-smoking throughout, extremely clean and with good service.

Symphony (Map pp90-1; ☎ 3326277; mains Rf40-190; 🔀) This long-time favourite for Male' residents has dim lighting, chilly air-con and a smart look. The menu is comprehensive and the Indian cuisine is especially good. It's off Majeedee Magu.

Trends (Map p94; ☎ 3323380; Boduthakurufaanu Magu; mains Rf50-100) At the Nasandhura Palace Hotel, Trends is an outdoor restaurant offering a varied menu of European, Indonesian, Thai, Chinese and Indian dishes. There's a huge choice and an equal variability in standards – we had a delicious Chinese meal here and an almost inedible sandwich here on two different occasions. However, it's always busy and the garden is charming.

Olive Garden (Map p94; ☎ 3312231; Fareedhee Magu; mains Rf40-90; 🔀) This is a mainly

Italian restaurant serving pasta and extremely mediocre pizzas in a room with Arctic air-con. Nothing special at all, but it remains popular with locals.

Self-Catering

The nearest supermarket to the airport ferry jetty is the **KPS Mart** (Map p94; Ameer Ahmed Magu), which has all the essentials of life on sale. Better choice can be had at the city's biggest supermarket in the **STO Trade Centre** (Map p94; Orchid Magu), which includes fresh fruit and veg. These stores are handy for self-catering, which is a sensible option during Ramazan.

ENTERTAINMENT

Nobody comes to a dry town for nightlife, let's face it, but despite the worrying sobriety of the Male′ populace, there's a surprising amount going on in the evenings. Dusk is the coolest time of day, and Male′ is popular with strolling couples and groups of friends who promenade along the seafront and Majeedee Magu until late in the evening. Thursday and Friday nights are the busiest, after prayers at sundown. There are even sporadic club nights put on, although there's nothing regular. Keep your eye out for notices along the seafront, as such events are always advertised.

The non air-con **Olympus** (Map p94; Majeedee Magu), opposite the stadium, shows Maldivian and Indian films as well as the occasional Hollywood blockbuster. The city's other cinema, **Star** (Map pp90-1; Majeedee Magu), was closed at the time of research and it was unclear whether it would be reopening soon or not.

The **National Stadium** (Map p94; Majeedee Magu) hosts the biggest football matches (tickets cost Rf15 to Rf30) and the occasional cricket match. More casual games can be seen any evening in the sports grounds at the east end of the island and near New Harbour.

SHOPPING

Most of the shops selling imported and locally made souvenirs are on and around Chandanee Magu, Fareedhee Magu and Orchid Magu. Many of the tourist shops have a very similar range of stock, but it's worth browsing in several if you're looking for something special.

The most popular purchases are T-shirts, sarongs, cotton clothing, postcards, picture books, small handicraft items (carved fish, lacquer boxes, coconut-shell spoons), and trinkets from India, Sri Lanka, Thailand and Indonesia. Prices are negotiable; they are generally cheaper in Male′ than in resorts, but more expensive than on village islands.

Male′ is definitely the best place to shop for more unusual antiques and Maldivian craft items – come here to look for old, wooden measuring cups, coconut graters, ceremonial knives, and finely woven grass mats. **Antique & Style** (Map p94) and **Gloria Maris** (Map p94), both upstairs on the east side of Chandanee Magu, are worth visiting. For less conventional souvenirs, such as giant fish-hooks, boat balers, hookahs (water pipes) and medicinal herbs, have a look in the local hardware, chandlery and general stores along the waterfront west of the fish market and down Fareedhee Magu.

The best range of surfboards, accessories and surf wear is available at **Atoll Surf** (Map p94; ☎ 3334555; Boduthakurufaanu Magu). Two of the best diving shops are next door to each other: **Dive Shop** (Map p94; Chandanee Magu) and **Water World** (Map p94; Chandanee Magu). Both supply a full range of equipment and are authorised dealers for big-name brands.

Several photographic shops stock quality film – **Photo Hi-Brite** (Map pp90-1; Fareedhee Magu) for Kodak products, **Villa Photo** (Map p94; STO Trade Centre, Orchid Magu) for Agfa, and **FDI Station** (Map p94; Fareedhee Magu) stocks Fuji.

GETTING THERE & AWAY

Air

All international flights to the Maldives use **Male′ International Airport** (www.airports.com.mv), which is on a separate island, Hulhule′, about 2km east of Male′ island. Domestic flights and seaplane transfers to resorts also use Hulhule′. Male′ is linked by daily scheduled flights to Colombo, Qatar, Dubai and Trivandrum and less frequently with Singapore, Kuala Lumpur, Vienna and Moscow. Charter flights connect Male′ several times a week with many western European capitals.

Boat

The airport functions as the biggest transport hub in the country, so if you want to travel to a resort from Male′, take the airport ferry and get a transfer to which-ever resort you want to visit. You'll need to book the transfer in advance and pay for it at the resort. Dhonis to/from the airport dock at the east end of Boduthakurufaanu Magu. This is also the best place to charter a dhoni for a day trip. Boats to Hulhumale', which is the overspill island for the capital and located on the other side of the airport island, depart from the brand-new ferry terminal east of the airport ferry dock.

Dhonis to nearby Viligili use the New Harbour on the southwest corner of Male'.

Safari boats and private yachts usually moor between Male' island and Viligili, or in the lagoon west of Hulhumale'. Safari-boat operators will normally pick up new passengers from the airport or Male', and ferry them directly to the boat.

GETTING AROUND
To/From the Airport
Dhonis shuttle between the airport and Male' all day and most of the night, de-parting promptly every 15 minutes. At the airport, dhonis leave from the jetties just north of the arrivals hall. In Male' they ar-rive and depart from the landing at the east end of Boduthakurufaanu Magu. The cross-ing costs Rf10 per person or US$1 if you don't have any local cash.

Bicycle
A bicycle is a good way to get around, but there's no place to rent one. Your guest-house might be able to arrange something. Be sure to lock it up and always use a light at night.

Taxi
The numerous taxis offer a few minutes of cool, air-conditioned comfort and a driver who can usually find any address in Male'. Many streets are one way and others may be blocked by construction work or stationary vehicles, so taxis will often take roundabout routes.

Fares are the same (Rf15) for any dis-tance. Taxis may charge Rf5 extra for lug-gage, and they cost Rf20 after midnight. You don't have to tip. There are quite a few taxi companies, but don't worry about the name of the company – just call one of the fol-lowing numbers: ☎ 3323132, ☎ 3325757 or ☎ 3322454.

AROUND MALE'

DIVING SITES
While the waters around Male' are said to be thick with rubbish and wrecked bicycles, there is some excellent diving within a short boat ride. The **Sea Explorers Dive School** (Map pp90-1; ☎ 3316172; www.seamaldives.com.mv; Bodufun-gadhu Magu) is a very well-regarded operation that does dive courses and trips for locals and the expat community. It costs US$40 per dive including all equipment and boat trip. If you do nine dives, the 10th dive is free. A PADI open-water course is US$410, and includes dives, equipment and certification.

Some of the best dives are along the edges of Vaadhoo Kandu (the channel between North and South Male' Atolls), which has two Protected Marine Areas. There is also a well-known wreck.

Hans Hass Place (also called Kikki Reef) is a demanding wall dive beside Vaadhoo Kandu in a Protected Marine Area. There is a lot to see at 4m or 5m, so it is good for snorkellers and less-experienced divers when the cur-rent is not too strong. There's a wide variety of marine life, including many tiny reef fish and larger species in the channel. Further down are caves and overhangs with sea fans and other soft corals.

Lion's Head is a Protected Marine Area that was once a popular place for shark feeding, and though this practice is now strongly discouraged, grey reef sharks and the occasional turtle are still common here. The reef edge is thick with fish, sponges and soft corals; although it drops steeply, with numerous overhangs, to over 40m, there is still much to see at snorkelling depth.

The wreck of the **Maldive Victory** is an im-pressive and challenging dive because of the potential for strong currents. This cargo ship hit a reef and sank on Friday 13 February 1981 and now sits with the wheelhouse at around 15m, and the propeller at 35m. The ship has been stripped of anything movable, but the structure is almost intact and pro-vides a home for a rich growth of new coral, sponges, tubastrea and large schools of fish.

VILIGILI
Probably the most obvious day trip from Male' is the short ferry ride to Viligili, the closest thing Male' has to a suburb, just

1km from the western shore of the capital. The short boat ride takes you into a different world. Far more relaxed than Male', Viligili has something of a Caribbean feel to it, with its brightly painted houses and laid-back pace. Here Maleans come to enjoy some space, play football and go swimming (usually fully clothed after the conservative fashion typically found on inhabited islands here – this is no place to be seen in a bikini). While it's still a great deal more cosmopolitan than most inhabited islands in the Maldives, if you only visit Male' and resorts, this is perhaps the best chance you'll have of seeing everyday life . There's nothing much to see but it's a pleasant excursion from Male'. The Symphony Garden, a pretty outdoor café by the harbour, is the most obvious place for refreshments. Viligili is easy to get to. Just catch one of the frequent dhoni ferries from New Harbour on the southwest corner of Male' (Rf3, 10 mins, every 5 mins).

HULHULE'

Better known as the airport island, Hulhule' was once densely wooded with very few inhabitants – just a graveyard and a reputation for being haunted. The first airstrip was built here in 1960, and in the early 1980s it had a major upgrade to accommodate long-distance passenger jets. Airport facilities have expanded to keep pace with the burgeoning tourist industry and now include a sizable terminal, workshops, administrative buildings, staff housing and the **Hulhule' Island Hotel** (p100; ☎ 3330888). Seaplanes land in the lagoon on the east side of the island. Everyone passes through on their way in and out of the country, but it's also a serious leisure option from Male' too due to the excellent swimming pool at the hotel, which is popular with expats who come to swim in the pool, drink in the bar or enjoy a good meal. The hotel runs a free transfer boat 14 times a day, from beside the President's Jetty (Jetty No 1) in Male'. Day membership that allows use of the swimming pool costs US$10; annual membership is available.

HULHUMALE'

One fascinating half-day trip from Male' is to easily accessible Hulhumale' – or, as many people see it – the future of the Maldives. Here, on the other side of the airport, 1.8 sq km of reef has been built up to create a brand new and entirely manmade island – the first phase of an ambitious project to relieve the pressure of growth on Male'. Sand and coral were dug up from the lagoon and pumped into big heaps on the reef top. Then bulldozers pushed the rubble around to form a quadrilateral of dry land about 2km long and 1km wide, joined by a causeway to the airport island. It's built up to about 2m above sea level to provide a margin of protection against the possibility of sea level rises.

This utopian project began in 1997 and now the northern section (about an eighth of the island's total area) is a fully functioning town, complete with rather Soviet apartment blocks, a school, an Internet café, pharmacy, an array of shops and a huge mosque – the golden glass dome of which is visible from all over the southern part of North Male' Atoll. There's even a surprisingly attractive artificial beach down the eastern side of the island. Coming here makes a fascinating contrast to the chaotic capital – here the planning is so precise and mathematical you could be on the film set of Brave New World. Walking across the acres of as yet empty plots of land towards the tiny conurbation on the far side is an eerie experience and a bewildering glimpse into the future of the Maldivian nation if sea levels continue to rise.

When the first-phase land is fully developed, by 2020, it will accommodate 50,000 people and have waterfront esplanades, light industrial areas, government offices, shopping centres, boulevards of palm trees, a marina and a national stadium. The basic layout has been carefully planned, but the details are still flexible, allowing for some natural, organic growth through multiple private developments. The second phase, a long-term proposal, involves reclaiming a further 2.4 sq km of land (engulfing all of Farukolhufushi, currently the Club Faru resort) and bringing the total population of Hulhumale' to around 100,000 people.

To visit Hulhumale' take the ferry (Rf5, 20 minutes, every 30 minutes) from the newly built terminal next to the airport ferry jetty and opposite the Maagiri Lodge.

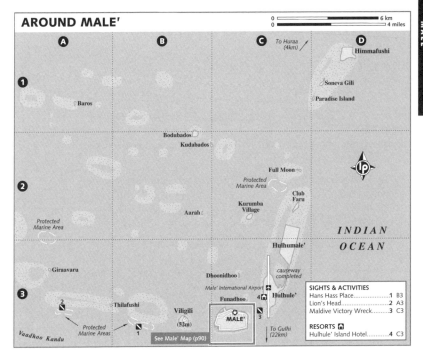

AROUND MALE'

On the island a bus service connects the ferry terminal to the settlement, but most people seem to enjoy the 10-minute walk.

OTHER ISLANDS

With so many small islands in the Maldives, it's not uncommon for individual islands to be allocated to specific activities or uses. One example is **Funadhoo**, between the airport and Male', which is used for fuel storage – it's a safe distance from inhabited areas, and convenient for both seagoing tankers and smaller boats serving the atolls.

One of the fastest-growing islands in the country, west of Viligli, is **Thilafushi**, also known as 'Rubbish Island'. It's where the capital dumps its garbage. The land is earmarked for industrial development, and its three conspicuous, round towers are part of a cement factory, which has just been built.

The island of **Dhoonidhoo**, just north of Male', was the British governor's residence until 1964. The house is now used for detaining people who may disrupt Maldivian society (political prisoners to you and me).

Slightly further north, **Aarah** is a small island used as the president's holiday retreat.

Another 3km further north, the island of **Kudabandos** was saved from resort development and became the Kuda Bandos Reserve, to be preserved in its natural state for the people's enjoyment. It has a few facilities for day-trippers, but is otherwise undeveloped – a small island encircled by a white beach. Tourists come to Kudabandos on 'island-hopping' trips from nearby resorts. Maldivian families and groups come on weekends and holidays. The **Bandos Island Resort's Male' office** (☎ 3325529) arranges a boat most Fridays for local people for about Rf30, including the Rf10 entry fee.

North & South Male' Atolls

At the centre of the country, the two atolls either side of Vaadhoo Kandu are the home of Maldivian tourism, where the first resorts cautiously developed in the 1970s. Today it's home to the Maldives' main international airport as well as to many of the country's most famous and best-established island resorts.

The dynamic national capital, Male', the economic and political centre of the country, lies between North and South Male' A tolls, and yet it's hard to imagine anywhere much more pristine than the islands that surround its bustle. Once you leave the area immediately around the capital and the airport, the nature of Maldivian geography means that even in the most developed part of the country there's little encroachment of the modern world on most islands.

Some excellent dive sites are found on these atolls, despite the coral bleaching caused by El Niño. Sites close to Male' have been heavily used, but in general they are in very good condition. Some of the most interesting sites are on either side of Vaadhoo Kandu, the channel that runs between North and South Male' Atolls. At the outer edge of the atolls, the dive sites are accessible from only a few resorts or by safari boat, and you'll probably have them all to yourself. Gaafaru Falhu Atoll, north of North Male' Atoll, has at least three diveable shipwrecks. Some of the Maldives' best surf breaks are also in North Male' Atoll.

This will be where many people experience the Maldives and both atolls are stunning visions of cobalt-blue water, white sand and island idyll – both worthy introductions to this most beguiling of countries.

NORTH MALE' ATOLL

North and South Male' Atolls together are officially known as Kaafu Administrative District and the capital island is **Thulusdhoo**, on the eastern edge of North Male' Atoll, with a population of about 800. Male' itself is not the capital as it is considered to be its own administrative district.

Thulusdhoo is an industrious island, known for *bodu beru* (big drums), traditional dancing and a government warehouse for salted fish. It is notable for producing Coca-Cola at the only Coke factory in the world where the drink is made from desalinated water.

The island of **Huraa** (population 700) is visited by tourists on island-hopping trips, but it's not yet as touristy as other North Male' islands. Huraa's dynasty of sultans,

founded in 1759 by Sultan Al-Ghaazi Hassan Izzaddeen, built a mosque on the island.

Many tourists visit **Himmafushi** (population 850) on excursions arranged from nearby resorts. The main street has two long rows of shops, where you can pick up some of the least expensive souvenirs in the country. Carved rosewood manta rays, sharks and dolphins are made locally. If you wander into the back streets, you quickly get away from the tourist strip to find an attractive, well-kept village with many modern amenities.

A sand spit has joined Himmafushi to the once separate island of **Gaamaadhoo**, where there used to be a prison. The surf break here, aptly called **Jailbreaks**, is a great right-hander, accessible by boat from nearby resorts.

The island of **Girifushi**, which has a military training camp, is off limits.

Further north, **Dhiffushi** is one of the most appealing local islands, with approximately 1000 people, three mosques and two schools. Mainly a fishing island, it has lots of greenery and grows several types of tropical fruit. Tourists from Meeru Island Resort are regular visitors.

Sights & Activities
DIVING
North Male' Atoll has been well explored by divers and has some superb dives. Some are heavily dived, especially in peak seasons. The following is just a sample of the best-known sites, listed from north to south.

Helengeli Thila, also called Bodu Thila, is long narrow thila on the eastern edge of the atoll famous for its prolific marine life. Reef fish include surgeonfish, bannerfish, butterflyfish and dense schools of snapper and fusilier. Larger fish and pelagics are also common – sharks, tuna, rays, jacks and a resident giant groper. Soft corals are spectacular in the cliffs and caves on the west side of the thila at about 25m. The large hard coral formations here are recovering from coral bleaching quite quickly, possibly because of the strong, nutrient-rich currents.

Also called Saddle, or Kuda Faru, **Shark Point** is in a Protected Marine Area and is subject to strong currents. Lots of white-tip and grey reef sharks can be seen in the channel between a thila and the reef, along with fusiliers, jackfish, stingrays and some impressive caves.

The alternative, less picturesque name of **Blue Canyon** is Kuda Thila, which means 'small thila'. A canyon, 25m to 30m deep and lined with soft, blue corals, runs beside the thila. The numerous overhangs make for an exciting dive, but require good buoyancy control. This site is recommended for experienced divers.

Bodu Hithi Thila is a prime manta-spotting site from December to March, with a good number of sharks and many reef fish. The soft corals on the sides of the thila are in excellent condition. If currents are moderate this site is suitable for intermediate divers, and the shallow waters atop the thila offer superb snorkelling. Nearby, the **Peak** is another great place to see mantas in season; it is also home to some large Napoleon wrasse.

The outer-reef slope of **Rasfari** drops down to a depth of more than 40m, but a couple of thilas rise up with their tops at about 25m. Grey reef sharks love it here – you might see 20 or 30 of them, as well as white-tip sharks, barracuda, eagle rays and trevally. It's a Protected Marine Area.

A curving cliff near a channel entrance forms the **Colosseum**, where pelagics perform. Sharks and barracuda are often seen here. Experienced divers do this as a drift dive, going right into the channel past ledges and caves, with soft corals and the occasional turtle. Even beginners can do this one in good conditions.

As the name suggests, **Aquarium** (a coral rock formation about 15m down) features a large variety of reef fish. A sandy bottom at 25m can have small sharks and rays, and you might also see giant wrasse and schools of snapper. It's an easy dive and suitable for snorkelling.

Across the kandu from the Aquarium, **Kani Corner** is the start of a long drift dive through a narrow channel with steep sides, caves and overhangs decorated with soft corals. Lots of large marine life can be seen, including sharks, barracuda, Napoleon wrasse and tuna. Beware of fast currents.

HP Reef, also called Rainbow Reef or Girifushi Thila, sits beside a narrow channel where currents provide much nourishment for incredibly rich growths of soft, blue corals, and support a large variety of reef fish and pelagics. The formations include large blocks, spectacular caves and a 25m vertical, swim-through chimney. It is a Protected Marine Area.

Also called Barracuda Giri, the attraction of **Okobe Thila** is the variety of spectacular reef fish that inhabit the shallow caves and crannies, including lionfish, scorpionfish, batfish, sweetlips, moray eels, sharks and big Napoleon wrasse.

The demanding dive at **Nassimo Thila** follows the north side of a fine thila, also known as Paradise Rock, which has superb gorgonians and sea fans on coral blocks, cliffs and overhangs. Numerous large fish frequent this site.

The best time to see the mantas for which **Manta Point** is famous is from May to November. Coral outcrops at about 8m are a 'cleaning station', where cleaner wrasse feed on parasites from the mantas' wings. Cliffs,

NORTH & SOUTH MALE' ATOLLS

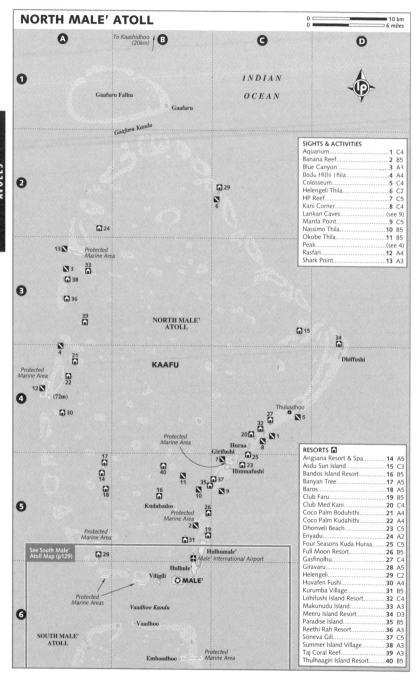

NORTH MALE' ATOLL

0 —————— 10 km
0 —————— 6 miles

To Kaashidhoo (20km)

Gaafaru Falhu

Gaafaru

Gaafaru Kandu

INDIAN OCEAN

NORTH MALE' ATOLL

KAAFU

Dhiffushi

Thulusdhoo

Protected Marine Area

Huraa
Girifushi
Himmafushi

Kudabados

Protected Marine Area

Protected Marine Area

See South Male'
Atoll Map (p129)

Protected
Marine Areas

Hulhumale'
Male' International Airport

Hulhule'
Viligili
MALE'

Vaadhoo Kandu

Vaadhoo

SOUTH MALE'
ATOLL

Emboodhoo

Protected
Marine Area

SIGHTS & ACTIVITIES
Aquarium	1 C4
Banana Reef	2 B5
Blue Canyon	3 A3
Bodu Hithi Thila	4 A4
Colosseum	5 C4
Helengeli Thila	6 C2
HP Reef	7 C5
Kani Corner	8 C4
Lankan Caves	(see 9)
Manta Point	9 C5
Nassimo Thila	10 B5
Okobe Thila	11 B5
Peak	(see 4)
Rasfari	12 A4
Shark Point	13 A3

RESORTS
Angsana Resort & Spa	14 A5
Asdu Sun Island	15 C3
Bandos Island Resort	16 B5
Banyan Tree	17 A5
Baros	18 A5
Club Faru	19 B5
Club Med Kani	20 C4
Coco Palm Boduhithi	21 A4
Coco Palm Kudahithi	22 A4
Dhonveli Beach	23 C5
Eriyadu	24 A2
Four Seasons Kuda Huraa	25 C5
Full Moon Resort	26 B5
Gasfinolhu	27 C4
Giravaru	28 A5
Helengeli	29 C2
Huvafen Fushi	30 A4
Kurumba Village	31 B5
Lohifushi Island Resort	32 C4
Makunudu Island	33 A3
Meeru Island Resort	34 D3
Paradise Island	35 B5
Reethi Rah Resort	36 A3
Soneva Gili	37 C5
Summer Island Village	38 A3
Taj Coral Reef	39 A3
Thulhaagiri Island Resort	40 B5

coral tables, turtles, sharks and numerous reef fish are other attractions, as are the nearby **Lankan Caves**.

The Protected Marine Area of **Banana Reef** has a bit of everything: dramatic cliffs, caves and overhangs; brilliant coral growths; big predators such as sharks, barracuda and groper; and prolific reef fish including jackfish, morays, Napoleon wrasse and blue-striped snapper. It was one of the first dive sites in the country to become internationally known. The reef top is excellent for snorkelling.

Resorts

Most of the resorts in North Male' Atoll are reached by speedboat from the airport, though some of the closest ones use a traditional and far slower dhoni. Some of the most distant ones offer optional seaplane transfers. Unless otherwise noted, airport transfers to the following resorts are by speedboat.

BUDGET

It's hard to think of anywhere more down-to-earth than little **Asdu Sun Island** (Asdhoo island; ☎ 6645051; www.asdu.com; s/d US$90/130; airport transfer 1½hr, US$110; 30 rooms). In an age of unbridled boutique luxury this charming resort retains the type of setting that originally kick-started the Maldivian tourist industry in the 1970s and 1980s: simple rooms free of TV and glass windows, no air-con and an informal atmosphere.

Divers, couples and families can be seen here in equal measure – there's some great surf nearby too and the resort organises trips for surfers to each spot. Beaches are lovely, with lots of healthy vegetation and huge palms. Much of the resort looks tired, but it's all part of its charm and if the repeating couples here are anything to go by, Asdu is easy to get hooked on.

Lohifushi Island Resort (Lhohifushi island; ☎ 6643451; www.lohifushi.com; s/d/t US$87/110/150; airport transfer by dhoni 1½hr, US$50, by speedboat 25min, US$80; 127 rooms; 🏊 🛥) is one of the best choices for an active water-sports holiday. As well as the usual sailing, windsurfing and water-skiing, there's a very surfable left-hand wave off the southeast corner of the island called Lohi's, overlooked by a surfers' bar and viewing deck. Other breaks are accessible by boat (US$10

per person for three hours, minimum four persons).

This is a big, modern resort on a long, narrow island. The standard rooms are fan-cooled, but have phones and hot water; air-con is available in more pricey rooms. There are tennis and squash courts, a football field, a volleyball court, a small swimming pool, a children's play area and a Japanese-style spa-massage centre.

Fishing enthusiasts can choose between sunrise fishing, night fishing and big-game fishing. Snorkellers can walk out on the jetty to get to the edge of the house reef, but for great snorkelling you'll need to take a boat trip.

Plenty of good dive sites are accessible, and the resort is quite popular with divers who are catered for by the five-star PADI dive centre.

Lohifushi is quite a big resort and somewhat impersonal, but you can get a great deal here on the rooms (particularly in triples) and it's great for young divers and surfers.

When we visited **Giravaru** (Giraavaru island; ☎ 6640440; www.giravaru.com; s/d US$125/145; airport transfer 15min US$45; 65 rooms; 🏊 🛥 🛥) the resort was planning to do a total refit and reopen in 2007 as a more upmarket place. However, such claims can often come to nothing, so check via the resort website to see if this has happened or not! The Giravaru people are believed to descend from the earliest inhabitants of the Maldives, and as such they are ethnically distinct from the rest of the population. About 30 years ago the number of people on the island declined to the point where they no longer included the 40 adult males required to support a mosque, so the islanders all moved to Male' and Giravaru became available for resort development. Sadly there's nothing left from the aboriginal Giravaran culture on the island.

As the resort was at the time of research, it would be hard to recommend unreservedly. Admittedly the diving school here is excellent and extremely friendly, with plenty of good diving sites nearby. Yet the whole place was pretty average otherwise – particularly suffering from its proximity to Thilafushi, or Rubbish Island as it's known to one and all. The main jetty and one of the island's two main beaches look out over the smoking stacks of Thilafushi in the distance, while rubbish washes up regularly on the otherwise lovely white beaches. The tiny swimming pool was also in a state of bad repair and going unused as a result. Lunch and breakfast were particularly lacklustre, although there was often a good choice at the big dinner buffet. The majority Italian guests seem entirely happy with the experience, however, even when being serenaded by instrumental versions of Tears in Heaven over breakfast. Let's hope the refit will include a music policy rethink.

Meeru Island Resort (Meerufenfushi island; ☎ 6643157; www.meeru.com; full board s/d/wb US$130/155/310; airport transfer 60min, $100, by seaplane 10min, $185; 227 rooms; ✶ ☐ ☎), a popular and highly recommended family and diving resort, has lots of laid-back charm and some functional style brought about by a late 1990s refit. It's at North Male' Atoll's most eastern point and travelling due east from here you'd hit nothing until Sumatra.

Meerufenfushi actually means 'Sweet Water Island' in Divehi, and the island's wells were used to replenish passing dhonis in the past. The unusual amount of ground water has created a large amount of natural vegetation and now some of the 28-hectare island is used for growing fruit and vegetables. Most guests are from Britain, Germany, France, Italy and other parts of Europe. The resort doesn't organise much entertainment, but the bars are busy most evenings, especially because many of the guests are on all-inclusive packages.

There's a huge choice of rooms – from standards in a U-shaped block near the swimming pool, to the Coral and Dolphin Suites – both at the end of their own private jetties and coming with a personal butler.

The house reef can only be reached by boat and these leave every two hours to take snorkellers and divers off to the outer reef where the aquatic life is fantastic.

All the usual water sports are offered, fishing trips are popular, and the vast lagoon is perfect for learning sailing and windsurfing. Meeru has its own safari boats, and two- or three-day cruises can be taken from the resort. Inexpensive excursions go to the fishing village on neighbouring Dhiffushi. Those interested in Maldivian history and culture will also appreciate the small museum at Meeru where there's a huge blue whale skeleton on display.

Ocean-Pro dive school (www.oceanpro-diveteam .com) is a large and efficient operation. A single dive is US$39 with tank and weights only, or US$42 including full equipment rental, plus US$10 per dive for the boat trip. A US$2 discount applies after seven dives, and there's a good six-day, no-limit dive deal. An open-water course costs US$619. A whole slew of great dive sites are accessible in the channels within 5km. Once known only as a budget resort and dive destination, Meeru now caters to a wide variety of interests and budget levels – it's a big resort but it's not crowded and has retained its personal, friendly feel.

Small, intimate and low-key, **Thulhaagiri Island Resort** (Thalhaagiri island; ☎ 6645930; www .thulhaagiri.com.mv; s/d/wb US$160/170/340; airport transfer 30min, US$80; 69 rooms; ✶ ☎) is an astonishingly pretty island with wide, sloping white beaches and a thick vegetation of palms. It represents a great choice for its price range, because although it's less expensive, its small size gives it a more exclusive feel than some of the bigger budget places. Guests are mainly German but hail also from Britain and other European countries.

The diving school offers a full open-water course including all equipment for US$470, and individual dives at US$37 each, plus equipment. The problem here is that each piece of equipment you borrow is charged separately and therefore quickly adds up – so if you want to do a lot of diving here, bring as many of the basics as possible. There's a good water-sports centre with catamarans and water-skiing available although the small, rather murky swimming pool is the only real evidence that this is a budget resort despite all other appearances. Rooms – like the slightly dated public areas – are in a rustic style featuring thatched roofs and wooden interiors. The 17 water villas have four-poster beds, colourful fabrics and coffee-making facilities – they're decent, but not especially great value at their high-season price. All meals are buffets, and they're very good for a resort in this range, offering plenty of variety and quality ingredients.

One of the largest resorts in the country, **Bandos Island Resort** (Bodubados island; ☎ 6640088; www.bandos.com; s/d/t/wb US$143/175/225/1212; airport transfer 20min, US$50; 225 rooms; ✶ ☐ ☎), has developed and expanded enormously since it opened as the second resort in the Maldives in 1972. It has an enviable range of facilities – a 500-seat conference centre, coffee shop, several restaurants, a disco, tennis courts, a billiard room, sauna, gym, swimming pool, beauty salon and spa-massage service. The childcare centre is free during the day, and only about US$5 per hour in the evening. With all these facilities, the island is quite intensely developed and resembles a well-manicured town centre rather than a typical tropical island.

Sailing and windsurfing are available, along with a full range of motorised water sports and an active big-game fishing centre. Fine, narrow beaches surround the island, and the house reef is handy for snorkelling and diving. Lots of fish and a small wreck can be seen here. The state-of-the-art dive centre does trips to about 40 dive sites in the area, and offers a full range of courses, including nitrox and rebreather training. A single boat dive costs US$57, including all equipment and boat charges, or US$49 with your own equipment. The diving health clinic here has a decompression chamber available to anyone who needs it (though it's very expensive). An open-water course costs US$520.

Bandos caters for evening visitors and day-trippers from Male', but currently does not provide a regular boat – call the resort if you want to arrange something. Airline crews and travel agents often use Bandos for short-term stays, as well as guests from all over Europe and Asia, so there can be a very mixed group here.

Rooms are modern, with red-tiled roofs, white-tiled floors, air-con, hot water, hair-dryer, minibar and phone. Other categories include the Jacuzzi Beach Villa and the luxurious new water villas, built in 2005. These include services such as a private butler, although the leap in price is quite staggering.

The main Gallery Restaurant does three international buffet meals daily. Other eateries include a fine-dining restaurant, the 24-hour Seabreeze Café with à la carte pasta and curries, and the Harbour Grill for steak and seafood. The Sand Bar hosts live bands, disco nights, cultural shows or karaoke several nights a week. This is one of the liveliest resorts in the country. Bandos is great for families and those who like big resorts where there's potential to meet lots of new people and to have a huge range of activities available. For a romantic break look elsewhere though; Bandos is not for you.

Helengeli (Helengeli island; ☎ 6642881; www .helengeli.net; s/d/t US$145/175/238; airport transfer by speedboat 2hr, US$110, by seaplane 20min, US$160; 50 rooms; ▨ 🖳 🦞), the most northerly resort in North Male' Atoll, is highly recommended for divers – almost 40 dive sites are accessible from here, and due to the resort's remote location most of them are used only by Helengeli guests and the occasional passing safari boat. The 2km-long house reef is excellent, so you need not venture far for snorkelling either, and qualified divers can do unguided scuba dives from the beach. Nearby Helengeli Thila is considered one of the best dive sites in the country. Dive costs are around US$60 for a boat dive with all equipment provided, or US$50 with tank and weights only. It's US$2 less after the seventh dive, and there's a good six-day, unlimited dive deal. An open-water course costs US$619. The **Ocean-Pro dive base** (www .oceanpro-diveteam.com) aims for personalised service and tries to keep guests with the same dive guides for their whole stay.

The resort was extensively renovated in 2004, and has modern rooms with air-con, hot water and open-air bathrooms. All rooms face the water; the best swimming beach is at the western tip of the island. Helengeli is a fair-sized island with plenty of natural vegetation, an uncrowded feel and secluded accommodation. The restaurant alternates between set-menu meals and buffets, including a weekly beach barbecue – the variety of food may sometimes be limited, but the atmosphere and service are good. There's no windsurfing, sailing or other water sports, but a few excursions are offered, including dolphin watching and trips to the inhabited island of Gaafaru nearby. Evening entertainment is very low-key, consisting mainly of a few drinks at the delightful beachfront bar, and an early night in preparation for the next day's diving activity.

Summer Island Village (Ziyaaraifushi island; ☎ 6641949; www.summerislandvillage.com; s/d/t/wb US$140/210/280/260; airport transfer by fast dhoni 1½hr, US$90; 108 rooms; ▨ 🖳), a long, thin island, is all about affordable fun and wins lots of repeat visits from German and British holidaymakers who enjoy the laid-back approach and profit from the good-value all-inclusive packages. The management has been making an effort to increase the vegetation and wildlife on the island – an aviary for rearing parrots was brimming with birds when we visited, and gardeners were working very hard on vegetable beds and planting new trees, all helping to make the resort more attractive.

Accommodation is a little spartan but clean and adequate, all rooms being on the beach and all having an extra bed and a spacious outdoor bathroom. The units are tightly packed together, and some rooms are in two-storey units. The modern-style water bungalows at the island's southern end are a recent addition. They're no great shakes, with no direct access to the water and just a small hole in the floor looking into the sea, but they're bigger and more comfortable than the standard rooms.

Sand floors in the public areas and friendly staff give the whole place a relaxed feel. Meals are buffets with a modest selection of curry, fish, salads and vegetables. Weekly theme nights feature Asian and international cuisine.

The lagoon is wide and shallow, so the resort is more suited to windsurfing, water-skiing and sailing than to snorkelling or swimming. The island has quite good beaches on both sides, though some stretches are protected by somewhat unattractive break-waters, which did at least ensure there was no significant tsunami damage here.

There are some great dive sites within about 5km – a single dive with equipment costs US$46; an open-water course costs US$483. The new Serena Spa has massages available from $30. A daily snorkelling trip is included in the package (excluding equipment), as are table tennis, volleyball and badminton. A decent, economical choice and rightly popular with divers.

MIDRANGE

Dhonveli Beach (Kanuhuraa island; ☎ 6640055; www.dhonvelibeach.com; s/d US$165/244; airport transfer 30min, US$70; 150 rooms; ✖ ▯ ☂) suffered full-scale devastation during the tsunami, being on the outer eastern rim of the atoll and totally exposed. Buildings and vegetation were destroyed and the resort has been in the process of rebuilding ever since. When we visited Dhonveli was up and running again, although work was still

being completed to make this an excellent and high-quality resort. This included the building of 24 brand-new and rather lovely water bungalows, a gorgeous new spa and the re-creation of several stretches of beach that were washed away by the tsunami.

This resort attracts surfers in big numbers from March to November – they even have their own bar area overlooking the island's private surf break, a consistent left-hander called Pasta Point. Outdoor tables here are great for a beer and a view of the surfing action.

The island is small, with scrubby natural vegetation and a few big banyan trees, but extensive landscaping is under way around the main beach, the bar and the swimming pool. The beach on the north side of the island is great for swimming and sunbathing, as well as being safe for children. The new rooms are fully equipped and come in various sizes, with designs that are more imaginative than at many resorts.

All meals are buffet style and feature a fair selection of good-quality food. Dhonveli is not a big diving destination, but there are lots of good dive sites nearby (the Protected Marine Area at HP Reef is very close).

Recovery from the disastrous tsunami should be complete by the time you read this, and Dhonveli is one of the classiest and most convenient surfing resorts anywhere in the country.

The wonderful **Makunudu Island** (Makunudhoo island; ☎ 6646464; www.makunudu.com; s/d US$220/250; airport transfer 50min, US$120; 36 rooms; ✖) remains one of our very favourite resorts in the country. Just 6 acres in area, the tiny island almost looks like it might sink under the sheer weight of lush vegetation on it – and the surrounding reef is so big that it's hard for unaccustomed speedboats to find their way into the dock through the shallow lagoon.

Things are extremely tasteful here, but almost unbelievably low-key as well, with individual thatched-roof bungalows hidden among the jungle-like foliage. All rooms face the beach and feature natural finishes, varnished timber, textured white walls, open-air bathrooms, and all facilities except the purposefully excluded TV. The service is of a high standard and the food is excellent, thanks to the French chef. Breakfast and lunch are buffets while most dinners are a choice of thoughtfully prepared set menus, served in the delightful open-sided restaurant. Beach barbecues are a weekly event and breakfast can be served in your room.

Guests are mainly German, British, French and Italian couples who come to relax, or who are on their honeymoon. Honeymooners from all over the world have planted the island with memorial trees with plaques. This has become too popular though, and the management has had to stop the practice due to a huge proliferation of trees growing everywhere.

There are excellent dive sites in the area, the house reef is great for snorkelling, and an introductory dive is free from the small diving school. Dive groups tend to be small and friendly. Windsurfing and sailing are free, as are shorter excursions. If you want a small, exclusive, natural-style resort, Makunudu is one of the very best in the Maldives.

Established in 1972, **Kurumba Village** (Vihamanaafushi island; ☎ 6642324; www.kurumba.com; s/d/t US$242/253/342; airport transfer 15min, US$45; 180 rooms; ⊠ 🖳 🏊) was the first resort in the Maldives. It was completely refurbished in 2003 and reopened as a very high-quality place with a relative sense of history. Some may feel its overly manicured gardens and foliage as well as its relentlessly modern architecture combine to make the resort feel a little sterile; others, however, will like its grand country-club style – golf buggies rule the roads here and the resort is big enough for this to be justifiable.

Kurumba is the closest resort to Male', and as such it caters regularly for business conferences and conventions as well as day-trippers from the capital who come for the renowned restaurants. If you're sensitive to aircraft noise, you may find it a little too close to the airport, although Male' International is hardly Heathrow or JFK.

The rooms come in a large range of categories – the pool villas being especially impressive, each with its own pool in a private back garden. For those wanting to splurge there are presidential villas and the Royal Kurumba Residence, which should satisfy even the most demanding international jet-setters.

There's no end to the facilities available, from a huge and well-equipped dive school (US$57 per dive with all equipment) to a

water-sports centre offering every conceivable discipline, tennis courts, baby-sitters, a gorgeous spa, two gyms, two pools and an incredible seven restaurants. Kurumba is a place for scale and grandeur rather than a desert island hideaway, but it remains a popular choice for both couples and families.

Once Club Med Faru before Club Med's lease expired, and just beyond the Male' overflow island of Hulhumale', **Club Faru** (Farukolufushi island; ☎ 6640553; www.clubfaru.com; s/d US$190/260; airport transfer 20min US$25; 152 rooms) reopened as a separate but similar-style resort in late 2005. It's all-inclusive and the rooms are basic but modern, all housed in two-storey blocks, not making it ideal for peace and quiet or privacy. Eventually the island will become part of the Hulhumale' development (see p104) and its future was not certain at the time of research.

Magnificently laid out with real style and class, **Full Moon Resort** (Furanafushi island; ☎ 6642010; www.fullmoonmaldives.com; s/d/wb US$286/286/418; airport transfer 20min, US$45; 156 rooms; ⊠ 🖳 🏊) has the ambience of an upmarket country club rather than remote tropical island. This is in part due to its proximity to the capital of course, but everything here is clearly aimed at the urbane sophisticate anyway, from the gorgeously understated public areas to the luxurious spa, housed on its own island linked to the resort by a footbridge.

The tsunami hit Full Moon hard, destroying all the water bungalows, although all 52 have now been rebuilt in grand style and are extremely impressive. The standard beachfront deluxe rooms are also charming and feature thatched roofs, shuttered windows and private gardens or terraces.

The Thai restaurant, Mediterranean restaurant and the Italian grill/pizza place serve more interesting food than the buffets at the main restaurant, so it might be best to take a bed and breakfast package and bring extra cash to spend in the speciality restaurants, although this will be more expensive, of course.

A full range of facilities is squeezed onto this small island, including an inviting swimming pool which has its own waterfall, tennis courts, a gym, spa and business centre. There are no motorised water sports, and the lagoon is unsuitable for snorkelling. The efficient dive centre charges about US$57 for a boat dive with all equipment, and US$555 for a complete open-water course. Windsurfing and sailing are available, as is big-game fishing. Full Moon is a great choice for a sophisticated break.

Located right at the top of North Male' Atoll, **Eriyadu** (Eriyadhoo island; ☎ 6644487; www .aaa-resortsmaldives.com/eriyadu; half-board s/d/t US$192/296/399; airport transfer 50min, US$80; 120 rooms; ✖) is pleasantly remote, which is a major incentive for divers who come here for the uncrowded diving. It's also wonderfully laid back without the fussy overservice that characterises so many Maldivian resorts.

After a bad fire it experienced at its power plant in 2005, the whole island is up and running again, having escaped the tsunami with only the loss of a few of its sunbeds.

The island is full of repeat visitors – the vast majority of which are German. Children aren't really encouraged as there are no facilities tailored to them, and this leads to a very quiet and undisturbed atmosphere.

The island is an oval shape, with a good reef all around it, great for snorkelling with turtles and dolphins regular fixtures just metres from the beach. There's no pool but a spa was under construction at the time of our visit.

The **Werner Lau Dive Centre** (www.wernerlau .com) is a very professional operation. A single boat dive is US$50 with all equipment, US$45 with tank and weights only, but the six-day no-limit dive package will cost US$390 – making it a great deal. An open-water course is US$560.

The rooms are divided into standards and superiors. The standards are in a block set back from the beach, while the superiors are in two-room blocks on the small but pretty beach. They're comfortable and with considerable rustic charm.

The island itself is quite heavily developed, but the buildings are interspersed with lots of shady trees and shrubbery, and there are fine, white beaches all around. Rooms have polished timber floors, TV, minibar and other mod cons. The sand-floor restaurant serves most meals in buffet style, with a varied selection of European dishes, curries and seafood.

The usual water sports and (expensive) excursions are available, as is some low-key evening entertainment, but this resort is mainly for diving, snorkelling and relaxing on the beach.

People who like Club Med tend to love Club Med – and the excited couples and families at **Club Med Kani** (Kanifinolhu island; ☎ 6643152; www.clubmed.com; full board s/d/wb US$155/310/620; airport transfer 30min, $US100; 225 rooms; ✖ ⬛ ✖), the only Club Med resort in the Maldives, seemed to be loving every minute when we visited. Indeed, you pretty much have to come through a Club Med package to stay here, as FIT (fully independent traveller) reservations aren't even accepted until 24 hours before arrival, making advance bookings impossible. French guests make up half of the resort's guests at any time while Italians are the second biggest group.

The resort is large and well set up for activities with a big pool, diving school and water-sports centre, and the place was humming with people coming and going from one activity to another when we visited, not to mention the nightly live entertainment and disco, which make it one of the livelier resorts in the country (though this is possibly not saying much given sleepy local standards).

Day passes are for sale for visitors from Male' – a full pass costs Rf1000 and gives access to the pool and beaches and a buffet lunch, while you can also buy dinner passes and evening entertainment passes (Rf190).

There are three room categories – the beachfront rooms cost a little more than garden rooms, and water bungalows are even more expensive. They're all comfortably furnished and feature lots of natural timber, air-con, a phone and minibar. The meals are very good with accompanying wine, beer or soft drinks included in the package price. Drinks at the bar cost extra (US$3 to US$8).

The island itself is quite large and well vegetated, and the beachside bar and entertainment areas are particularly spacious. The wide lagoon is a good place to learn sailing or windsurfing (both included in the price), but not as good for snorkelling (though snorkelling trips to other reefs are also included). Fitness sessions, one daily scuba dive, volleyball and other games and activities are all included, but you pay extra for excursions and spa treatments.

The less exclusive of the two Taj resorts in the Maldives, **Taj Coral Reef** (Hembadhoo island; ☎ 6641948; www.tajhotels.com; s/d/wb US$290/

310/515; airport transfer 45min, US$95; 65 rooms; 🌊 💻 🏊) is a popular and well-run place at the northern end of North Male' Atoll. The orange roof tiles here may jar somewhat with the Robinson Crusoe look most visitors expect from the Maldives, but the excellent beaches look so good that they more than compensate.

Popular with Japanese divers and European honeymooners, the resort offers plenty for both: some excellent diving nearby with the **Blue In dive centre** (www.blueinmaldives.com), including a great shipwreck at 22m at the end of the main jetty, and romantic, beautifully attired bedrooms for honeymooners; the beachfront rooms are big, comfortable and fully furnished with TV, in-house movies, minibar and the works. The 35 water bungalows are even bigger and the deluxe lagoon villas are especially lovely.

All meals are buffet, with theme nights featuring Chinese, Italian, Maldivian or other cuisines. In addition, a small, à la carte beach restaurant specialises in Indian food. Beach erosion is a problem in places, with beach wideness changing according to the time of year and somewhat unsightly protective walls dotting the lagoon around half the island, though there's an interesting and accessible house reef on the other side, and a good beach at one corner.

Paradise Island (Lankanfinolhu island; ☎ 6640011; www.villahotels.com; s/d/wb US$310/320/550; airport transfer 20min, US$60; 260 rooms; 🌊 💻 🏊) is something of a byword for massive impersonal resorts in the Maldives, the island offering a huge range of facilities and services to travellers from all over the world looking for a bargain. Indeed, pulling into the cobalt-blue waters of the large harbour, the beaches at least do live up to the resort's name.

The facilities are all perfectly good, even if the public areas are rather dated. Extras from diving to drinking add up quickly here, so be careful if your package price sounds too good to be true.

Rooms are clean, with white tiles, white walls, air-con and satellite TV. Water bungalows are a bit bigger but were closed for refurbishment at the time of research. Full board is definitely worth it: you get a decent buffet for every meal and the other three restaurants are nothing to shout about so you won't find yourself wanting to eat elsewhere that much.

The island is well landscaped and has good beaches and a swimming pool. Some rooms are a long way from the restaurant, and some don't have much of a view. Activities include gym, squash, badminton, tennis and billiards – everything costs extra except darts and table tennis. Snorkelling is excellent in the lagoon and on the house reef, which is full of fascinating marine life. The **Delphis dive centre** (www.delphis.com.mv) is very friendly but not the cheapest around. However, there are plenty of excellent diving sites nearby and the location is unquestionably a highlight of the resort.

Paradise is a popular, activity-packed resort with great beaches. It's pervaded by a sense of the naff, but it's good value and always busy.

Understated, sophisticated class jumps out at you from the moment you arrive at **Baros** (Baros island; ☎ 6642672; www.baros.com; s/d/wb US$430/440/742; airport transfer 25min, US$95; 75 rooms; 🌊 💻), one of the most popular resorts in the country. Closed for much of 2005 and refitted as a result of a long-planned renovation rather than any tsunami damage, Baros reopened a magnificently rejuvenated place the same year and is definitely a classic luxury resort at surprisingly decent prices.

The centrepiece of the new resort is the impressive Lighthouse Restaurant, a white circus top–style fine-dining and cocktail bar establishment, where guests have to book and which has the feel of a terribly exclusive yacht club. Other dining can be had at the far less formal Cayenne Restaurant, overlooking the reef, where you can have your food cooked anyway you choose by the fleet of chefs. All guests are on a bed-and-breakfast basis, allowing them to enjoy the different eating opportunities throughout their stay (although this adds up quickly of course).

The atmosphere is intimate and quiet, with children under six not allowed – this is upmarket European honeymoon territory through and through. There's 'gentle' jazz and Maldivian music three times a week, and that's about the scope of the nightlife. During the day most people seem to be enjoying diving, swimming and treatments in the luxurious new spa. The three room categories are all beautiful. Even the standard 'luxe villa' is a 95 sq metre dark woodwork of gorgeous refinement with a sumptuous outdoor bathroom, while the water bunga-lows are proper holiday-of-a-lifetime stuff.

Baros is one of many upmarket resorts that has made a conscious decision not to have a swimming pool. This is a superbly rejuve-nated resort that has rightly earned a huge following of loyal visitors and is a superb choice for a luxurious romantic getaway.

TOP END

You'll be greeted with both a scoop of homemade coconut ice cream and an ice-cold towel when you arrive at **Angsana Resort & Spa** (Ihuru island; ☎ 6643502; www.angsana.com /maldives; half-board s/d US$759/767; airport transfer 30min, US$99; 45 rooms; 🗶 🖵), a perfect way for the management to say that they don't do things around here like they do everywhere else.

Just across the water from its sister resort Banyan Tree, Angsana opened five years ago and characterises itself, much like Ban-yan Tree, by an innovative management team who combine luxury with thought. It has raised its standards and service consid-erably, although it still generally works out cheaper to stay here than at Banyan Tree.

With its canopy of palm trees and sur-rounding a gorgeous white beach, Angsana conforms exactly to the tropical-island stere-otype and often features in photographs pub-licising the Maldives. The house reef forms a near perfect circle around the island, bril-liant for snorkelling and shore dives. Look near the jetty for the 'barnacle', the oldest of several metal structures on which a small electric current stimulates coral growth.

All nonmotorised water sports are free, including all snorkelling equipment. The best dive sites are some distance away on the edges of the atoll, but boats take divers out morning and afternoon.

The stylish rooms are all decorated in contemporary style, with black furniture, lime-green fabrics and designer bathrooms. There's a modern look in the restaurant too, but most guests prefer to eat dinner on the deck overlooking the sea. The spa consists of eight treatment rooms, almost all dou-bles, and the treatments are almost identical to the unmitigated luxury of Banyan Tree. Angsana offers a very Banyan Tree mix of cuisine, comfort and indulgence, but it's somewhat more relaxed and informal.

The intriguing **Banyan Tree** (Vabbinfaru island; ☎ 6643147; www.banyantree.com/maldives; half-board

s/d US$833/841; airport transfer 25min, US$99; 48 rooms; 🗶 🖵) is a wonderful mix of shameless lux-ury and ecotourism project. Part of the in-ternational Banyan Tree chain, it's actually about as un-chainlike as can be imagined. Remote enough from Malc' to feel like the true desert island experience, Banyan Tree offers a refreshing take on the top-end ex-perience given that it doesn't have many of the features (such as a swimming pool) that many resorts would take for granted. This is intentional and ties in with the overall guid-ing policy that tourism must be sustainable and eco-friendly.

This is a romantic resort, extremely quiet and popular with couples. The most unique feature of the resort is the marine laboratory on the island. This is no gimmick, but a seri-ous research facility run by a charming team of marine biologists. Guests are able to help out in various capacities – from planting their own coral in the coral garden, helping with reef cleans and even monitoring the sharks and turtles kept under observation in cages just off the island shore. All of these activities are free and marine biology lessons are given twice a week to any guest whose in-terest in the sea has suddenly been aroused.

The rooms are similarly unique, with the use of lots of wood imported from Indonesia; they have a gorgeous feel with terrific and unusual outdoor bathrooms. The tsunami did not affect the island so all buildings date from when Banyan Tree first opened here in 1995.

The house reef is excellent for snorkel-ling and diving, but the very best dive sites are some distance away on the edges of the atoll. A single boat dive is very pricey, how-ever, at US$98 with all equipment (pack-ages of dives become much cheaper); an open-water course is US$628.

Guests come from all over Europe and Asia, and the superb buffet meals satisfy their varied tastes. Lunch under the palm trees is a delight, with barbecued fish, succulent steak, fresh salads and delicious desserts – even a cheese platter. The restaurant and bar are both casually elegant, open-sided spaces with sand floors and quality furniture.

This was one of the first resorts to have a spa, billed as a 'sanctuary for the senses', where Thai-trained therapists offer you everything

(Continued on page 125)

Many students come to Male' to finish their high-school education (p27)

Theemuge (p97) is the president's official residence

The Male' produce market (p95) is full of tropical flavours

DENNIS WISKEN

Blue waters, white sands and coconut palms (p40) – the typical Maldivian scene

DENNIS JONES

Try your hand at windsurfing, one of many water sports (p53) on offer at Maldivian resorts

Over-water villas (p48) are a feature of almost every resort in the Maldives

JAMES L'

JAMES LYON

Enjoying the sea outlook at Club Faru (p113) on Farukolufushi island

Heading out to one of the Maldives' many surf breaks (p80)

JOHN BORTHWICK

Catamaran sailing off
Farukolafushi
island (p113)

DENNIS JONES

MICHAEL AW

The infinity pool is one indicator of a fashionable
resort (p126)

Maldivian resorts are the destination of choice for many couples and honeymooners (p49)

JAMES LYO

One of the few island settlements (p28) in the atolls

Another spectacular sunset in the Maldives

MICHAEL AW

Tuna fishing (p27) is one of the country's biggest sources of income

JOHN BORTHWICK

Islam (p30) is the official religion of the entire population

A rubber ring, water and youthful exuberance – water sports (p53) are a way of life in the Maldives

JOHN BORTHWICK

Children of a local madrasa (primary school; p26), Male'

Traditional Maldivian boat or dhoni (p29)

Minaret of a local mosque in
Eydhafushi (p152), the capital of
Baa district

Smoking a hookah (water pipe; p102), Male'

Sail-powered *vedis* (p186) are used for trade between Male' and the outer atolls

Trade for tourists – drinks, shark jaws and concha shells

(Continued from page 116)

from a 60-minute turmeric and honey body rub to a Hawaiian Lomi Lomi for two. For the more active, night fishing, windsurfing, sailing and snorkelling are included in the price.

Angsana, Banyan Tree's 'little sister' resort, is just across a small channel next door – a boat goes back and forth every half-hour, allowing guests at each resort to enjoy the other's facilities.

Redefining the luxury market for the Maldives when it opened in 2005, One & Only at **Reethi Rah Resort** (Medhufinolhu island; ☎ 6648800; www.oneandonlyresorts.com; s/d/wb $900/900/1400; airport transfer by luxury yacht 50min, $100, by seaplane 10min, price varies; 130 rooms; ✗ ☐ ☎) is the kind of place where you expect to see only movie stars and royalty. Indeed, when we arrived we were immediately asked not to take to photographs, as there were 'top celebrities' on the island.

Reethi Rah ('pretty island') is nothing short of astonishing. One of the longest islands in the country, the resort is scattered with secluded and spectacular villas, 32 of which are over water, all offering privacy and sophisticated luxury.

Far more so than the other One & Only property in the Maldives (see p157), Reethi Rah is about glamour and style, and shamelessly so. If you aren't comfortable with almost mind-boggling pampering and fly anything other than first class, this probably isn't the place for you.

Rooms have every possible convenience, and are some of the most enormous in the country, beautifully furnished in a modern style that picks and mixes different Asian designs. Some have their own pools.

All guests get around by bicycle, although those unable to ride can call club cars from reception to take them around – the island is rather too large to be covered comfortably on foot. There are several gorgeous beaches and even a charming canal that was built through the island for the sea to flow through. Vegetation is improving quickly – with 16,000 trees and two million plants planted since One & Only took over the resort from a low-budget, far smaller island a few years ago. To put this in perspective, the island was just 39 acres when One & Only got it, and it now stands at an incredible (for the Maldives, at least) 109 acres. Most impressively of all, it's hard to see that this is land reclamation as it has been done so well.

There are three superb restaurants: the main one, Reethi Restaurant; a chic Japanese restaurant, Tapasake; and perhaps the most magical, the open-air Fanditha, at the northern tip of the island, an informal Middle Eastern–style restaurant where cuisine from Lebanon to Iran is served on luxurious day beds and massive cushions, described by One & Only as 'shipwreck chic'.

The enormous ESPA-run spa features 10 treatment rooms, and is predominated by Asian treatments – Ayurvedic therapies and Balinese, Thai and Shiatsu massage, for example. Other attractions include two tennis courts and pro-tennis trainers, a superb diving school and a full water-sports program. The house reef is superb and great for snorkelling. Guests from Germany, the UK and Japan predominate, many of whom are honeymooners.

Book as far in advance as you can; it can be impossible to get a room at short notice. Reethi Rah remains the most talked about resort in the Maldives, as exemplified by its notice from *Condé Nast Traveller*, which included the resort on its 2006 Hot List.

Huvafen Fushi (Nakatchafushi Island; ☎ 6644222; www.huvafenfushi.com; s/d/wv US$1100/1116/1600; airport transfer 30min, US$120; 43 rooms; ✗ ☐ ☎), a recent Per Aquum addition the Maldivian luxury market, opened in 2004 to massive acclaim, making it onto *Condé Nast's* 2005 Hot List and generally lauded as a milestone in boutique luxury in the Maldives.

Understated and more than a little fabulous, Huvafen Fushi is the last word in privacy and modern romance. The rooms are stunning in their simplicity, space and design savvy, all somehow still managing to feature 40-in plasma-screen TVs, Bose surround systems, iPod plug-in points, espresso machines and remote-control everything. The water villas are some of the most impressive in the country – each with its own sizeable plunge pool on an enclosed deck overlooking the sea, with access to the lagoon down a staircase. The bedrooms and bathrooms are massive and both masterpieces of understatement despite including luxuries such as rain showers and the largest king-sized beds we've ever come across. Linen is from Frette and furniture by names such as Frank Gehry – the vibe is architect-designed through and through.

Despite this the atmosphere within the resort itself is informal and relaxed. The international clientele is made up mainly of honeymooners and couples, who spend the day by the enormous infinity pool overlooking the sea, lunching in one of the three superb restaurants (Celsius for international, Salt for fish and seafood and Raw for Japanese) and being treated at the spa – unique for having the only underwater treatment room in the world, which really is something you have to see on a trip here.

Diving and water sports are catered for amply, and the entire place feels eerily empty even at full capacity, such is the way in which the resort has been laid out. This is a great place for a honeymoon or a romantic break, but families are welcome too. Definitely one of the most amazing resorts in the country and highly recommended.

Probably our favourite resort in the whole of the Maldives on the grounds of its unique design and utter luxury, **Soneva Gili** (Lankanfushi island; ☎ 6640304; www.sixsenses .com/soneva-gili; wb US$1145; airport transfer 20min, US$110; 44 rooms; ⚌ ▯ ▨) is essentially Swiss Family Robinson meets *Condé Nast Traveller* and we're smitten. Closed by the havoc wreaked by the tsunami in 2004, Soneva Gili reopened in mid-2005 and is as amazing as ever.

Where to begin? All villas (for there are no mere rooms here) are over water, ranging from the standard Villa Suite that has three rooms as well as a sea garden, a sun deck and bed on the roof for stargazing, to the incred-ible Private Reserve, a freestanding lagoon complex sleeping nine people in the lap of luxury a short boat ride from the island.

All the buildings are made from natural materials – wood imported from elsewhere in Asia is the main material used – and all villas are as open to the elements as possible – it's only the bedroom that is air conditioned, the rest of the villa is open-air. The attention to detail is incredible with luxurious treats everywhere discreetly hidden away under natural fibres in what is one of the Maldives' most environmentally conscious resorts.

The island itself is very pretty, criss-crossed with sand pathways through which guests can cycle to the main communal areas – the infinity pool overlooking the beach, the charming bar and beachside restaurant where elaborate buffets and à la carte menus are equally impressive. The diving school allows you to dive from a luxury dhoni complete with waiters and a plush leather upholstered sun deck. The water-sports centre offers all nonmotorised sports for free and the lagoon is great for snorkelling a little further out by 'one palm island' – a gorgeous desert island belonging to the resort. Staff are positively obsequious – this is not a good place for those who don't like fussy and unrelenting service where all the staff appear to know your name – but this is the sum total of any gripe we could have with this intelligent place.

When we visited Chelsea FC owner Roman Abramovich's yacht was moored just off the island – his family had dropped by for the day. An indication of price, yes, but

---

HOW TO SPOT A FASHIONABLE RESORT

In case you have any doubts about where you're staying, this checklist should help you confirm you're in the very smartest of Maldivian resorts:

- You will not be given a fruit cocktail on arrival, but an iced ginger tea, homemade ice cream, homemade lemonade or melon juice, served in dainty earthenware cups.
- Exclusively dark wood interiors, no light wood whatsoever.
- Infinity pools all the way, hopefully even a private one for your own sun deck.
- No glass floors in water villas – you should have your own sea garden or at least a staircase into the sea from your veranda.
- You have more towels than you know what to do with in your room.
- Staff members you have never even seen magically address you by your first name.
- Every time you leave your room a fleet of staff will swarm in to clean it.

ALSO IN NORTH MALE' ATOLL

Four Seasons Kuda Huraa (Kudahuraa island; ☎ 6644888; www.fourseasons.com; 106 rooms; 🏊 💻 🏋)
Badly damaged by the tsunami, the Four Seasons Kuda Huraa Resort was still closed for huge-
scale refurbishment at the time of research. The Four Seasons brand ensures that this will be
one of the most luxurious and stylish resorts in the country, and the Maldivian tourism industry
was waiting with bated breath at the time of writing.

    Coco Palm Boduhithi (Boduhithi island; www.cococollection.com) Twinned with next-door Kudahithi,
Boduhithi will reopen in 2007 as part of the Coco Collection suite of properties in the Maldives.

    Coco Palm Kudahithi (Kudahithi island; www.cococollection.com) The smaller of the two islands to
have been taken over by Coco Collection, due to reopen in 2007.

    Gasfinolhu (Gasfinolhu island; ☎ 6642078; airport transfer 40min, free; 40 rooms; 🏊) Catering exclu-
sively to the Italian market, Mahureva offers transfers, most activities and some drinks included.
All bookings are by the week, through the Italian tour company **Valtur** (☎ in Italy 39-6-47061;
www.valtur.it).

---

hardly typical of the clientele, the majority of
whom are honeymooners and smart but not
necessarily plutocratic couples enjoying an
absolute trip of a lifetime at one of the world's
most sumptuous and inspiring hotels.

KAASHIDHOO

Though in the Kaafu (Male') administrative
district, the island of Kaashidhoo is way out
by itself, in a channel between much larger
atolls. The island has a clinic, a new secondary school, and over 1500 people, which
makes it one of the most populous in Kaafu.
Some of the ruins here are believed to be
remains of an old Buddhist temple. Local
crops include watermelon, lemon, banana,
cucumber and zucchini, but the island is
best known for its *raa* – the 'palm toddy'
made from the sap of a palm tree, drunk
fresh or slightly fermented.

Local boats going to or from the northern atolls sometimes shelter in the lagoon
in Kaashidhoo in bad weather. Dive boats
on longer trips might stop to dive Kaashidhoo East Faru, a good place to see large
pelagic marine life.

GAAFARU FALHU

This small atoll has just one island, also called
Gaafaru, with a population of 850. The channel to the north of the atoll, Kaashidhoo Kuda
Kandu, has long been a shipping lane, and
several vessels have veered off course and finished on the hidden reefs of Gaafaru Falhu.
There are three diveable wrecks – SS *Seagull*
(1879), *Erlangen* (1894) and *Lady Christine*
(1974). None is anywhere near intact, but
the remains all have good coral growth and
plentiful fish. Dive trips are possible from

Helengeli and Eriyadu, but most visitors are
from live-aboard dive boats.

SOUTH MALE' ATOLL

Crossing the Vaadhoo Kandu, the awesome
channel between North and South Male'
Atolls, you'll quickly notice that South
Male' Atoll has a very different feel from
its busy northern neighbour. This is partly
due to the lack of population – there are
only three inhabited islands here, all of
which are on the eastern edge of the atoll
and none of them with a big population –
and partly to do with the fact that the even
the uninhabited islands here are spread out
and so you really feel that you're remote
from the hustle and bustle of Male' and its
surrounding islands.

The biggest island in South Male' Atoll
is **Maafushi** (population 1150), which has
a prison and a reformatory, providing
skill training and rehabilitation for way-
ward youths. A State Trading Organisation (STO) warehouse here buys salted fish
from the local fishing villages and packs it
for export.

Guraidhoo island, which with around 1400
people is the atoll's most populated, has a
lagoon with a good anchorage, used by both
fishing dhonis and passing safari boats. Sultans from Male' sought refuge here during
rebellions from as early as the 17th century.
Island-hopping visitors come here from the
resorts, and a score or so of shops sell them
souvenirs, sarongs and cool drinks.

The island of **Gulhi**, north of Maafushi,
is not large but is inhabited by around 670
people. Fishing is the main activity, and
there's also a small shipyard.

Sights & Activities

DIVING

Some of the best dive sites are around the Vaadhoo Kandu, which funnels a huge volume of water between the North and South Male' Atolls. Various smaller kandus channel water between the atoll and the surrounding sea, and also provide great diving. Some typical, well-known sites are listed here.

The rugged **Velassaru Caves** and overhangs, on the steep wall of the Vaadhoo Kandu, have very attractive coral growth. You may see sharks, turtles and rays on the bottom at around 30m. This dive is not for beginners, but if the current isn't too strong there's excellent snorkelling on the reef edge.

Vaadhoo Caves consists of a row of small caves, plus a bigger one with a swim-through tunnel, as well as excellent soft corals, gorgonians, jackfish and the odd eagle ray. If the current is strong, this is a demanding dive; if not, it's great for snorkelling.

Embudhoo Express is a 2km drift dive through the Embudhoo Kandu, which is a Protected Marine Area. With the current running in, rays, Napoleon wrasse and sharks often congregate around the entrance. The current carries divers along a wall with overhangs and a big cave. The speed of the current makes for a demanding dive, but also provides the ideal environment for soft corals and a large variety of fish. The reef top is good for snorkelling.

Also called Yacht Thila, the attraction of **Kuda Giri** is the hulk of a small freight ship, deliberately sunk here to create an artificial reef. Sponges and cup corals are growing on the wreck, and it provides a home for morays, gropers and large schools of batfish. A nearby thila has recovering coral growth and lots of reef fish to be seen at snorkelling depths. Sheltered from strong currents, this a good site for beginners and for night dives.

Vaagali Caves is an exciting dive and not especially demanding. It's in a less-exposed location and has many caves on its north side, at around 15m, filled with sponges and soft corals. There is good coral regrowth and lots of fish on the top of the reef, much of it visible to snorkellers.

A central reef splits **Guraidhoo Kandu** into two channels, with many possibilities for divers, even those with less experience. There are numerous reef fish, larger pelagics near the entrance and mantas when the current is running out. The kandu is a Protected Marine Area.

Resorts

Most resorts in the South Male' Atoll are reached by speedboat from the airport, but some of the closer, cheaper resorts may offer a slower, less-expensive transfer by dhoni. Unless otherwise specified, all transfer prices are by speedboat.

BUDGET

Embudu Village (Emboodhoo island; ☎ 6644776; www.embudu.com; s/d/wb US$86/144/250; airport transfer by dhoni 45min, US$40; 124 rooms; 🖳) is a very popular and enduring budget resort with a heavy focus on divers and couples. It's as relaxed as its sand-floor reception suggests, and has lots of thoroughly unpretentious charm. This is a resort where people make friends and socialise without it really being a party island – it's just a friendly and straightforward place. Clearly this is resort is predominantly European as, unusually for the Maldives, everything is priced in euros. The island has lots of shady trees, some gorgeous beaches and a very accessible house reef.

All accommodation is on a full-board basis, with buffet meals. The standard rooms are fan-cooled, but still very acceptable. Superior rooms, with air-con, hot water, fridge and phone, cost about US$20 more. There are also 16 deluxe over-water bungalows, although budget water bungalows are always something of a disappointment – these are bare and functional and you may be disappointed if you're after romance. An 'all-inclusive' option, for US$25 per person per day, includes most drinks and afternoon snacks.

The food is amazingly good for an inexpensive resort, with a varied, well-presented selection and very fresh fruit and vegetables. Entertainment is organised one night per week, but the main attraction is watching the sunset from the casual beach bar.

Diving is popular here, thanks to the very professional **Diverland** (www.diverland.com) and the great dive sites in the area (over 90 different sites are reached on a regular basis). A single dive is US$46 with all equipment (and there are good discounts for multidive packages). A full open-water course costs US$316 – extremely good value; nitrox and rebreather courses and facilities are available. Windsurfing is also popular, and there's a good range of excursions to Male' and various other islands. Massage is available at the new, somewhat improvised, spa. If you're not looking for luxuries but an unpretentious beach and diving holiday, Embudu Village is a really excellent and enjoyable resort.

Fihalhohi Resort (Fihaalhohi island; ☎ 6642903; www.fihalhohi.info; s/d US$125/145; airport transfer 75min, US$80; 128 rooms; 🔌), open since 1981, is a charming budget place that retains its unpretentious appeal, a world away from the necessity of having your own butler or private plunge pool. Its dual attractions are its low prices and fantastic reef, making it a great budget diving resort.

The island itself is lovely, with white beaches almost all the way around it and a gorgeous lagoon in front. The house reef is very good for snorkelling, and is also used for night and individual dives. The Ocean Venture dive centre charges US$45 for a single boat dive with tank and weights, or US$53 with all equipment. Open-water courses are US$390.

Meals at the Palm Grove restaurant are mostly buffet, and for variety there's a fun theme meal almost every night, from Middle Eastern to Mexican, flambé to fish and chips. Rooms have been progressively upgraded; all have hot water, but a few have no air-con. Deluxe rooms, in two-storey blocks, have extras like a hairdryer, safe and

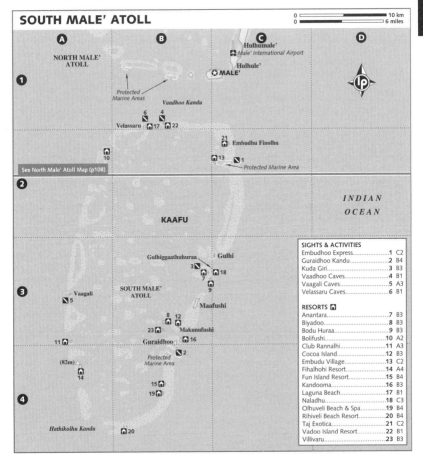

SOUTH MALE' ATOLL

SIGHTS & ACTIVITIES	
Embudhoo Express...............1	C2
Guraidhoo Kandu.................2	B4
Kuda Giri.............................3	B3
Vaadhoo Caves....................4	B1
Vaagali Caves......................5	A3
Velassaru Caves...................6	B1

RESORTS	
Anantara..............................7	B3
Biyadoo...............................8	B3
Bodu Huraa..........................9	B3
Bolifushi...........................10	A2
Club Rannalhi.....................11	A3
Cocoa Island.......................12	B3
Embudu Village...................13	C2
Fihalhohi Resort..................14	A4
Fun Island Resort................15	B4
Kandooma...........................16	B3
Laguna Beach.....................17	B1
Naladhu.............................18	C3
Olhuveli Beach & Spa..........19	B4
Rihiveli Beach Resort...........20	B4
Taj Exotica.........................21	C2
Vadoo Island Resort............22	B1
Villivaru.............................23	B3

minibar. Fihalhohi is a fun resort, and a good choice for families, FITs and divers.

For the price range it's in, **Laguna Beach** (Velassaru island; ☎ 6645903; www.lagunamaldives .com; s/d/t/wb US$165/175/236/405; airport transfer 20min, US$60; 132 rooms; ✂ ▢ ▣) punches impressively above its weight – this is a very good, modern resort offering full facilities and efficient service. Despite the quite dense development, the island is very attractive with lots of trees and gardens and very pretty beaches. Some rooms are in two-storey blocks, others are individual bungalows with a split-level design; there are also water bungalows. All are bright white and equipped with everything from coffee-making facilities to satellite TV.

The main restaurant buffets have a large selection of fine, but not outstanding, dishes. For a change, try the special Italian or Chinese restaurants, or the outdoor barbecue/grill. The bar has entertainment almost every night in the form of live bands, a cultural show or a disco. Guests are mostly from Europe – a mixture of young couples, older couples and families. The resort offers childcare and a children's swimming pool, as well as rooms with interconnecting doors, which are good for families.

Excellent dive sites are nearby, on both sides of the Vaadhoo Kandu. The dive centre charges average rates. Snorkelling is wonderful on the edge of the house reef, but it's hard to get to and subject to currents. The lagoon is good for learning windsurfing and sailing, and excursions to Male' and other islands are popular. There are no motorised water sports.

The atmosphere at Laguna is a little formal, rather than casual and laid back, but it's still a good choice for top-end comforts at a reasonable price.

MIDRANGE
Bolifushi (Bolifushi island; ☎ 6643517; www.bolifushi .com; s/d/wb US$208/244/403; airport transfer by speedboat 30min, US$65; 55 rooms; ✂) is a supremely relaxing, intimate and laid-back resort. It's a tiny island peopled with honeymooners, families and divers from all over Europe who come for the two exceptionally pretty beaches and a good house reef close to shore.

Half of the rooms are fairly uninspiring standards, housed in blocks of two, while there are also 13 beach bungalows with terraces overlooking the sea and 15 water bungalows – nothing particularly sophisticated here but very pleasant.

The PADI dive centre runs trips to the excellent dive sites in the area and there's also good diving on the house reef, including a small wreck. Diving prices are very reasonable.

Water sports are also big here: the island is surrounded by sheltered waters and is well placed for cat sailing and not-too-strenuous windsurfing. Other activities from waterskiing to pedalo hire are available.

The restaurant serves a basic buffet breakfast, set-menu lunch and a reasonable buffet dinner. If you want to do a little snorkelling, diving and relaxing, and you're not looking for high style or *haute cuisine*, Bolifushi is a good choice.

On the western edge of the atoll, **Club Rannalhi** (Rannalhi island; ☎ 6642688; www .aitkenspencehotels.com; s/d/t US$230/264/352; airport transfer 45min, US$100; 116 rooms; ✂ ▢) is an Italian club-style resort. It's an attractive island with tall palm trees, fine beaches and good snorkelling on the house reef, but it's so built up that there's hardly any open space left. The rooms are in two-storey blocks, modern and well finished with all the amenities, and there are 16 spacious water bungalows. The big, airy restaurant serves all buffet meals, and they're very good – plenty of pasta of course, as well as other Italian staples.

Many of the guests dive, sometimes commuting to the dive sites in South Ari Atoll. A single boat dive costs about US$44 with tank and weights, US$57 with all equipment. Open-water courses are inexpensive at US$375. Snorkelling is good on the house reef, especially the excellent coral growth on the thila 100m off the service jetty. The main attraction though, if it's your thing, is the programme of animation activities, which start with morning aerobics, continue with volleyball and dance competitions, and finish late at night with amateur theatrics and karaoke. Nearly all guests come through the Italian agent Viaggi del Ventaglio (Club Venta), but there's also a sprinkling of French, British and FITs. Club Rannalhi has an enthusiastic, animated ambience, which will put off most non-Italians, but it's a good place to come if that's your cup of tea.

The extremely friendly **Vadoo Island Resort** (Vaadhoo island; ☎ 6643976; www.vadoo.net; s/d/wb US$228/272/590; airport transfer by dhoni 1hr, US$50, speedboat 20min, US$100; 31 rooms; ✗) has traditionally attracted divers, but today it pitches itself more as a relaxation centre. Diving remains popular though, mainly because of the resort's great location right beside Vaadhoo Kandu, with access to great dive sites in both North Male' and South Male' Atolls. While Vadoo's main market is the Japanese, there's a strong European presence too.

The resort has a wonderfully relaxed feel to it, its rustic rooms are simple and clean and its charmingly old-fashioned water bungalows – the first in the country, built in 1988 – have lots of retro charm and feature traditional furnishings while still being extremely comfortable, with great touches.

The beaches are delightful, the public areas are basic but stylish and the new Ayurveda Health Centre is the full deal, with a doctor on hand seven days a week, two treatment rooms, a traditional steam bed and a pharmacy. Packages start from US$174 per day (minimum three days) and a full week's therapy comes in at US$878.

The house reef is great for snorkelling, and qualified divers can make unguided dives here. It's not a great place for beginners as rental charges for basics are high – one dive with tanks and weights will cost US$33, but to include all other equipment will set you back an additional US$36! This is unfortunate – we've never seen anywhere in the Maldives charge US$9 per dive for a dive computer – Vadoo needs to correct this urgently.

The six days' unlimited diving deal is quite a bit cheaper at US$330. Dive courses feature very personalised instruction, with one instructor per two students, but you should reserve a dive course at least three weeks ahead. An open-water course costs US$625.

The rooms are all reasonably new, and quite well finished (no TV or minibar) – the cheapest ones are in the Sunrise Wing, which is a block with rooms on two storeys. Each has either a veranda or balcony. All in all, Vadoo is a highly recommended resort, full of unpretentious, easy-going charm.

Olhuveli Beach & Spa (Olhuveli island; ☎ 6642788; www.olhuveli.com; s/d/wb US$340/360/495; airport transfer 50min, US$120; 129 rooms; ✗ ▢ ▣) is a fantastic resort following major post-tsunami renovations and repairs. Its reopening in late 2005 has heralded the arrival of a very upmarket midrange resort in South Male' Atoll.

The main market here is Italian, followed by German and a smattering of Japanese and British visitors. The rooms are spread out along the beach in two-level blocks, but they are extremely tastefully done, furnished throughout with dark-wood four-poster beds and all featuring balconies or patios which lead straight out to the gorgeous beaches on either side of the island. There are also two rings of extremely swish water bungalows stretching over the lagoon.

The new Serena spa is popular for its Ayurvedic treatments, aromatherapy and massage. Although narrow, the beaches are attractive, and the wide lagoon is good for sailing, windsurfing and being towed around behind a motorboat. This is one of the first resorts to offer kitesurfing lessons and equipment. Snorkelling is excellent off the end of the jetty, at the edge of the reef, where turtles are common. The first-class **Sea-Explorer dive centre** (www.sea-explorer.net) does lots of drift dives in nearby channels, as well as doing wreck and night dives.

Overall, Olhuveli offers excellent value. It's the perfect compromise between budget prices and high standards, between romance and diving. There are some extremely good week-long accommodation packages offered through its website, so check for these too.

Rihiveli Beach Resort (Mahaana Elhi Huraa island; ☎ 6643731; www.rihiveli-maldives.com; s/d/tr US$261/427/597; airport transfer 1hr, US$145; 48 rooms) is the personal creation of a Frenchman who lived here for 20 years. He has now moved on, and a legion of loyal guests are hoping that the resort will retain its natural, informal charm and quality. So far, so good. While the resort remains popular with French and Swiss visitors, it's in no fear of being overrun anytime soon.

Consisting of just 48 little bungalows, all built in a rustic style from now-illegal coral stone and with traditional thatched roofs, they have all the basics for comfort such as hot water but nothing considered superfluous, such as air-con, fridges, phones or a TV set. This is the secret of its success – Rihiveli ('silver sand') will never be overrun with your run-of-the-mill package group.

The open-air bar has a sand floor and shady trees overhead, while the restaurant is built over the lagoon and has a lovely view as well as truly mouthwatering cuisine.

The usual water sports (windsurfing, sailing, canoeing, even water-skiing) plus tennis are all included in the room price. You can wade across to two other, uninhabited islands where the resort organises regular barbecue lunches. Regular boat trips to other reefs make up for the lack of snorkelling sites next to the resort. The main diving destinations are around nearby Hathikolhu Kandu, and there's a small wreck to explore. A single boat dive organised by the **Eurodivers Dive School** (www.euro-divers.com) costs about US$41 with all equipment. An open-water course is US$355.

With its relaxed ambience, French style and natural appeal, Rihiveli is a unique and special resort for those who appreciate the simple things. The resort was closed in summer 2006 for renovations, so it will probably be even better by 2007.

TOP END

Reopening in late 2005 after being disastrously affected by the tsunami, the **Taj Exotica** (Embudhu Finolhu island; ☎ 6642200; www.tajhotels.com; s/d/wb US$850/900/1000; airport transfer 20min, US$75; 62 rooms; ⚅ ▯ ♨), the most exclusive of the Indian Taj chain's two resorts in the Maldives, is already experiencing full occupancy again.

This elegant, understated resort is all about quiet luxury and indulgence. The resort was one of the original pioneers of fine à la carte dining in the Maldives – the main Asia-Pacific restaurant here wouldn't know a buffet if it hit it in the face. Everything here is ordered and individually cooked from a sumptuous and expensive menu. This is one place where full board would come in handy – the meals here add up very quickly. The second restaurant is built out over the lagoon and is only open in the evenings – one feature here is an open hole into the water, where fish flock in the evening attracted by the light.

ALSO IN SOUTH MALE' ATOLL

Anantara (Dhigufinolu island; ☎ 3341708; www.anantara.com; 110 rooms; ⚅ ▯ ♨) Still a full-scale building site when we visited, the Thai Anantara group will have opened its first resort in the Maldives by the time you read this and it promises to set people talking. The beautiful island, previously a fairly downmarket resort, has been razed to the ground and is being built from scratch. The beach villas and water bungalows we saw were stunning and we fully expect this to become a big success in the luxury market.

Naladhu (Veliganduhuraa island; ☎ 3341708; www.anantara.com) Anantara's second project in the Maldives and next door to the Anantara resort, little Veliganduhuraa is to be developed into a super-luxury hotel of the six-star style, provisionally named Naladhu. Work had yet to begin when we visited, but once it does this will doubtless be something quite special.

Bodu Huraa (Boduhuraa island; ☎ 6640172; www.hotelplan.it; airport transfer 45min; 36 rooms) This relatively new resort offers accommodation in over-water bungalows. The resort is 100% booked by the Italian Hotelplan group and does not accept FITs or anyone who does not come through Hotelplan.

Biyadoo (Biyadhoo island; ☎ 6647171; www.biyadoo.com.mv; 96 rooms) The lease at Biyadoo expired in 2004 and the resort was still shut for refurbishment at the time of research, due to reopen in 2007. The island itself is very attractive, with several fine beaches and an excellent house reef.

Villivaru (Viligilivaru island; ☎ 6647070; 60 rooms) The sister resort of Biyadoo is also due to be re-leased, refurbished and repositioned further upmarket.

Fun Island Resort (Bodufinolhu island; ☎ 6644558; www.villahotels.com) This big, popular and well-run resort had been operating since the mid-1980s but was badly damaged in the tsunami and was still closed for a complete refit and upgrading at the time of research. The resort will reopen in 2007.

Kandooma (Kandooma island; ☎ 6644452; www.kandoom.info) Badly damaged by the tsunami, charming little Kandooma, a budget island on the eastern edge of South Male' Atoll, was being totally renovated at the time of writing and was due to open in late 2006.

Other public area features include a DVD and book library, a well-stocked games room, the Grand Jiva Spa with six treatment rooms (four of which are doubles) and a gorgeous infinity pool.

The beach is best on the western side of the island; the tsunami decimated the beach on the eastern side of the island but it's gradually being returned to its original condition with the help of sand pumps. All categories of rooms are supremely smart, many of which have their own plunge pools overlooking the beach. The bathrooms in the lagoon villas have wonderful bathtubs next to huge windows allowing you to contemplate the sea as you soak.

All in all, Taj Exotica is a great choice; even though it's a small island, with only a meagre amount of vegetation, it excels with its wonderful style, atmosphere and superb food.

Since its lavish rebranding at the hands of the COMO group, whose diverse hotels include the Metropolitan in London and the Parrot Cay Resort in the Turks and Caicos Islands, **Cocoa Island** (Makunufushi island; ☎ 6641818; www.cocoa-island.com; wb US$680; airport transfer 1hr, US$180; 30 rooms; 🗷 🖳 🕿) has been a much talked-about luxury resort.

The ethos is one of escape and pampering here, at the very southern tip of South Male' Atoll.

The rooms here are quite something else, all over water, but built in the shape of traditional Maldivian dhoni boats. Inside they look like a glossy magazine editorial – all clean lines, white cotton and dark wood. Every amenity you could need is catered for in the rooms and they are some of the best designed and most consciously fabulous we've seen.

Elsewhere the island is typical of the luxury market: superb beaches, great diving, water sports and a COMO Shambhala spa are all absolutely top quality. There's a fantastic à la carte menu at the resort's main restaurant, with emphasis on seafood cooked in the Keralan style as well as other dishes combining Indian and Sri Lankan cooking. Alternatively, the COMO Shambhala cuisine available is for the health-conscious (no cow or soya milk here, just blended nut milks, honey instead of sugar), featuring raw vegetables and fish dishes for those on total detox.

This is an original, boutique place that will thrill anyone wanting a luxurious, healthy and unusual getaway.

Ari Atoll

Second only to North Male' Atoll as the centre of the Maldivian tourist industry, Ari Atoll sits to the west of the capital, a vast oval lagoon dotted with reefs and as sumptuously inviting as anywhere else in the country. Like Male' Atoll, Ari is known universally by its traditional name rather than its official name of Alif, a usage we have followed here.

To the east, Ari Atoll is separated from South Male' Atoll by a 40km-wide channel, perhaps 500m deep; to the west, the sea floor drops precipitously to over 2000m. Abundant marine life in the atoll creates nutrient-rich water that flows out through channels, attracting large creatures from the open sea and divers from all over the world.

Despite its importance for the tourism industry, Ari Atoll is not a particularly developed part of the country. The regional capital, Mahibadhoo, has a population of just 1750 and there are only 18 inhabited islands in the entire atoll. The Indian Ocean tsunami did not massively affect the atoll, due to North and South Male' Atolls bearing the brunt of the wave. All resorts that were affected here have long since been up and running again.

The 28 resorts here are some of the best-established in the country and include the Hilton Maldives, frequently winner of various 'best hotels in the world' accolades, as well as Dhoni Mighili, one of the most extraordinary resorts in the whole country, where guests stay aboard their own customised luxury dhoni. Whatever you seek from the Maldives you'll find it in Ari Atoll.

THODDOO ISLAND

Though administratively part of Ari Atoll, Thoddoo is actually a single, separate, oval island about 20km from the northern edge of the main atoll. It's about 1km across, and has a population of over 1300. The principal activity is fishing, but Thoddoo is also known for its market-garden produce (watermelons and betel leaf especially) and its troupe of traditional dancers, who sometimes perform in tourist resorts.

There is evidence that Thoddoo has been occupied since ancient times. A Buddhist temple here contained a Roman coin minted in 90 BC, as well as a silver bowl and a fine stone statue of Buddha, the head of which is now in the National Museum in Male'.

Safari boats can stop here, but usually don't because of the lack of sheltered anchorages. You could also arrange a day trip here from one of the Rasdhoo Atoll resorts.

RASDHOO ATOLL

The small atoll of Rasdhoo lies off the northeastern corner of Ari Atoll proper. The main island of the atoll, also called **Rasdhoo** (population 830), is the administrative capital of North Ari Atoll, despite ironically not being within the atoll itself. Rasdhoo has an attractive little village with a junior secondary school, a health centre, four mosques and a score of souvenir shops – it's often visited as a day trip from the nearby resorts. The island has been settled for many centuries and there are traces here of a Buddhist society predating the arrival of Islam.

Sights & Activities
DIVING
The medical centre at Kuramathi has a decompression chamber and trained hyperbaric specialists.

Accessible from the shore, **Kuramathi House Reef** is good for beginning divers

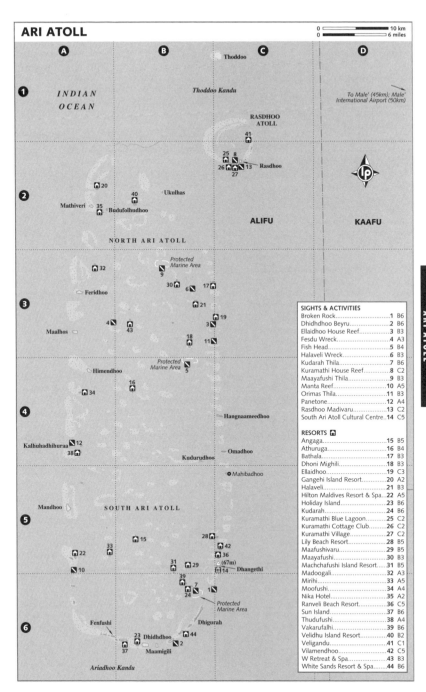

ARI ATOLL

0 — 10 km
0 — 6 miles

INDIAN OCEAN

Thoddoo

Thoddoo Kandu

RASDHOO ATOLL

To Male' (45km); Male' International Airport (50km)

Rasdhoo

ALIFU

KAAFU

Mathiveri · Budufolhudhoo
Ukulhas

NORTH ARI ATOLL

Protected Marine Area

Feridhoo

Maalhos

Himendhoo

Protected Marine Area

Kalhuhadhihuraa

Omadhoo

Kudurudhoo

Mahibadhoo

Mandhoo   SOUTH ARI ATOLL

Dhangethi

Protected Marine Area

Fenfushi   Dhigurah

Dhidhdhoo

Maamigili

Ariadhoo Kandu

ARI ATOLL

SIGHTS & ACTIVITIES

Broken Rock..............................1 B6
Dhidhdhoo Beyru....................2 B6
Ellaidhoo House Reef.............3 B3
Fesdu Wreck............................4 A3
Fish Head.................................5 B4
Halaveli Wreck........................6 B3
Kudarah Thila..........................7 B6
Kuramathi House Reef............8 C2
Maayafushi Thila.....................9 B3
Manta Reef.............................10 A5
Orimas Thila...........................11 B3
Panetone................................12 A4
Rasdhoo Madivaru.................13 C2
South Ari Atoll Cultural Centre..14 C5

RESORTS

Angaga...................................15 B5
Athuruga................................16 B4
Bathala...................................17 B3
Dhoni Mighili.........................18 B3
Ellaidhoo.................................19 C3
Gangehi Island Resort............20 A2
Halaveli...................................21 B3
Hilton Maldives Resort & Spa..22 A5
Holiday Island.........................23 B6
Kudarah..................................24 B6
Kuramathi Blue Lagoon..........25 C2
Kuramathi Cottage Club.........26 C2
Kuramathi Village...................27 C2
Lily Beach Resort....................28 B5
Maafushivaru..........................29 B5
Maayafushi.............................30 B3
Machchafushi Island Resort.....31 B5
Madoogali...............................32 A3
Mirihi.....................................33 A5
Moofushi.................................34 A4
Nika Hotel...............................35 A2
Ranveli Beach Resort..............36 C5
Sun Island...............................37 B6
Thudufushi..............................38 A4
Vakarufalhi.............................39 B6
Velidhu Island Resort.............40 B2
Veligandu...............................41 C1
Vilamendhoo..........................42 C5
W Retreat & Spa.....................43 B3
White Sands Resort & Spa.......44 B6

and snorkellers. A small dhoni and a 30m freighter have been sunk off the island to provide an attraction for divers. Sea fans and featherstars decorate the reef wall, while sharks, stingrays and turtles might also be seen.

Also known as Hammerhead Point, **Rasdhoo Madivaru** is a more demanding dive on an outer reef where hammerhead sharks, mantas and other large pelagics are frequent visitors. Outside this reef the depth drops rapidly to over 200m and the water is exceptionally clear. It's a fine snorkelling site if conditions permit.

Resorts

Kuramathi Maldives (Kuramathi island; ☎ 6660527; www.kuramathi.com; 288 rooms; airport transfer 2hr, US$120; ✗ ☐ ✈) is a unique island in the Maldives, as it houses no less than three resorts, in apparent contravention of the government's beloved 'one island, one resort' policy. In fact, Kuramathi's three resorts are all run by the same management team and are all owned by Universal Resorts, but the island's size has allowed three separate entities aimed at different crowds to spring up here. Kuramathi island itself was once inhabited but population decline lead in 1970 to the mass relocation of the remaining islanders to next-door Rasdhoo, leaving Kuramathi ripe for development.

Kuramathi Village (s/d US$190/198), the largest and least expensive Kuramathi resort, is where the younger, party crowd come to stay. Rooms are basic, high-ceilinged affairs with hot showers and air-con but little else in the way of comforts and are frequented by British and German travellers. The superior and deluxe rooms offer some improved comforts although they're still fairly average.

Kuramathi Cottage & Spa (s/d/wb US$197/205/285) is in the middle of the island and is a spa resort whose guests come for treatments, pampering and total relaxation. There are an incredible 50 water bungalows here, which are beautifully attired.

Kuramathi Blue Lagoon (s/d/wb US$232/240/305), at the quiet end of the island, is quieter and more upmarket. It features 20 water bungalows (favoured by honeymooners), and 36 beach cottages, which are popular with families.

The three resorts share all facilities and so these are great choices if you want a huge amount of activities and facilities. There's a marine biology centre here that provides guided snorkelling and diving as well as giving guests informative introductions to various aspects of the natural underwater world, from coral formation to reef structure.

Rasdhoo Atoll Divers (www.rasdhoodivers.com) serves all three resorts, charging US$60 for a boat dive with all equipment, US$52 with tank and weights only, and US$420 for an open-water course. There's a four-berth decompression chamber on the island as well.

The lagoon is the perfect place for learning windsurfing and sailing. Motorised water sports, including wakeboarding, are available. Stingrays come into the shallows on the beach every evening. All in all Kuramathi offers a lot and it's particularly good for a group of people who might want different things, as you can easily combine diving, spa treatments and partying here in a way that few other resorts can offer.

A charming island fringed with white beaches and featuring a huge 80m sandbank at one end, **Veligandu** (Veligandu island; ☎ 6660519; www.veliganduisland.com; full board s/d/t/wb US$240/282/381/425; airport transfer by seaplane 20min, US$175; 73 rooms; ✗) is all about nature and true escape.

Well vegetated with plenty of coconut palms and located on the beautiful lagoon within Rasdhoo, this is a midrange place built in a traditional Maldivian style, although the rather modern rooms smash any genuine shipwreck fantasies before they can fully set in.

There are no TVs in the rooms, which adds to the 'no shoes, no news' atmosphere, as do the rustic outdoor bathrooms. There's a second bed in each room, so each can potentially be a twin, double or triple. The reception area, bar and restaurant have sand floors, cane furniture and a delightfully casual feel. The meals are mostly buffets, offering a limited variety of very good quality dishes. Guests are mainly German, Austrian and Italian couples.

There are a couple of excellent dive sites nearby, including very common hammerhead shark sightings. The Swiss-run

Ocean-Pro dive base (www.oceanpro-diveteam.com) charges very reasonably. The edge of the house reef is not very accessible and is not great for snorkelling. But Veligandu isn't primarily a diving or water-sports resort – the main attractions are the natural ambience, rustic simplicity and fine beaches.

ARI ATOLL

The geographic entity of Ari Atoll (as opposed to the administrative regions of North and South Ari) is about 80km from north to south and 30km wide. The most populous island is **Mahibadhoo**, the capital of South Ari, with some 1700 people. Fishing and fish processing are the main industries – there's a cold storage and processing plant here. Safari boats might stop here, but there are no resorts nearby.

Other inhabited islands, typically with a population of a few hundred, are dotted around the edges of the atoll. Few of them are accessible from resorts, but safari boats may be able to stop at some of these islands, which are little visited by tourists. Quite a few islands have ruins or artefacts of ancient Buddhist and Hindu settlements.

Maamigili, in the south of the atoll, has over 1500 people, many of whom work in nearby resorts, or in tourist shops that cater to island-hopping visitors. The island of **Fenfushi** (population 550), on the southwest corner of the atoll, supplies sand and coralstone for buildings in Male' and elsewhere, and is noted for coral carving. **Dhangethi** (population 700), on the southeastern edge of the atoll, is worth visiting for its Cultural Centre.

Sights & Activities
DIVING

All of the resorts have diving operations and some are known as destinations for serious divers. During peak season some sites may have several groups diving on them at one time, but good dive masters will know how to avoid the crowds at popular sites and where to find equally attractive but less popular sites. The following is a brief description of some well-known sites (from north to south), to give an idea of the possibilities.

Maayafushi Thila is a classic round thila known for the white-tip reef sharks that circle it. Caves and overhangs around the thila have lots of gorgonians, soft corals and schools of reef fish. It's a Protected Marine Area.

The well-known **Halaveli Wreck** was created when a 38m cargo ship was deliberately sunk in 1991. It's famous for the friendly stingrays enticed here by regular feeding – keep your fingers away from their mouths.

Fesdu Wreck is a 30m trawler with a good covering of corals at a depth of 18m to 30m. Moray eels and groper live inside the hull, which is easily entered and has good growths of soft corals and sponges. Divers can also check the adjacent thila, which has hard and soft corals as well as lots of fish.

Only accessible to Ellaidhoo's guests, the excellent **Ellaidhoo House Reef** has a long wall just 25m from the beach. It has a row of caves with sea fans, whip corals, schools of bannerfish, Napoleons, stingrays and morays, and even a small wreck. This reef is popular with night divers.

Overhangs, caves, crevices, canyons and coral heads make **Orimas Thila** an exciting dive. Marine life includes good growths of soft corals, sea fans, anemones and clown fish. The top of the thila is only 3m down, and can be easily enjoyed by snorkellers if the conditions are calm. It's a Protected Marine Area.

Also called Mushimasmingali Thila, **Fish Head** is one of the world's most famous dive sites. Its steep sides are spectacular, with multilevel ledges, overhangs and caves supporting many sea fans and black corals; its top is heavily encrusted with anemones. Beware of stonefish. The prolific fish life at this Protected Marine Area includes fusiliers, large Napoleons, trevally and schools of hungry barracuda. The main attraction, however, is the numerous grey reef sharks, which can be seen up close. Strong currents can make this a demanding dive, and extreme care should be taken not to damage this superb but heavily used site.

The north side of Kalhuhadhihuraa Faru is subject to strong currents, so the caves and overhangs of **Panetone** are thick with soft coral growth. As well as the many reef fish, there are giant trevally, sharks, barracuda and turtles. From December to

April, mantas feed around the outside of the channel; March to November are the best months to see sharks. There's excellent snorkelling in light currents.

Also called Madivaru, **Manta Reef** is at the end of a channel where powerful currents carry plankton out of the atoll during the northeast monsoon (December to April) – fast food for manta rays. Mantas also come to be cleaned. Reef fish include Napoleon wrasse, snapper and parrotfish, while pelagics such as turtles, tuna and sharks visit the outer reef slope. It's for advanced divers only, but great for snorkellers in the right conditions.

Kudarah Thila is a very demanding but exciting dive – if there is a current running, this is strictly for experienced divers. There are gorgonians, whip corals, black corals and a whole field of sea fans swaying in the current, surrounded by sharks and trevally from the open sea. In the gaps between large coral blocks, bluestriped snapper, tallfin, batfish, goby and other unusual small fish can be seen. It's a Protected Marine Area.

In the mouth of the Dhigurashu Kandu, **Broken Rock** is bisected by a canyon up to 10m deep and only 1m to 3m wide. Swimming through the 50m canyon is unforgettable, but extreme care is needed not to damage the coral formations on either side. Rock formations around the thila are decorated with sea fans and superb corals, and are inhabited by abundant marine life.

From May to September, whale sharks cruise almost continually along the 10km-long **Dhidhdhoo Beyru** on the southwestern edge of the atoll, which extends from Ariyadhoo Kandu north to the tip of Dhigurah island. There's plenty of fish life on the reef, and mantas also cruise the area. The reef drops off steeply into deep water, and it's quite exposed and subject to ocean currents.

Resorts

While some resorts nearer to Male' operate speedboat transfers to and from the airport, the majority of resorts use seaplane transfers due to the distances involved. These take anything from 20 to 45 minutes. Bear in mind that as seaplanes do not fly at night, if you arrive after dark at Male' airport you'll have to stop over in Male' until the next morning for your seaplane transfer. This is usually done at the airport hotel, which is a good international-standard business hotel. However, it's not the ideal start to a holiday, so it's always best to land in good time before dusk.

BUDGET

One of the best resorts in the country for diving, **Bathala** (Bathalaa island; ☎ 6660587; www .bathala.com; full board s/d/tr US$170/200/270; airport transfer by seaplane 20min, US$180; 46 rooms; ☒) is a small, pretty island which has a loyal tribe of repeat guests from all over Europe.

The cabaña-style cottages are simple and rustic, but with all the essentials such as air-con and warm running water in their outdoor bathrooms. The style is very much Robinson Crusoe – you won't be in danger of any over-attentive pampering here (although there is now a small spa) and most people come for the superb diving.

The attitude towards diving is extremely passionate here – the dive school actively encourages beginners to take one of their full open-water courses, which are spread out over five days and limited to a maximum of three students per group.

Dive costs are relatively low, but more costly if you need to rent full equipment, again making this a good choice for experienced divers. Multidive packages are available. Bring your own wetsuit if possible. The edge of the house reef drops off steeply all around, and is accessible from the beach or more readily from the jetties – it's a good dive site in itself.

An immaculate beach goes right around the island, as does the house reef. The good mix of clientele, including more than average numbers of FITs (fully independent travellers) gives the whole resort a very laid-back feel.

Maayafushi (Mayafushi island; ☎ 6660588; maaya@ dhivehinet.net.mv; s/d US$150/178; airport transfer by seaplane 25min, US$235; 60 rooms; ☒) offers very good value for an unpretentious island holiday. The island is small and quite intensively developed; soft sandy beaches surround it, and the house reef is a beauty. Rooms all have basic furnishings, air-con, hot water, TV, phone and beach frontage. Most of the guests are divers from Germany, Switzerland or Austria, but there are a few families with young children who get on well here. Most meals are set menu (with Indian dishes and lots of fresh fish), but there are a couple of buffet nights each week.

The dive school offers a wide range of courses, night dives and trips to the famous dive sites nearby, all for average prices. Once it was a low-cost divers island, but now Maayafushi has been upgraded and its rooms improved, though it's still a pretty laid-back resort.

More than just a typical Italian resort, **Halaveli** (Halaveli island; ☎ 6660559; www.halaveli .com; s/d US$145/190; airport transfer by seaplane 20min, US$178; 56 rooms; 🔀) may be booked predominantly by package giant Gran Viaggi, but it's open to other nationalities and has a fair share of divers and FITs as well.

The island is the shape of a crescent moon with beaches all around and plentiful vegetation. The rooms are individual coral-and-thatch bungalows with outdoor bathrooms, air-con, phone and heavy wood furniture.

A full animation program is provided every afternoon and evening, as befits Italian resorts, and the majority Italian guests are into it with enthusiasm. The breakfast and lunch buffets are a pretty fair selection of tasty dishes with an Italian bias. Dinner is partly à la carte.

The house reef is accessible for snorkelling at several points and it has a variety of fish, but not much coral regrowth. Some of the Maldives' most famous dive sites are in easy reach, and the **TGI dive centre** (www .tgidiving.com) is keen to show them off. Prices are low, but better deals can be got by booking online via the diving school website before you arrive.

With a reputation as the most hardcore diving destination in the Maldives, **Ellaidhoo** (Ellaidhoo island; ☎ 6660586; www.travelin -maldives.com; s/d US$134/168; airport transfer by seaplane 20min, US$210, by speedboat 80min, US$115; 156 rooms; 🔀) has over 100 dive sites within a half-day trip, making it one of the top choices in the country for keen divers. Recently it has upgraded its facilities and added extra services to broaden its appeal, but divers still predominate. One reason is the Ellaidhoo house reef, only a few metres offshore and offering some great snorkel-

ling and diving with a 750m wall, lots of caves, corals, rich marine life (turtles, sharks, mantas and eagle rays) and even a small shipwreck. The Sub-Aqua dive centre organises a huge array of trips at reasonable prices. It also runs courses in marine biology.

The rooms were all upgraded in 2001 and feature air-con, hot water and even satellite TV. The main restaurant now serves all meals as buffet style, and there's a coffee shop as well. A new sports centre has a gym, sauna, spa and facilities for billiards, squash, tennis and tension-relieving Thai-style massage. Water sports (like windsurfing, jet skiing and wakeboarding) are provided on a neighbouring island with a wider lagoon.

It looks like Ellaidhoo will continue to attract real diving enthusiasts, but nondivers will now find it's a more enjoyable, all-round destination.

MIDRANGE
Velidhu Island Resort (Velidhoo island; ☎ 6660551; www.johnkeellshotels.com; s/d/t US$210/240/300; airport transfer by seaplane 20min, US$200; 100 rooms; 🔀) is a sizable island with some great beaches and a good house reef. It's not the best-looking resort, with uninspired architecture, haphazard landscaping and rooms with very ordinary interiors, but the food and service are quite good. The new overwater bungalows are the classiest accommodation available (US$75 extra). The **Euro-Divers dive centre** (www.eurodivers.com) is very professional and enthusiastic about the diving in this part of the atoll. A single boat dive is US$51 with tank and weights only, or US$61 with full equipment. To do an open-water course costs about US$510. The six-day, no-limit package is a good deal if you dive a lot. Nitrox courses (US$60) and nitrox diving (US$5 extra) are available. Velidhu could be a good choice for keen divers who are not looking for luxury, and its low-season prices can be very good value.

Another almost implausibly perfect island, **Madoogali** (Madoogali island; ☎ 6660581; www.skorpion-maldives.com; full board s/d/tr US$185/ 255/315; airport transfer by seaplane 20min, US$250; 50 rooms; 🔀) is richly verdant, has gorgeous beaches all the way around its circular shore and is set on a stunning lagoon.

ARI ATOLL

The ethos here is rustic Maldivian relaxation – the coral-walled architecture with thatched roofs and wooden interiors may have air-con, but that's one of the few concessions to the modern world.

The large majority of guests are Italian, but the resort has slowly moved from being an Italian-only place to having a large range of European guests, many of whom are repeat visitors.

The house reef is excellent for snorkelling, and as Madoogali is the only resort in this part of the atoll, there is easy access to lots of little-used dive sites. The Albatros dive centre charges reasonable rates and has professional multilingual staff offering all the usual courses. Madoogali is a natural-style resort with a European atmosphere and all-round appeal.

White Sands Resort & Spa (Dhidhdhoofinolhu island; %6680513; www.maldiveswhitesands.com; half-board s/d/wb US$275/348/470; airport transfer by seaplane 20min, US$300, by speedboat 2hr, US$156; 139 rooms; ⌘) manages to combine all major resort aspects confidently on its lovely 2km island; honeymooners are accommodated in the excellent water bungalows, while divers have the pick of lots of great local dives and activities on the island abound – tennis, badminton, volleyball, the Balinese spa, the great beaches and four restaurants all provide enjoyable pastimes.

The older rooms at one end of the island are a reminder that this resort was once called Ari Beach, a very casual, inexpensive place with a reputation as a party island. At the other end, a long jetty leads to a restaurant and 47 water bungalows perched over the lagoon, all in sophisticated-rusticated nautical style. In between, in price and geography, are the 'superior' rooms, the dive school and spa.

Standard rooms are basic boxes and feel somewhat worn, but they're quite OK – they have air-con and a phone, but no hot water. The over-water bungalows are among the most charming and unusual in the Maldives. The sloping walls, wooden finishes, white fabrics and uninterrupted water views make you feel you're in an old yacht, but all the modern accessories are provided, from hairdryers to cable TV. The over-water bar and restaurant also have a shipboard feel, as you eat and drink on shaded decks with water on every side. The

meals here are also excellent, all served buffet style, with quality ingredients and dishes that are not too elaborate but perfectly prepared.

The island itself is long and narrow with natural, somewhat scrubby, vegetation and long white sandy beaches. The lagoon is wide on all sides, and a good place to learn windsurfing or catamaran sailing. Water-skiing, wakeboarding and fun rides on the banana are also available. For snorkelling, take one of the free boat trips to the reef edge – these go every afternoon. The island has always been popular with divers, especially for the whale sharks that cruise the outside edge of the atoll here from May to November, and the mantas on the west side of the atoll from December to May. The very efficient **Euro-Divers dive centre** (www.eurodivers.com) is involved in whale shark research. A single boat dive is US$45 with tank and weights only, or US$50 with full equipment. An open-water course costs US$346. Nitrox courses (US$70) and nitrox diving (US$6 extra) are available.

Villa Hotels have a bad habit of naming their resorts with such dreadful names that they seem naff before you even arrive, which is a real pity as **Holiday Island** (Dhiffushi island; ☎ 6660011; www.villahotels.com /holiday; full board s/d/t US$305/315/425; airport transfer by speedboat 2½hr, US$140, by seaplane 35min, US$260; 142 rooms) is beautiful – wide beaches, lush vegetation and a gorgeous lagoon make this every bit the picture-perfect Maldivian island. Like most of Villa Hotels' resorts this is a midlevel resort but the accommodation is basic, and the whole place rather crowded, though it's not nearly as awful as it sounds.

The rooms are in blocks of two (some with interconnecting doors for families), surrounded by cultivated gardens and fitted out with everything from satellite TV to hot water in the bidet. All meals are served buffet style in the main restaurant – the selection is limited, but the quality is good. The Italian animation includes disco nights, karaoke and fitness sessions, avoided like the proverbial plague by all the non-Italians on the island.

Recreational activities such as table tennis, badminton, billiards, tennis and use of the gym are free. Windsurfing, catamaran sailing and motorised water sports are available too. The beaches are lovely around most of the island, but snorkelling is not good in the lagoon, and boat trips out to the reef edge and beyond are charged as an extra. Diving is well catered for by the Villa Diving dive school; there are lots of good dive sites around and a single boat dive costs US$44 with tank and weights, or US$48 with all equipment.

While Holiday Island is good value for the quality of its accommodation and meals, it's still a place for a bog-standard package break. However, if so-called animation and its adherents frighten you like they do us, avoid.

Gangehi Island Resort (Gangehi island; ☎ 6660505; www.clubvacanze.it; 25 rooms; 🗶 🖵 🖳) is a gorgeous, upmarket place that is only marketed in Italy through Club Vacanze. FITs cannot stay here (and nor can kids under 12 for that matter). All stays are all inclusive, with loads of extras including free diving and excursions – keeping the guests as busy as ever in the inimitable Italian fashion. The island is pretty, with lots of palm trees, but unfortunately has suffered from sand movements, so the seafront rooms have no beach and the over-water bungalows are surrounded by a sandbar.

Meaning 'the island of roots' in Divehi, **Moofushi** (Moofushi island; ☎ 6680517; www.moofushi .com; s/d US$237/263; airport transfer by seaplane 20min, US$270; 62 rooms; 🗶) is heavily vegetated with mangroves. Opened in 1990 under the Italian management that continues to run the island today, this is a small, smart resort where the staff to guest ratio is 1:1. As it's popular with Italian package travellers, expect to be animated.

The resort has spacious, natural-style, thatched rooms and 17 water bungalows, all of them filled by Italians. It's a pretty island, but the beach is suffering from erosion and some of the breakwaters are unsightly.

The dive centre offers the full range of courses and equipment. Nearby Moofushi Kandu has some good dive sites and makes a great snorkelling trip. The main attractions of Moofushi are the low price and the diving.

Widely marketed through the big package markets of Europe, **Athuruga** (Athuruga island; ☎ 6660508; www.planhotel.ch/athuruga; s/d

US$335/470; airport transfer by seaplane 25min, US$210; 46 rooms; 🗶) is one of two Planhotel properties in Ari Atoll (Thudufushi is the other one) and it's an all-inclusive resort, including most drinks, excursions and unmotorised water sports in the daily rate. The air-con rooms are spacious and comfortable and all face onto the superb beach. Guests are mostly from Italy, Switzerland, Germany and the UK, in that order, and the atmosphere is casual. The meals are consistently very good. Other facilities include a Serena Spa, water sports and animation areas.

The house reef offers easy snorkelling and a lot to see, and there are some good dive sites nearby, though it's an hour by boat to the exciting dives on the western rim of the atoll. The **Crab dive base** (www .thecrab.com) charges about US$60 for a boat dive with tank and weights, US$68 with all equipment and US$600 for an open-water course, making it not the most competitive place if you plan to dive a lot.

Athuruga is quite densely developed, but it still has lots of palm trees and a good beach all round – it's a good-value resort with a mainly Italian ambience.

The second Planhotel resort in Ari Atoll, **Thudufushi** (Thudufushi island; ☎ 6660583; www .planhotel.ch/thudu; s/d US$360/480; airport transfer by seaplane 25min, US$240; 47 rooms) was closed at the time of research for a refit, expecting to open again in late 2006.

The island itself is just beautiful, especially the beaches. In high season the majority of guests are Italian, but at other times there are also Germans and Brits. The dive centre management and prices are the same as at Athuruga, but Thudufushi may be better placed for dives on the atoll edge. The house reef is superb, and accessible for snorkelling and diving.

It's hard not to be charmed by tiny **Mirihi** (Mirihi island; ☎ 6680500; www.mirihi.com; s/d/t/wb US$510/550/635/584; airport transfer by seaplane 25min, US$240; 35 rooms; 🗶 🖵). Named after the yellow flower that grows around the island, this gem of a resort keeps it simple and natural. The wonderful beach that rings the thick vegetation in the centre of the island and the fantastic house reef beyond are both first class.

Redeveloped in classy, contemporary style, Mirihi is a tiny island, but 30 of the rooms are built over the water so it's not too crowded – in fact, if anything, it feels positively spacious.

The beach villas have eye-catching décor, polished timber finishes, white linen furnishings, rich red accents and every facility, including a CD player, TV and espresso machine. The over-water rooms have all this plus water views and very private sun decks. The main restaurant presents a lavish gourmet buffet for nearly every meal, usually eaten on a sun deck or on the sand. Some nights feature à la carte specials or theme dinners. Another restaurant, on a jetty over the water, specialises in grills and seafood.

Use of the gym is free of charge, as are activities like board games, windsurfing and kayaking. The small spa has a range of massage and holistic treatments. Divers come here for access to dive sites all over South Ari Atoll. The **Ocean-Pro dive centre** (www .oceanpro-diveteam.com) charges US$39/55 per dive with/without equipment and US$619 for an open-water course.

Mirihi is remarkable for making the most of a small island without overdeveloping it. It's equally attractive as a stylish resort, romantic retreat or quality dive island.

Angaga (Angaagau island; ☎ 6660510; angaga@ dhivehinet.com; s/d US$230/240; airport transfer by seaplane 25min, US$200; 50 rooms; ✖) was Ari Atoll's first resort and has been operating since 1989. It's a gorgeous and obvious-choice island. White beaches fringe the island, and the house reef is great for diving and snorkelling – the corals have recovered from the bleaching well here. The thatchroofed bungalows, with a traditional swing seat (undholi) out front, show a little more character than many of the midrange resorts available.

The spacious sand-floored bar and restaurant also show some style – they are built in a distinctive fish shape. All meals are buffet, and include a good selection of Asian and European dishes – seafood barbecues are a regular event. The house wines are inexpensive, but all-inclusive packages are still good value if you indulge. Entertainment is nothing elaborate, but there are plenty of water sports and excursions on offer. Nearby Angaga Thila is a top dive site, but others are some

distance away on the edge of the atoll. The dive centre charges reasonably for a range of diving packages and courses. Angaga is popular with Germans, Swiss, Brits and other Europeans, many of whom are repeat visitors.

Consistently being recommended as a great place for a good-value Maldivian holiday, **Lily Beach Resort** (Huvahendhoo island; ☎ 6660013; www.lilybeachmaldives.com; s/d/tr/wb US$203/256/344/356; airport transfer by seaplane 25min, US$200; 85 rooms; ✖ ✖) inspires popularity that springs from its all-inclusiveness, which generally means guests spend very little on the extras that can be so shockingly expensive at other resorts.

Lily Beach Resort has all its guests on an all-inclusive price plan, which includes all meals, snacks, coffee, beer, wine, whisky, gin, vodka, rum, water sports (except diving), tennis and one island-hopping excursion. If you're keen on windsurfing or drinking, this plan could save you US$10 or US$20 per day compared with other resorts. Most guests are European, including a strong British contingent, and quite often families with children (there's a children's play area).

This is an unpretentious resort and the architecture is neat but nothing fancy – squarish white buildings with green tiled roofs. The vegetation is a bit sparse, but there are good beaches on two sides of the island – the main drawback is the circle of ugly breakwaters that protect the beaches. Resort facilities include a good swimming pool, tennis court, gym and games room. Sand floors in the bar and restaurant go with the friendly and informal atmosphere. All meals are buffet, with a varied selection including pasta and some very tasty Chinese dishes. The standard rooms have air-con, phone and outdoor bathroom with hot water, while the 16 water bungalows are in fact only half over the water, but are markedly larger than the standard rooms.

The house reef is very good (turtles are common) and easily accessible for snorkelling – you can do night snorkelling here too. Keen divers come for the many South Ari dive sites such as the famous Kudra Thila, especially in the whale shark season. The **Ocean-Pro dive base** (www.oceanpro-diveteam .com) offers competitive rates and is extremely friendly. Lily Beach is quite a well-managed resort that offers great value for those who want to eat, drink, dive and relax.

Vilamendhoo (Vilamendhoo island; ☎ 6660637; www.aaa-resortsmaldives.com/vilamendhoo; s/d US$265/340; airport transfer by seaplane 25min, US$210; 154 rooms; 🛄) is a very lush, well-vegetated island that still has some sense of space. The beaches are narrow around most of the island, but there's a big sandy area at one end, or both ends, depending on the season. The house reef is particularly good for snorkelling, and marked channels make it easy to reach the reef edge.

The rooms are divided into three categories; all are air-conditioned, spacious, clean and comfortable, with a thin toupee of thatch as a concession to natural style. The restaurant has a tiled floor, a timber ceiling and no walls, so it's cool and breezy. All meals are buffet style, and offer a wide choice of satisfying dishes, with theme nights for variety and several options for vegetarians. The main bar is the heart of the resort, and the guests on all-inclusive packages make sure it keeps beating.

There are over 40 accessible dive sites in the area, including some of the very best in the Maldives. The **Werner Lau dive centre** (www .wernerlau.com) provides equipment, training and guides at reasonable prices. For non-divers there are numerous excursions, a tennis court, windsurfing and water-skiing, but no pool.

Vilamendhoo is efficiently managed, but friendly and informal, and it attracts a good mix of visitors, mostly from Germany, Italy and the UK. It's recommended for divers.

Fervently focused on diving, **Machchafushi Island Resort** (Machchafushi island; ☎ 6664545; www .machchafushi.com; s/d US$125/175; airport transfer by seaplane 25min, US$190; 64 rooms; 🛄) has a fantastic array of dive and snorkelling sites nearby including the extraordinary Kudarah Thila. The house reef is also superb. Diving is good value, and nearly all the guests here are divers – mainly from Germany and Austria.

The rooms are perfectly adequate and comfortable although guests seem to spend almost no time in them. The restaurant does breakfast and lunch buffets and a set meal for dinner – nothing special, but good

food for hungry divers. There's a swimming pool and tennis court too. This is a great choice for a well-located, easy-going divers' resort.

Simple but stylish, **Vakarufalhi** (Vakarufalhi island; ☎ 6680004; www.vakaru.com; full board s/d/t US$286/336/454; airport transfer by seaplane 25min, US$225; 50 rooms; 🛄) is a fairly run-of-the-mill place – it offers as good a beach as anywhere else (and better than most) – it's wide, white, soft and surrounds the island.

The bar and restaurant at Vakaru (as anyone who's been here for more than five minutes calls it) also feature sand floors, in keeping with the natural style. All the individual bungalows are clean and modern inside, with tiled floors, air-con, hot water and open-air bathrooms; on the outside, they have thatched roofs and a canopy of palm trees. Breakfast and lunch always offer a big buffet selection, while dinners alternate between à la carte menus and theme nights featuring Maldivian specialities (expect fish and curries) or a beach barbecue.

The house reef has caves, overhangs and lots of fish life, sometimes including large visitors from outside the atoll. It's accessible for snorkelling and diving, off the jetties or off the beaches, by day or night. The Pro-Divers dive centre is in fact very professional, and charges standard prices for diving.

A good range of excursions is on offer, along with a little low-key evening entertainment. Vakarufalhi would suit anyone who wants a comfortable beach holiday in a natural environment, with great diving and snorkelling as a bonus.

Ranveli Beach Resort (Viligilivaru island; ☎ 6660570; www.ranveli-maldives.com; s/d US$260/340; airport transfer by seaplane 25min US$205; 56 rooms) seems distinctly overbuilt, with too many rooms on a small island. The main restaurant is offshore, in an elegant pavilion on a pier over the lagoon, and serves a rich variety of quality meals. The house reef is good for snorkelling, excellent dive sites are nearby, and there's a lot of white sandy beach. The guests are all from Italy, and Ranveli offers lots of animation and club-style activities.

Entirely booked through the Italian travel company Turisanda, **Maafushivaru**

(Maafushivaru island; ☎ 6660596; www.turisanda.it; s/d US$350/390; airport transfer by seaplane 30min, US$230; 38 rooms) is a modern-style resort crowded onto a rather small island. The beaches are attractive, but the circle of sea walls, which protects them, is not. The rooms are boxy and modern, with distinctive blue tiled roofs, but comfortable and well furnished. All meals are buffet, well prepared and presented. The house reef is good for snorkelling and lots of fine dive sites are close by. But the main attraction at Maafushivaru is the sociable atmosphere and the lively Italian crowd.

TOP END

Another Villa Hotels product, **Sun Island** (Nalaguraidhoo island; ☎ 6660088; www.villahotels.com/sun; full board s/d US$524/534/721; airport transfer by speedboat 2½hr, US$140, by seaplane 35min, US$260; 350 rooms; 🍴 🖥 🛒) is perhaps more in the style of the Caribbean than the Maldives – this most massive of resorts (the largest in the country) is no place for re-enacting Swiss Family Robinson fantasies – Sun Island is entirely modern, smart and not a particularly charming place.

The rooms themselves are large and have quality indoor-outdoor bathrooms, bidets, minibars, and minisafes. Everything is very modern although it's hardly cutting-edge style and has none of the deeply considered charm of the true luxury market.

If it's an activities-packed holiday you want, though, with endless choice, Sun is a good option. There are 11 bars, five restaurants and the fullest possible choice of water sports, diving, spa treatments, excursions and sports (including a putting range and tennis court), a video arcade and a good gym.

The Sun Island Diving School is quite a big operation with reasonable prices. Most dives are done at nearby sites, and groups can be quite large. Snorkelling is doable at the reef edge off the end of the main jetty. Elsewhere the lagoon is wide, and only good for swimming and water sports.

Nika Hotel (Kudafolhudhoo island; ☎ 6660516; www.nikamaldive.com; full board s/d/wb US$570/680/750; airport transfer by seaplane 20min, US$240; 26 rooms; 🖥) is possibly the finest old-style, natural resort in the country. Individual villas are spacious and imaginatively designed in a seashell shape. This is utter luxury, but genuinely eco-friendly (no pool and no air-

conditioning –just the sea and natural ventilation) to the point that it looks spookily like a traditional Maldivian fishing village populated by well-heeled Europeans.

Tastefully decorated with thatched roofs and handcrafted timber furniture, the villas have private gardens and preserve a rustic image – cooling is by natural ventilation through wooden louvre windows; the wine cellar is the only place to feature air-con. The meals are Italian/international style and excellent, served in the sand-floored dining room or outside on a seaside deck.

Dive costs here are much higher than at other resorts, but groups are small, attention is personal, and the guests can afford it. Fishing, windsurfing, tennis and most other activities are included. Guests are mostly European or Japanese, and value the privacy that Nika provides. Though several new luxury resorts are more sumptuous and have fancier features, Nika is still doing the designer desert island thing to perfection.

Kudarah (Kudarah island; ☎ 6660549; www.club vacanze.it; s/d $455/530; airport transfer by seaplane 25min, $260; 30 rooms; 🍴 🖥) is a small, elegant luxury resort catering exclusively to the Italian market. With white walls, columns, arches and tiles, even the buildings look Italian and the entire feel is Mediterranean rather than tropical. Rooms are large with conservative, quality furnishings, and resort facilities include a tennis court and swimming pool. The dive centre provides personal service with basic dive costs included in the price. The resort is superbly located just minutes from superb diving at Kudarah Thila. It's a Club Vacanze resort, and has a sociable atmosphere, but entertainment and animation are very understated. The beaches are not great, however – there is only one decent stretch that does get very busy, though this doesn't seem to bother any of the numerous repeat visitors.

Sumptuous barefoot luxury is the name of the game at the **Hilton Maldives Resort & Spa** (Rangali island; ☎ 6660629; www.hiltonmaldives resort.com; s/d/wb US$404/808/1435; airport transfer by seaplane 35min, US$270; 150 rooms; 🍴 🖥 🛒), the Hilton Group's long-standing Maldivian resort. It was established long before the rest of the international chain gang arrived. It's hard to imagine anywhere less like the Hiltons you see in major cities around the world; this is one of the very best resorts the country has to offer. British glamour model and tabloid fixture Jordan might have spent her high-profile honeymoon here, but nonetheless this is a classy place and one often booked up months ahead.

The Hilton actually occupies two islands in this atoll – the heart of the resort, with the main lobby, restaurants, bars, water sports, dive centres and 100 beach villas, is on Rangalifinolhu; on the second island, Rangali, are two other restaurants plus a bar, a separate reception area, and 52 water villas in their very own class of exclusivity. A walkway bridge connects the two islands across a broad lagoon.

With seven restaurants running the whole gamut of cuisines from local Maldivian to Japanese and European, you have plenty of choice. Most amazing is the Ithaa Undersea Restaurant where diners eat in a glass-domed restaurant underwater, an experience quite unlike any other in the country. Other restaurants at the resort include the Sunset Grill for fresh seafood (check out the live lobster pond); Vilu Restaurant, serving up creative Euro-Asian fusion dishes; Koko, an outdoor teppanyaki grill; and the Wine Bar, an epicurean education hosted by the ebullient resident sommelier in a climate-controlled cave surrounded by some 5000 bottles of selected wines.

The rooms are varied and beautifully conceived; the standard beach villas are up to 150 sq metres, all are set on the beachfront with sea views; they have outdoor terraces and outdoor bathrooms as well as sea views from the bath. The spectacular water villas all enjoy their own private terraces, gorgeous wooden interiors and, in the more luxurious, glass floors.

All needs are catered to: tennis courts, a swimming pool, excellent beaches, gorgeous gardens and two spas offering massages, Ayurvedic treatments and beauty-salon service. The over-water spa is especially serene, with a glass floor looking into the lagoon. All the public areas are superbly finished with natural materials and an understated island feel.

Diving, water sports, excursions and light entertainment are all on offer, but the real attractions at the Hilton are the unobtrusive, efficient and friendly service, the incredible food and wines, and the ultra-attractive water villas.

At the heart of Ari Atoll, the delightful **W Retreat & Spa** (Fesdhoo island; ☎ 3329489; www .whotels.com; s/d US$816/824; airport transfer by seaplane 25min, US$275; 78 rooms; ✖ 🖳 🏊), which was known as a fairly budget resort for over two decades, has been redeveloped by the W Hotel brand – a boutique, luxury group who is clearly intent on producing something very special for its first Maldivian venture.

The resort was still being built at the time of writing and so we were unable to visit the island during research, although it will definitely be operational by the time you read this book. The resort's central concept is aimed at young, fashionable groups of friends, couples and – shock, horror – single people. While most single people feel a growing sense of nausea and/or exclusion in the Maldives, W is actively encouraging single people and groups of single friends to come here, luring them with such attractions as a 24-hour underground bar (15'Below) where the party never stops (something hard to imagine in the Maldives, admittedly) and a sociable beach-barbecue restaurant where young, single, well-heeled gorgeous things can make new friends. Each 'retreat' (for these are no mere rooms at 188 sq metres for a standard!) comes with its own plunge-pool, day bed and lounge area. Full spa, diving and water-sports facilities complete the picture. It's certainly an interesting concept and will doubtlessly be executed beautifully by the truly boutique W group.

There appears to be at least an interim winner in the war of luxury being waged in the Maldives and **Dhoni Mighili** (Mushimasmingili island; ☎ 6660751; www.dhonimighili.com; s/d US$1295/2590; airport transfer by luxury dhoni 4hr $400, by seaplane 30min $300; 6 dhoni & room pairings; ✖ 🖳) is it. The concept is simple – on the island there are six luxury bungalows and each one is paired with a luxury customised dhoni. As well as your standard *thakuru* (butler; no longer such a status symbol in the Maldives, rather astonishingly) you get your own dhoni captain and two crew on permanent 24-hour alert. You can sleep aboard your dhoni or in your beach bungalow – frankly, you can do whatever the hell you like at these prices.

Both the dhonis and the bungalows are incredible pieces of design and craftsmanship; 20m-long bespoke crafted sailboats fitted with an engine for longer trips (your dhoni can even meet you at Male' airport so you can step off the plane and straight into your hotel room!), they include all possible amenities from king-sized beds to Smeg kitchens and Philippe Starck bathroom fittings. They are definitely rather different to the Male' airport ferry.

On the island the beach bungalows are spread out generously to ensure total privacy. Of the six, four have plunge pools, but all are stunning – featuring private courtyards, incredible outdoor showers, bathrooms decked out in metallic slate and every luxury from Bose surround sound to espresso machines.

The island itself is charming, with gorgeous wide beaches, a luxurious spa, dive centre, DVD and CD library and a full suite of excursions and entertainments that can be arranged whenever a guest snaps their fingers.

You can't bring children under 16 here unless you book out the entire resort – at a mere $12,000 per night (understandably this is a favourite with celebrities on the run from the paparazzi). For utter, shameless luxury you can't currently beat Dhoni Mighili, but it's probably only a matter of time until someone tries.

Northern Atolls

The least developed region of the Maldives, the Northern Atolls are pure tropical island escapism territory. While traditionally the tourism zone has only ever included the three atolls directly to the north of North Male' Atoll, there are a further six even further north that are gradually opening up to tourism as new islands are earmarked for development by the cautious central government. These atolls remain almost totally unknown by foreigners, and this is a great place to visit for a taste of untouched, traditional Maldivian life.

Maldivian history owes much to this part of the country – Muhammad Thakurufaanu, the man who drove the Portuguese out in the 16th century, was born on the island of Utheemu in Haa Alif Atoll, which remains a place of historical pilgrimage today for Maldivians who come to see his small wooden mansion.

There's also huge diving potential throughout the region; there are known to be wrecks along the western fringe of the atolls, but these are only now being properly explored and documented.

In the Northern Atolls there are only 11 functioning resorts at present, making this an un-crowded and truly remote part of the country to visit. Tourism is slowly set to expand here, but at the moment it's still about as remote from elsewhere in the country as you can get.

About 200km beyond Ihavandhippolhu Atoll at the country's northern tip lie the Lak-shadweep Islands, which have had a long association with the Maldives. Formerly known as the Laccadives, these islands are now Indian territory, but geologically they are part of the mostly submerged Laccadive-Chagos ridge that underlies all of the Maldives and extends down to the Chagos Archipelago.

HAA ALIF

Traditionally known as Ihavandhippolhu and North Thiladhunmathee Atolls, the very northern tip of the Maldives is generally known to one and all as Haa Alif Atoll, even though this refers to an administrative district that actually comprises the small, trapezoid shaped Ihavandhippolhu Atoll and the northern tip of North Thiladhunmathee Atoll, which together have 16 inhabited islands and a population of just over 14,000. On Minicoy, the largest island of the Lakshadweep Islands, people speak a language very similar to Divehi and readily understand the Maldivian language themselves.

The second northernmost island, **Uligamu** (population 326) is the 'clear-in' port for private yachts – it has health and immigration officers as well as National Security Service (NSS) personnel, so yachts should be able to complete all formalities here (see p184). The Sailor's Choice store (on VHF) has basic supplies and some diesel (US$0.50/L). Following a feasibility study, the government has decided to establish a yacht marina in the Northern Atolls, but Uligamu has been ruled out for financial and environmental reasons.

The capital island is **Dhidhdhoo** (population 3400), which offers good anchorage for passing yachts. **Huvarafushi**, the next largest island (population 2800), is noted for its music, dancing and sporting activities, and it also has a fish-freezing plant.

The island of **Utheemu** (population 760) is the birthplace of Sultan Mohammed Thakurufaanu who, with his brothers, overthrew Portuguese rule in 1573. A memorial to this Maldivian hero, with a small museum and library, was opened in 1986. Thakurufaanu's wooden palace has been restored and Maldivians come to pay homage to the great man.

Kelaa (population 1900) was the northern British base during WWII, mirroring Gan at the other end of the archipelago. The mosque here dates from the end of the 17th century. Yams and *cadjan* (mat made of coconut palm leaves) are the island's products.

Resorts

In the increasingly unsubtle war of luxury being waged by major hotel brands in the Maldives, there's one place conspicuous in its silence and relatively rarely mentioned by the media – **Island Hideaway** (Dhonakhli Island; ☎ 6501515; www .island-hideaway.com; s/d/wb US$810/810/1930; airport transfer by plane then speedboat 65 mins, $275; 43 rooms; ⧫ 🖵 ⧫), which, true to its name, is located about as remotely as you can imagine in the Maldives' most northerly atoll. This is about as far from the bucket-and-spade brigade as you can get.

Opened in 2005, this is utter boutique luxury, a gorgeous crescent-shaped island with beaches 1.5km long on both sides. One of its big selling points is its marina, the first in the Maldives. Here there are 30 berths for yachts up to 80m – all state of the art and installed by Walcone Marine.

The five categories of rooms start with the standard Funa Pavilions on the beach – which at 176 sq metres are still rather large – white-walled houses with separate bedrooms and living rooms, teak floors throughout, slate and onyx-finished outdoor bathrooms, all possible conveniences from DVD players to espresso machines and each featuring their own gardens. The astonishingly grand two water villas and the incredible two Hideaway Palaces (1420 sq metres of faintly ridiculous exclusivity coming in at around US$3000 per night) make up the top end of the resort's accommodation.

The pampering extends to the Mandara Spa (sorry, the Hideaway Spa by Mandara…pretentious, moi?), the infinity pool, a range of restaurants that will effectively serve up bespoke meals 24 hours a day and a range of boutiques for retail therapy (as if you haven't had enough). The pristine reefs around the island and the untouched sites further afield make another great reason to come here – the **Meridis Diving School** (www.meridis.de) is exceptionally smart with luxury boats and tiny groups, but inevitably expensive.

To confirm exactly who it's aimed at, the resort offers landing facilities for private jets at the nearby regional airport of Hanimaadhoo. Those poor things without their own planes will get their own Island Aviation Services charter from Male', or – eek – can even arrive by the daily scheduled IAS flight. For most of us, a trip here is just a fantasy, but if it's anonymous, boutique luxury and pampering you're after this is the place to come.

Alidhoo was allocated in 2004 for development in the near future as the atoll's second island resort.

HAA DHAAL

Haa Dhaal is an administrative district comprising some 17,000 people spread over 17 islands and made up of South Thiladhunmathee Atoll – the central section of an elongated reef and lagoon formation extending over 150km north to south – and the far smaller Maamakunudhoo Atoll, a narrow oval of reefs, about 20km to the west.

Kulhuduffushi is the capital island and also the most populous, with 7500 people. It has been chosen by the government as the Maldives' northern regional centre, and has a hospital, a secondary school and all basic services. A new harbour was being completed at the time of research. The traditional specialities here are rope making and shark fishing. The regional airport is on Hanimaadhoo (population 1300). Island Aviation has flights from Male' and back on most days – and this is the only runway in all the Northern Atolls, so flights are busy.

The highest natural point in the Maldives, at about 3m above sea level, is on **Faridhoo** (population 230), where there are ancient Buddhist ruins. On **Kumundhoo** there's a stone circle that seems to be the

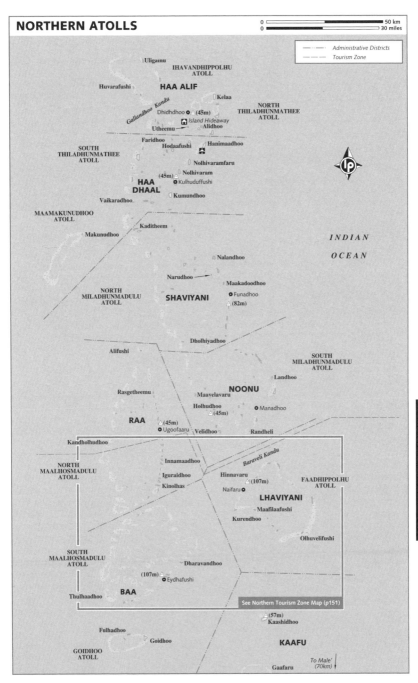

NORTHERN ATOLLS

0 — 50 km
0 — 30 miles

— · — · — Administrative Districts
— — — — Tourism Zone

Uligamu

IHAVANDHIPPOLHU ATOLL

Huvarafushi

HAA ALIF

Kelaa

NORTH THILADHUNMATHEE ATOLL

Gallandhoo Kandu

Dhidhdhoo ○ △(45m)

Island Hideaway

Uttheemu

Alidhoo

Faridhoo

SOUTH THILADHUNMATHEE ATOLL

Hodaafushi

Hanimaadhoo

Nolhivaramfaru

Nolhivaram

HAA DHAAL

(45m)△

○ Kulhuduffushi

Vaikaradhoo

Kumundhoo

MAAMAKUNUDHOO ATOLL

Kaditheem

Makunudhoo

INDIAN

OCEAN

Nalandhoo

Narudhoo →

Maakadoodhoo

NORTH MILADHUNMADULU ATOLL

SHAVIYANI

○ Funadhoo

△(82m)

Dholhiyadhoo

Alifushi

SOUTH MILADHUNMADULU ATOLL

Landhoo

Rasgetheemu

NOONU

Maavelavaru

Holhudhoo

△(45m)

○ Manadhoo

RAA

△(45m)

○ Ugoofaaru

Velidhoo

Randheli

Kandholhudhoo

NORTH MAALHOSMADULU ATOLL

Innamaadhoo

Baraveli Kandu

Iguraidhoo

Hinnavaru

△(107m)

FAADHIPPOLHU ATOLL

Kinolhas

Naifaru ○

LHAVIYANI

Maafilaafushi

Kurendhoo

Olhuvelifushi

SOUTH MAALHOSMADULU ATOLL

Dharavandhoo

(107m)△

○ Eydhafushi

Thulhaadhoo

BAA

See Northern Tourism Zone Map (p151)

Fulhadhoo

△(57m)

Kaashidhoo

Goidhoo

KAAFU

GOIDHOO ATOLL

To Male'
(70km)

Gaafaru

NORTHERN ATOLLS

base of Buddhist stupa, and *hawitta* (artificial mound) remains can still be seen on **Vaikaradhoo**.

The area around Haa Dhaal suffers severe storms, and quite a few vessels have gone down in these waters. Maamakunudhoo Atoll is the graveyard of several ships, including the English ships *Persia Merchant*, wrecked here in 1658, and the *Hayston*, which ran onto a reef in 1819. In each circumstance, survivors were rescued by local people and treated with kindness, a source of great local pride.

The island of Hodaafushi has been allocated as a resort and plans are currently being worked on to create a 9-hole golf course here.

SHAVIYANI

Looking at a modern map, the Shaviyani administrative district, made up of Miladhunmadulu Atoll and Thiladhunmathee Atoll, appears to be part of one elongated atoll enclosing a single, very long lagoon. Shaviyani administrative district comprises 15 inhabited islands with a total of 11,406 people. This atoll is most famous today as a major breeding ground for turtles, who breed successfully on its pristine beaches.

The capital is **Funadhoo** (population 1330), a pretty island with the ruins of an ancient mosque and 13th-century tombstones. The most populous island, with 1600 inhabitants, is **Komandhoo**. **Narudhoo** island is tiny but has a natural freshwater lake on it – one of the very few open places in the whole country where water collects.

The main mosque on the island of **Kanditheem** (population 1160) incorporates the oldest known example of the Maldives' unique Thaana script – it's an inscription on a doorframe, which notes that the roof was constructed in 1588. Another famous island is uninhabited **Nalandhoo**, where the Thakurufaanu brothers hid their boat between guerrilla battles with the Portuguese.

The beautiful crescent island of Dholhiyadhoo has been allocated as the atoll's first resort island.

NOONU

The southern end of the Miladhunmadulu-Thiladhunmathee Atoll complex is called South Miladhunmadulu, and it forms the Noonu administrative district, comprising 13 inhabited islands with a combined total of 11,000 people. The capital island, **Manadhoo**, has 1500 people, but **Holhudhoo** (population 1900) and **Velidhoo** (population 2100) are more populous.

On the island of **Landhoo** (population 850) are the remnants of a *hawitta* supposedly left by the fabled Redin, a people who figure in Maldivian folklore. The *hawitta* is a 15m-high mound known locally as *maa badhige* ('great cooking place'). Thor Heyerdahl writes extensively about the tall, fair-haired Redin in his book *The Maldive Mystery*. He believes them to have been the first inhabitants of the Maldives, as long ago as 2000 BC.

Two islands, Maavelavaru and Randheli, have been allocated for development as the first two resort islands in Noonu Atoll.

RAA

Raa administrative district, with 15,000 people dispersed throughout 16 inhabited islands and one resort, is made up of North Maalhosmadulu Atoll and the island of Alifushi. Development is slow but sure here – diving safari boats are starting to venture into this area, and new dive sites are being documented.

The sea to the west of Raa has some of the best fishing areas in the country. The capital island **Ugoofaaru** (population 1250) has one of the largest fishing fleets in the country. On the west side of the atoll the tiny island of **Kandholhudhoo** (also spelt Kandoludhu) is the nearest to the rich western waters, and has 3600 people crowded onto it – a candidate for the most densely populated island in the country.

The island of **Alifushi** (population 2250), which is actually in a small, separate atoll to the north of Raa proper, is reputedly the home of the finest dhoni builders in the country. The government-owned Alifushi Boat Yard continues the tradition, producing a modern version of the dhoni. **Iguraidhoo** (population 1500) and **Innamaadhoo** (population 700) are also boat-building and carpentry centres that are accessible for excursions from Meedhupparu Island Resort.

According to local legend, the now uninhabited island of **Rasgetheemu** is where Koimala Kaloa and his princess wife landed after being exiled from Sri Lanka and before

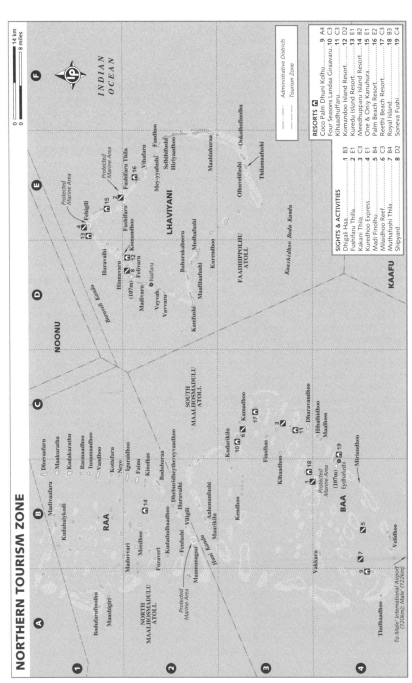

NORTHERN ATOLLS

moving to Male' to found a ruling dynasty. Another important visitor to the atoll was the Arab seafarer Ibn Battuta, who landed at **Kinolhas** in 1343 and then moved on to Male'.

The channel between Baa and Raa, locally known as Hani Kandu, is also named Moresby Channel after the Royal Navy officer Robert Moresby, who was responsible for the original marine survey of the Maldives made from 1834 to 1836. There's good diving on both sides of the Moresby Channel, as it funnels water between the atolls, bringing pelagic fish and promoting coral growth. Mantas abound in October and November. The channels entering the atoll are studded with interesting thilas, and reefs dot the inside of the atoll.

Resorts

Raa Atoll is home to just the one resort – many more are planned but the combination of tourism downturn and the tsunami have held up a lot of development projects.

You are truly remote at the **Meedhupparu Island Resort** (Meedhupparu island; ☎ 6587700; www .meedhupparu.com; full board s/d/t US$210/250/335; airport transfer by speedboat 4hr, US$170, by seaplane 45min, US$300; 215 rooms; ✖ ☒), the only island resort in the whole of Raa Atoll; and Meedhupparu does not disappoint, with its gorgeous wide white beaches sloping down to the lagoon. While once colonised by the Italian market, Meedhupparu today is mainly marketed in the UK and Germany, whose citizens make up the bulk of the guests here. Italians and Russians make up the other main groups.

Unaffected by the tsunami, Meedhupaaru's buildings all date from 2000 when it opened. The resort also features an Ayurvedic Village made up of 24 houses, popular with German guests, as well as an area known as the 'Water Villas' that functions as a resort within a resort, aimed at wealthier clients. The Water Villas complex is marketed separately and non-Water Villa guests are not allowed into the Water Villa area of the island, which includes an exclusive Balinese spa and a charming garden full of Sri Lankan flowers. The rooms elsewhere in the resort are perfectly fine if lacking in character and the rooms in the Ayurvedic Village are identical, but simply feature thatched roofs.

Water sports and diving are big attractions here – the water-sports activities available include two catamarans and the diving is so diverse due to the remote location of the resort that new diving spots are constantly being discovered! Over 27 dive sites are visited regularly by the resort's dive boats and there's a huge variety of species to see. However, the diving isn't as cheap as it is at most resorts. There's a huge pool, gym, tennis and badminton courts and a big choice of bars and restaurants to keep people entertained.

All in all Meedhupparu is a great opportunity to escape from it all and combines remote location with plenty of activities and all-round good value.

BAA

The Baa administrative district includes South Maalhosmadulu Atoll and the small Goidhoo Atoll, 10km further south. Its inhabitants number roughly 11,000 people in 13 inhabited islands and a handful of resorts. Fishing is the most important activity, but Baa is also famous for its lacquer work and the fine woven-cotton sarong, called a *feylis*. **Eydhafushi**, the capital and principal island (population 2700), is also the *feylis* centre. **Thulhaadhoo** (population 2400) is the second largest island and the main centre for the production of lacquered boxes and jars. Both of these islands can be visited on excursions from nearby resorts.

Because of its isolation, **Goidhoo** has traditionally been a place for castaways and exiles. In 1602 Francois Pyrard, a French explorer, found himself on the island of **Fulhadhoo** after his ship, the *Corbin*, was wrecked. Incredibly, in 1976 a German traveller was banished here for the murder, in Male', of his girlfriend – he refused offers of extradition, converted to Islam and later married a local woman.

Sights & Activities
DIVING
Strong currents flowing through the Kamadhoo Kandu provide an environment for soft corals, which thrive on **Milaidhoo Reef**, on the north side of an uninhabited island. The reef top, at 2m, is great for snorkelling, and it drops straight down to about 35m. This cliff has numerous caves and overhangs with sea fans and sponges.

The north side of **Kakani Thila**, at 25m to 30m, retains coral formations in excellent condition, and colourful soft corals fill the overhangs. It's also home to lots of fish, including Napoleons, jackfish and Oriental sweetlips.

The small **Dhigali Haa**, though well inside the atoll, commonly attracts pelagic species (barracuda) and grey reef sharks. Other fish include jacks, batfish and trevally. It's also a good place to see nudibranch, yellow and orange soft corals and anemones (with clown fish).

The sandy **Madi Finolhu** has large coral blocks on which black corals grow. Stingrays can be seen on the sand, and mantas also pass through. This is a good beginners' dive (20m).

Overhangs at **Muthafushi Thila** are home to soft corals and anemones. Many hard corals are in good condition and very colourful, soft corals can also be seen. There are large schools of blue-striped snapper.

Resorts

MIDRANGE

The Reethi Beach Resort (Fonimagoodhoo island; ☎ 6602626; www.reethibeach.com; s/d/t US$125/179/242; airport transfer by seaplane 35min, US$240; 100 rooms; ⬚ ⬚) is all about well-heeled ecotourism, and even through it's very much a smart midrange resort, the management does a great job of making guests feel like it's still a haven for nature and stripped-down pleasure.

This good-sized island has plenty of natural vegetation, soft white beaches, an accessible house reef and an expansive lagoon. The buildings, all with thatched roofs, are designed to blend with the environment, and also incorporate some Maldivian design elements like the deep horizontal mouldings used on the old Friday Mosque in Male'. Rooms are very well finished and have air-con, TV, minibar, IDD phone, quality bathrooms and polished timber floors. The deluxe villas are more spacious and have better beach frontage, while the water villas are decent but nothing show-stopping.

Guests are mostly British, German and Swiss, many on half-board packages that let them try the weekly barbecue and the two speciality restaurants (Chinese and Maldivian) as well as the excellent selection in the main buffet.

For the sporting guests, there's a swimming pool, gym, squash, badminton and tennis. Windsurfing, sailing and other water sports are popular here because of the wide lagoon. Kitesurfing is the latest thrill on offer. Motorised activities like parasailing, wakeboarding and jet skis are available only at certain hours. The spa offers a full range of massage and beauty treatments. The **Sea-Explorer dive centre** (www.sea-explorer.net) is very professional and reasonably priced. Qualified divers can make dives off the house reef, and with few resorts in the area you'll probably have good dive sites to yourself.

Reethi Beach is an excellent resort all round – attractive, well managed, with great food, where you can relax completely or have a full-on action holiday.

Marketed as Kihaad Maldive for an exclusively Italian market, **Kihaadhuffaru** (Kihaadhuffaru island; ☎ 6606688; www.valtur.it; airport transfer by seaplane 35min, US$220, by speedboat 3hr, US$140; 100 rooms; ⬚ ⬚) is a very stylish resort on a gorgeous island that enjoys lots of vegetation and some great sand spits out into the lagoon. Italian guests are on packages that include meals, some drinks and lots of activities. The rooms are new, fully equipped (air-con, TV, minibar etc) and attractively designed; deluxe rooms have hi-fi systems, and water villas are also available. The restaurant serves a rich selection of Italian and international dishes: buffet for breakfast and lunch, table service for dinner. The resort has a first-class swimming pool, disco, spa, kids' club and water-sports centre, and the island itself is a delight, with shady palm trees, perfect beaches, a lovely lagoon for sailing and a house reef that's accessible for snorkelling and diving. Bookings are all through the Italian operator **Valtur** (☎ in Italy 39-6-47061; fax 39-6-4706334) and rack rates are unavailable.

Royal Island (Horubadhoo island; ☎ 6600088; www.royal-island.com; s/d/t US$422/432/583; airport transfer by seaplane 35min, US$285; 152 rooms; ⬚ ⬚) is Villa Hotels' flagship upmarket resort (their others such as Paradise Island, Sun Island and Holiday Island are distinctly lower down the food chain) and it is clearly lucky to have avoided being saddled with a terribly naff sounding name, judging by the fate of its sister resorts. In fact, this is a classy place with attentive staff, an impressive spa and plenty of leisure activities.

The island is long and narrow, with magnificent long stretches of white beach and a brilliant house reef. Most of the natural vegetation has been preserved, including many coconut palms, pandanuses, screw pines and seven big banyan trees. An old bathing pool and some mosque ruins have also been preserved.

The modern-looking rooms are nestled in trees and front onto the beach. Inside they have pine walls, hardwood floors and all the gadgets from air-con and IDD phone to electric kettle and satellite TV. The airy main restaurant offers a huge variety of styles – Italian, Indian, Mexican, Maldivian and others – all served as buffets. A second restaurant specialises in à la carte Mediterranean meals, while several bars serve snacks and drinks. Alcohol is a bit pricey here (about US$5 for a beer; US$7 for a glass of house wine), but many 'extras' are included in the room rate – mineral water, gym facilities, daytime tennis, windsurfing and snorkelling gear. The Royal Araamu Spa is a luxury facility with a relaxing ambience. Eight therapists perform a range of beauty and 'wellness' treatments from face massage to pedicure.

The Delphis Diving Centre is keen to have divers explore the many sites in Baa Atoll, and they're very good guides. A single boat dive is US$45 with tank and weights, or US$57 with all equipment. An open-water course costs US$595.

Though the style here is much more natural than at other Villa properties, it doesn't have the character of many older, smaller resorts. But with its high-quality facilities and food, beautiful beaches and fantastic snorkelling and diving, Royal Island represents great value for money.

TOP END

The original Soneva resort in the Maldives, opening in 1995, the stunning **Soneva Fushi** (Kunfunadhoo island; ☎ 6600304; www.sixsenses.com /soneva-fushi; s & d US$640; airport transfer by seaplane 30min, US$330; 65 rooms; 🏊 🖥 🐟) has been somewhat eclipsed by its even more fabulous sister resort Soneva Gili in North Male' Atoll, but this is still an incredible and alluring place. Whereas Soneva Gili is about water, Soneva Fushi is about the jungle and the incredible, dense vegetation of this island is one of the first things that strikes you on arrival.

Soneva Fushi is housed on the biggest resort island in the country (more than 1.5km long) but has just 65 luxurious villas. Each one is like a small house built with natural materials, fitted with designer furnishings and finished in rustic style. All the deluxe features are included (air-con, hairdryer, minisafe, CD player etc) but 'modern' items are concealed – no plastic is visible. Villas are well spaced around the edges of the island, affording complete privacy – they're reached by sandy tracks that wind through the lush vegetation, which is kept as natural as possible. There's a big range of villas as well as prices and even if the 15 'standard' Rehendi Rooms come in comfortably below four figures a night, prices quickly rise as you move up the categories. The most expensive option, the Jungle Reserve, a vast Swiss Family Robinson–style retreat for the mega-rich, has to be seen to be believed.

The reception, bar and restaurant areas all have sand floors and cane furniture, and the chickens are free to wander anywhere. The food is superb, with the freshest, finest ingredients, beautifully prepared and presented. It could be called European-Asian fusion cuisine, with a bias towards light and tropical flavours. Lunch and sometimes dinner are buffet style, but the offerings change daily, and the wine list is wonderful. Meals are often served alfresco, and in-room dining is also available.

Picnics on isolated islands are popular, as are the dozens of different massages and treatments offered at the Six Senses spa. The atmosphere is completely relaxed and delightfully unpretentious – leave your jewellery and your dinner jacket at home.

There is the usual range of resort recreations, many of them complimentary. The **Soleni dive school** (www.soleni.com) has years of experience diving the sites around Soneva. A single boat dive is US$69 with tank and weights, or US$81 with all equipment. An open-water course costs about US$695.

For back-to-nature meets *haute couture*, you'll find nowhere better than Soneva Fushi.

Four Seasons Landaa Giraavaru (Landaa Giraavaru island; ☎ 6600888; www.fourseasons.com/maldiveslg; s/ d/wb US$800/800/990; airport transfer by seaplane 30min, US$295; 102 rooms; 🏊 🖥 🐟), the second Four Seasons resort in the Maldives, was, like it's badly tsunami-hit sister, still not operational at the time of research. Unlike the Four Seasons at Kuda Hura, however, this property is brand new and promises to raise the bar again in the struggle for ultimate luxury in an already crowded market.

The accommodation is divided into thatched-roof beach and water villas, each replete with teak furnishings and rustic yet modern décor. Private plunge pools come with many of the rooms, as do personal butlers and the full range of amenities you'd expect from a five-star international chain.

Coco Palm Dhuni Kolhu (Dhunikolhu island; ☎ 6600011; www.cocopalm.com.mv/dhunikolhu; s/d/wb US$452/495/914; airport transfer by seaplane 30min, US$295; 100 rooms; ✕ ☐), one of the most architecturally interesting resorts, has large tentlike thatched pavilions for reception, restaurant and bar areas. The beach villa rooms are circular with high, thatched, conical roofs, quality furnishings and open-air bathrooms, while the deluxe rooms have, in addition, an individual, free-form plunge pool. The 14 over-water bungalows are even more luxuriously appointed, and combine privacy with uninterrupted sea views.

The island itself is quite large with soft, white beaches all around and a very accessible house reef. The vegetation has a very natural look, although it's a little sparse and scrubby – they're working to thicken it up. Another highlight is the food. All meals are buffet, but the variety, quality and freshness is hard to believe – it's one of the few resorts with perfect avocados.

With no other resorts around, divers here have access to almost untouched sites. Diving is run by **Ocean-Pro** (www.oceanpro-diveteam.com), which offers professional, personal service. A single boat dive is US$51 with tank and weights, or US$70 with all equipment. An open-water course costs about US$646. Nitrox courses cost US$207 and nitrox dives cost no extra.

Whale watching is an option in October and November, when the animals migrate through the channel between Baa and Goidhoo Atolls. Excursions include a visit to Thulhaadhoo, an island well known for producing lacquer work, which you can see and buy. For recreation there's a gym, a spa, tennis courts, and a billiard table, as well as the Mandara Spa for Balinese-style massage.

Coco Palm has developed a well-deserved reputation for being an ideal honeymoon and couples' hideaway and is maturing into a sophisticated home away from home.

LHAVIYANI

The single atoll of Faadhippolhu makes up the administrative district of Lhaviyani, where fishing is the main industry and tourism is gradually becoming more important. It has a population of about 10,000 living on just five inhabited islands. On the capital island, **Naifaru** (population 4350), the people have a reputation for making attractive handicrafts from coral and mother-of-pearl, and for concocting local medicines. **Hinnavaru** (population 4300) is also densely settled and the central government is promoting the development of **Maafilaafushi** as an alternative, but so far only about 100 people have settled there. Maafilaafushi had a much greater population in the 17th century, but it was later abandoned, though remnants of the old mosque can still be seen. Day trips from the resorts visit all these islands, as well as **Felivaru**, which has a modern tuna-canning plant.

Sights & Activities
DIVING
Usually done as a long drift dive through the channel next to the Kuredu resort, **Kuredhoo Express** is a demanding dive in strong currents but also offers brilliant snorkelling on the eastern side. Napoleon wrasse, grey reef sharks and trevally frequent the channel entrance, while inside are overhangs dripping with soft corals. Look for morays, turtles and stingrays. It's a Protected Marine Area.

Shipyard is another demanding dive, with two wrecks within 50m of each other. Strong currents around these ships have promoted rapid growth of soft and hard corals, which now form a habitat for many types of reef fish. Moray eels and sweepers live inside the wrecks, while nurse sharks cruise around the bottom.

When the current is strong, **Fushifaru Thila** is no place for beginners, but when the currents are slow the top of the thila is superb for snorkelling. The thila, with lovely soft corals, sits in the centre of a broad channel and attracts mantas, eagle rays, sharks, groper, sweetlips and turtles. Cleaner wrasse abound on the thila, which is a Protected Marine Area.

Resorts
Though Kuredu has been open for over 25 years, the other resorts are more recent (late 1990s), and reflect the upmarket trend in Maldives tourism.

BUDGET
Kuredu Island Resort (Kuredhoo island; ☎ 6620337; www.kuredu.com; s/d/wb US$120/140/320; airport transfer by seaplane 40min, US$250; 330 rooms; 🖭 🖳 🖳) is about as close as you can get to a resort city in the Maldives – this truly is the resort that has everything, and people will love it or loathe it in equal measure for this very reason. Since a comprehensive refit a few years ago Kuredu has managed to go impressively upmarket while retaining its very reasonable prices and it's now a great chance to enjoy a midrange style resort at distinctly budget prices.

Established as a diving camp in 1976, Kuredu is favoured by British and German visitors – the former make up some two thirds of the guests while the latter are the second biggest nationality represented. You can effectively have whatever kind of holiday you're after here – the sheer number of activities and facilities available is mind-boggling. From the only golf course in the Maldives (six holes and 250m driving range) and kite-boarding, to a decompression chamber and a football pitch, Kuredu has it all.

The beach bungalows are recently renovated with air-con, phone, hot water and minibar, but are still very affordable. The new, all-wood beach villas face the best beach, have an open-air bathroom, stereo and coffeemakers, and cost up to US$30 more. Spa beach villas are more expensive again, and the spacious Sangu water villas, made with the honeymooners in mind, are suitably grand. In fact the Sangu Resort is an exclusive resort within a resort: the restaurant here does first-class buffet meals with live cooking stations as a special attraction and 'wedding' ceremonies or renewal-of-vows services are held here.

The main reception, restaurant, bar, swimming pool, shops and dive centre are all near the centre of the island, and cater

for the generally younger, livelier crowd in the less expensive rooms. The buffets in the main restaurant are pretty good, with a fair selection of Asian and international dishes. In addition there are three à la carte restaurants specialising in Italian pizza, Thai food and grills. There's even a teashop where you can get typical Maldivian short eats at typical tourist prices (it's more popular with staff than guests). The big Babuna Bar is the busiest place in the evening and hosts movies, discos, cultural shows, games nights and live bands. Other bars offer poolside drinks or a more intimate atmosphere.

Recreation facilities include a gym, tennis courts, a well-used beach volleyball court and the aforementioned golf course. For water sports there are windsurfing, kitesurfing, catamarans, water-skiing, wakeboards and the ubiquitous banana. A new and palatial spa offers hour-long Swedish, Thai and Oriental massages as well as two-hour lessons so you can learn to massage your partner. Excursions go to a variety of local fishing villages, resorts and uninhabited islands. There's a day cruise on a traditional wooden yacht (US$75) and a choice of fishing trips too.

Excellent dive sites are accessible to Kuredu and just a few other resorts. The **ProDivers centre** (www.prodivers.com) offers a full range of courses, and does a good job matching divers with others of similar experience and interest. A single boat dive costs US$49 with tank and weights, or US$65 with all equipment. An open-water course is US$595. A nitrox course costs US$99, and nitrox dives are available at no extra cost. Rebreather courses and dives are also available. Much of the house reef is accessible, and you can do good dives directly from the shore. ProDivers also runs a complete snorkelling program, with instructors taking groups for fish spotting, photography and wreck-snorkelling trips.

It's a well-run resort that has always been popular with young Europeans, giving it a lively, sociable atmosphere. Now it also has more honeymooners, older couples and families. The island is very big and has been intelligently developed to cater for a variety of needs. If you want high-style luxury or intimate island atmosphere, this resort may not be for you. But for activities such as diving and snorkelling, relaxation, recreation, families and fun, Kuredu is hard to beat.

MIDRANGE

Komandoo Island Resort (Komandhoo island; ☎ 6621010; www.komandoo.com; s/d/wb US$270/280/420; airport transfer by seaplane 40min, US$270, by speedboat 4hr, US$120; 65 rooms; ✕ ☐) , the smaller and more stylish sibling of Kuredu, shares the same management. The feel at this resort couldn't really be more different, though – instead of crowds of excitable holidaymakers going from activity to activity, at Komandoo the pace is far more relaxed and the resort ethos is one of pampering and relaxation. There are no children allowed here, making this a favourite spot for honeymooners and other couples enjoying a romantic break.

The round island is ringed by a strikingly beautiful beach, although the sea breaks that surround much of the island obscure the desert-island perfection somewhat. The visitors here are mainly British and German.

The hexagonal rooms, prefabricated in pine from Finland, come complete with aircon, phone, four-poster bed, minibar, safe and CD player, and they all front directly onto a pure white beach. Fifteen water bungalows were added in 2006 and they are suitably impressive.

The four reefs accessible through two channels from the island have a wide variety of marine life (256 fish species have been documented) and recovering corals, so are ideal for snorkelling from the beach. The very professional **ProDivers** (www.prodivers .com) runs the dive centre, as on Kuredu, but with smaller groups and slightly higher prices – US$52 for a single boat dive with tank and weights and US$665 for an openwater course. Nitrox is available.

Perhaps Komandoo's most charming feature is its own uninhabited island just a short boat ride across the lagoon. This is almost too picture perfect to be believed, a perfect circle of heavily vegetated heaven with virgin beaches and total peace and quiet.

The island is not lush, but is impressively landscaped. The main restaurant and bar buildings have sea views, sand floors and tropical-island atmosphere. The food and service get rave reviews, and the new Etoile spa adds another opportunity for indulgence. If you want a small, quiet, quality resort, Komandoo is ideal.

Famous throughout the atoll for being a particularly beautiful island, triangular **Palm Beach Resort** (Madhiriguraidhoo island; ☎ 6620087; www.palmbeach-maldives.com; full board s/d/t US$248/364/489; airport transfer by seaplane 40min, US$330; 100 rooms; ✕ ☐ ☎) enjoys some of the best beaches in the atoll. The bungalows dotted along both sides of the island are quite big and have air-con, phone, TV, in-house movies, minibar and other mod cons, though the white walls, tiled floors and bamboo furniture aren't especially stylish. Most of the resort facilities (restaurant, bar, pool, spa, sports centre) are towards one end of the island, quite a way from some of the rooms. Electric carts and bicycles are available to help people get around.

The main restaurant serves all meals as buffets with an Italian bias, and they're very good. Seven bars are dotted around the island. Live music, discos and other entertainment happens in the pool bar. Tennis, squash and most water sports are free, as are some excursions and snorkelling trips (the lagoon isn't good for snorkelling). The Macana Diving School charges very reasonable diving rates and runs the full gamut of courses for beginners.

Palm Beach Resort is operated by Sporting Vacanze and most guests come from Italy, but it's not really a club-style resort and the animation is low key. In fact the whole resort has a very casual atmosphere. It attracts all age groups, and quite a few families with children, so it's perfectly possible to stay here as a FIT (fully independent traveller), unlike at many Italian package resorts.

TOP END

One & Only's first Maldivian resort, **One & Only Kanuhura** (Kanahuraa island; ☎ 6620044; www.oneandonlyresorts.com; s/d/wb US$664/698/1140; airport transfer by seaplane 40min, US$309; 100 rooms; ✕ ☐ ☎) is a sumptuous, charming, impressive place with magnificent beaches, stunning accommodation and top-notch food. This place manages to get it right on so many levels – it's classy and stylish without being too formal, it's romantic without being too quiet and it's welcoming to families without allowing the kids to run riot. If you want a laid-back, high-end beach holiday with considerable style, this may be for you.

The rooms combine classical luxury and elegant simplicity. The beach villas have four-poster beds, a separate dressing area, fabulous indoor outdoor bathroom, lots of polished timber and a frontage onto the perfect beach. They're equipped with the works – air-con, safe, stereo, satellite TV, DVD, espresso machine, minibar, bathrobes, umbrellas and even slippers. The more expensive suites and water villas are even bigger and feature several rooms, private spas, sun decks and direct sea access.

The resort's public areas are focused around the expansive infinity pool near the main jetty. This has the main Thin Rah restaurant at one end, the Olive Tree Italian restaurant to one side and the wonderfully Arabesque bar at the other. Also near the pool is the One & Only Spa, a serene space that's central to the resort's concept, with some 40 treatments on offer. There's also a gym, aerobics studio, karaoke bar, cigar lounge, games room and library with free Internet access. Other facilities around the island include the Nashaa nightclub, several boutiques, a coffee shop, tennis and squash courts, and an excellent kids' club. This is a complete resort.

At the other end of the island is the high-end outdoor dining option of the Veli Café – overlooking the resort's very own desert islet of Jehunuhura. A complimentary boat shuttles guests back and forth between the two, the main attraction of Jehunuhura being the gorgeous Cove's Beach restaurant, open for lunch, but there's also the beds scattered about the undergrowth for lovers to lounge in while pretending to be in an upmarket version of *Lost*.

Kanahuraa is a big island, about 1km long, and assiduous landscaping is augmenting the natural vegetation with local species. The environment is a priority here – garden waste is composted, water is recycled, sewage is reprocessed and solar panels provide the hot water. Lovely, squeaky beaches go right around the island, and the wide lagoon makes for smooth sailing – you can follow the reef for 5km and make your own stops at several tiny uninhabited islands along the way. Water-skiing is an option; jet skis are not. Field trips here vary from dolphin watching to one of the most unusual we've come across – a trip to the tuna-tinning factory on nearby Felivaru.

The house reef is not suitable for snorkelling, so take one of the special snorkelling excursions run by the **Sun Dive Centre** (www .sundivecenter.com), a PADI Gold Palm facility that caters for youngsters, beginners and advanced divers. Over 40 dive sites are accessible. A single boat dive costs US$65 with tank and weights, or US$75 with all equipment, and an open-water course costs US$660. Nitrox dives costs US$5 extra, and a nitrox course is US$280.

One & Only Kanuhura is a treat and a half, a full resort thought out by a company fanatical about getting everything right. On all fronts it scores maximum points – stay here if you are lucky enough to have the chance.

Southern Atolls

All eyes are currently on the southern Maldives to provide the islands for the future development of tourism in the Maldives. The already-crowded central Maldives and the bad transport links to the northern atolls mean that the pristine south is, in the words of many a developer, ripe for it. There are three regional airports with daily connections to Male' already here and the new international airport at Gan will begin taking long-haul flights from Europe and Asia during the lifetime of this book, so tourism arrivals to this relatively untouched area of the country are set to dramatically increase.

Until a few years ago, the atolls south of Male' and Ari Atolls were isolated and had scarcely seen a foreigner. The exception was Gan, in the far south of the country, where the British had established military facilities in WWII and an air-force base that operated from 1956 to 1976. Even 30 years after the British departed Gan still has an unusually British feel.

Staying at the budget Equator Village remains one of the best ways to experience real life in the Maldives, as a new road has connected Gan to three other inhabited islands that tourists are free to explore by bicycle or taxi without the usual restrictions.

Development is set to be huge over the next decade here: the tourism zone looks set to be expanded to cover all five southern atolls that are currently off-limits to non-permit-holders, safari boats are regularly exploring dive sites as far south as the Huvadhoo Kandoo (famously known as One-and-a-Half-Degree channel), and surfing trips are going to the remotest breaks of Gaaf Dhaal. Despite this, the region is almost totally pristine and a wonderful place to visit.

VAAVU

The Vaavu administrative district is made up of Felidhoo Atoll (also spelled Felidhe and Fulidhoo) and the small, uninhabited Vattaru Falhu Atoll. This is the least populous area of the country, with around 2000 inhabitants spread over just five inhabited islands. As the area is just south of Male' and thus well served by transport links, this is an area set to be developed far more heavily in the near future than the two resorts currently functioning here.

The main industry is fishing, and there is some boat building as well as two tourist resort islands. The capital island is **Felidhoo**, which has only about 500 people, but visitors are more likely to go its neighbouring island, **Keyodhoo** (population 650), which

has a good anchorage for safari boats. At the northern edge of the atoll, **Fulidhoo** (population 370) is an attractive island, regularly visited on day trips from the resorts – you may see some impressively large boats under construction here. **Rakeedhoo** (population 360), at the southern tip of the atoll, is used as an anchorage by safari boats taking divers to the nearby channel.

Sights & Activities
DIVING
There are at least 24 recognised dive sites in the atoll and only two resorts in the area. Some of them are not readily accessible, even from the resorts, and are mostly visited by safari boats. The following sites are

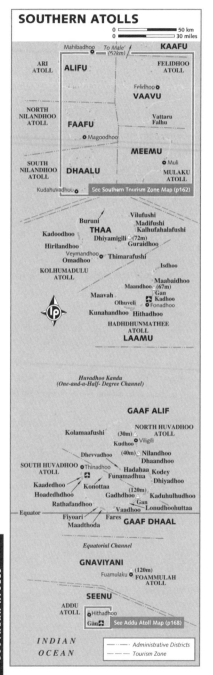

SOUTHERN ATOLLS

rated as amongst the best in the Maldives, and they all offer superb snorkelling.

Devana Kandu is a not-too-demanding drift dive in a channel divided by a narrow thila; it's a great snorkelling area too. There are several entrances to the channel, which has overhangs, caves, reef sharks and eagle rays. The southern side has soft corals and lots of reef fish. Further in, the passages join up and there is a broad area of hard corals, the deeper parts being less affected by bleaching. The whole channel is a Protected Marine Area.

Fotteyo is a brilliant dive and snorkelling site in and around a channel entrance – it's worth making several dives here. There are numerous small caves, several large caves and various arches and holes, all decorated with colourful soft corals. Rays, reef sharks, groper, tuna, jackfish, barracuda, turtles and even hammerhead sharks can be seen. Inside, the channel floor is known as 'triggerfish alley'.

Rakeedhoo Kandu is a challenging dive in a deep channel – the east and west sides are usually done as separate drift dives. Broad coral shelves cover overhangs and caves, which have sea fans and black corals. Turtles, Napoleon wrasse, sharks and schools of trevally are often seen and the snorkelling on the reef top is brilliant.

Vattaru Kandu, a remote channel dive on the southern edge of Vattaru Falhu, is now a designated Protected Marine Area. It is not too demanding unless the currents are running at full speed. The reef next to Vattaru island is a fine snorkelling area. Around the entrance are many caves and overhangs with soft corals, sea fans and abundant fish life – barracuda, fusilier and white-tip reef sharks. Turtles are sometimes seen here, and manta rays from December to April.

Resorts

Dhiggiri (Dhiggiri island; ☎ 6700593; mmtours@ dhivehinet.net.mv; s/d US$330/358; airport transfer by seaplane 20 min US$200, by speedboat 1½hr, US$130; 45 rooms; ⚿) was completely renovated in the late 1990s and caters exclusively to the Italian market. It's a club-style resort, and all guests are on packages that include activities, a couple of excursions, all meals (with beer and wine) and nonmotorised water sports. The rooms have air-con, TV, phone, minibar and satellite TV; 10 of them are water bungalows. It's a small island, a little bit cramped, splendidly isolated, with good dive sites nearby and a house reef that's accessible for snorkellers.

As its name suggests, **Alimatha Aquatic** (Alimathaa island; ☎ 6700575; safari@dhivehinet.net.mv; s/d US$270/295; airport transfer by seaplane 20 min US$200, by speedboat 1¾hr, US$130; 102 rooms; ⚒) is a resort devoted to the pleasures of diving, snorkelling and water sports. Like its sister resort Dhiggiri, Alimatha was completely renovated in the late 1990s. It's also an Italian club-style resort with the guests on inclusive packages. It's essentially a bigger, more attractive version of Dhiggiri. The lagoon is quite wide and more suited to sailing and windsurfing (included in the package price) than snorkelling.

MEEMU

Meemu administrative district (traditionally called Mulaku) has only about 5000 people living on its nine inhabited islands. **Muli** (population 760) is the capital island, and now gets a few visitors from the newly established resorts. Nearby **Boli Mulah** and **Kolhuvaariyaafushi** islands, in the south, are more populous, with about 1400 and 1200 people, respectively. Both these islands grow yams, which are an important staple in more fertile islands, and an alternative to rice that must be imported.

The atoll was included in the tourism zone in the late 1990s, and has lots of sites that are recently explored and named, both in the kandus on the edges of the atoll, and inside the atoll around the numerous thilas and giris.

Sights & Activities
DIVING
Shark's Tongue is east of Boli Mulah, in the mouth of the Mulah Kandu. White-tips sleep on the sandy plateau, and grey reef sharks hang around a cleaning station at 20m. In strong currents, black-tip, grey and silver-tip sharks cruise through the coral blocks, but this is no place for beginner divers.

Giant Clam is an easy dive around two sheltered giris, where several giant clams are seen between 8m and 15m, even by snorkellers. Numerous caves and overhangs are rich with anemones and home to lobsters, groper and glassfish. Colourful butterflyfish and clown triggerfish are easily spotted, but look hard for well-camouflaged stonefish and scorpionfish.

Resorts
Hakuraa Club (Hakuraahuraa island; ☎ 6720014; www .johnkeellshotels.com; wb US$270; airport transfer by seaplane 45 min, US$255; 70 rooms; ⚒) reopened in 2005 after a US$3.2 million post-tsunami refit and the results are something. Traditionally a water-sports destination, Hakuraa Club is still a resort of choice for those who like sailing, windsurfing, snorkelling and diving, but it is now marketing itself as a romantic place to do these things too.

Catering mainly to British and German guests on all-inclusive packages, Hakuraa offers only over-water bungalows in a massive swathe of construction spread out over the lagoon. The lagoon is not good for snorkelling, though snorkelling gear and twice-daily snorkelling trips are included in the package. Use of windsurfers is also included, but at low tide the lagoon becomes too shallow for windsurfing and sailing – so it's a strange choice for a specialist water sports resort!

The dive school is good value and offers what so few centres in the Maldives can these days – access to truly pristine dive sites. With so many little-visited dive sites in the area, diving might be the best reason to stay at Hakuraa Club.

The lovely island resort of **Medhufushi** (Medhufushi island; www.aaa-resortsmaldives.com/medhufushi) was closed at the time of research for a total refit. It is expected to reopen in mid-2007. No further details were available at the time of writing.

FAAFU

The administrative district of Faafu, also known as North Nilandhoo Atoll, has about 3800 people living on its five inhabited islands. The capital island, **Magoodhoo** (population 630), is a small fishing village with a very traditional Islamic community.

Sights & Activities
On the southern edge of the atoll, **Nilandhoo** (population 1500) has the second oldest mosque in the country, Aasaari Miskiiy,

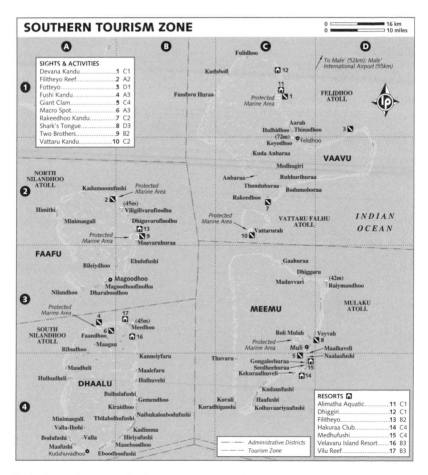

SOUTHERN TOURISM ZONE

SIGHTS & ACTIVITIES	
Devana Kandu	1 C1
Filitheyo Reef	2 A2
Fotteyo	3 D1
Fushi Kandu	4 A3
Giant Clam	5 C4
Macro Spot	6 A3
Rakeedhoo Kandu	7 C2
Shark's Tongue	8 D3
Two Brothers	9 B2
Vattaru Kandu	10 C2

RESORTS	
Alimatha Aquatic	11 C1
Dhiggiri	12 C1
Filitheyo	13 B2
Hakuraa Club	14 C4
Medhufushi	15 C4
Velavaru Island Resort	16 B3
Vilu Reef	17 B3

built during the reign of Sultan Mohammed Ibn Abdullah (1153–66). It is made of dressed stone and the interior is decorated with carved woodwork. It's possible that the stones were recycled from the ruins of earlier, pre-Islamic structures.

Thor Heyerdahl's book *The Maldive Mystery* has an entire chapter about this island. His expedition unearthed many phallic stone carvings, like the lingam associated with the Hindu god Shiva in his manifestation as the creator. Some of these images can be seen in the National Museum in Male'. Heyerdahl's expedition also found ruins apparently from an ancient gate, one of seven surrounding a great pagan temple complex. You can visit Nilandhoo on

a full-day excursion from Filitheyo resort, but the ruins are mostly unexcavated. As Heyerdahl wrote:

> Five teams of archaeologists could dig here for five years and still make new discoveries. The magnitude of this prehistoric cult centre seemed quite out of proportion to the size of the island.

The diving in the area is the other main attraction.

Filitheyo Reef, the kandu south of Filitheyo resort, is now a Protected Marine Area and has several diving possibilities. Only accessible by boat, the house reef on the southeast corner of the resort descends in big steps where great clouds of fish school. Swarms of batfish and several Napoleons are resident, while grey reef sharks, rays and trevallies are frequent visitors.

The **Two Brothers** are two thilas placed in a narrow channel. The big brother (north) tops out at 3m and is covered with soft corals and sponges, and attracts snorkellers. Many turtles reside here. Big pelagics cruise around both brothers and there are lots of nudibranch, pipefish, gobies and other small marine life.

Resorts

Filitheyo (Filitheyo island; ☎ 6720025; www.aaa -resortsmaldives.com/filitheyo; s/d/wb US$268/276/390; airport transfer by seaplane 35min, US$245; 125 rooms; 🅿 🖳 🏊) is a beautifully designed and finished resort on a large, well-vegetated, triangular island. The public buildings are spacious, open-sided Balinese-style pavilions with palm-thatch roofs and natural finishes. The main restaurant is especially attractive and serves a wide assortment of wonderful food at buffets for every meal. Even at lunch, expect canapés, soup, several types of fish, chicken, a couple of curries, fresh-cooked pasta and a few vegetarian options. Drinks are very reasonably priced here, and at the main bar and sunset bar (beers US$3 to US$4; house wine US$4 per glass; spirits US$4 to US$6), but all-inclusive options are available.

Most rooms are comfortable timber bungalows facing the best beach, nested amongst the palm trees, and equipped with phone, minibar, TV, CD player, open-air bathroom and personal sun deck. Interconnecting rooms are perfect for families. Deluxe villas provide extra space and style, while the water villas have sea views and private balconies. Resort facilities include a gym, small spa, horizon pool, reading room and shops. Some low-key evening entertainment is organised, and there's an interesting programme of excursions and fishing trips.

Beaches are pretty all around, but the lagoon is shallow on the south side, and not suitable for swimming on the east side. The north side has it all – soft sand, good swimming, and an accessible house reef that's great for snorkelling. Qualified divers can do unguided dives off the house reef too.

Filitheyo is a first-class resort with great food, friendly and efficient service and a lovely setting. It doesn't cater for party-goers or pampering. It suits families and those looking for relaxation, and is ideal for diving, snorkelling and other outdoor and water activities.

DHAALU

The administrative district of Dhaalu is made up of the South Nilandhoo Atoll and has about 5000 people living on its eight inhabited islands.

The biggest and most interesting island is the capital, **Kudahuvadhoo** (population 1450), which has an ancient and mysterious mound. The mound is now just sand, but originally this was the foundation of a structure made of fine stonework. The building stones were later removed to build part of the island's mosque. Heyerdahl said the rear wall of this mosque had some of the finest masonry he had ever seen, surpassing even that of the famous Inca wall in Cuzco, Peru. He was amazed to find such a masterpiece of stone-shaping art on such an isolated island, although the Maldivians had a reputation in the Islamic world for finely carved tombstones. Kudahuvadhoo is a long way from the resorts on this atoll, so a visit would be difficult. The waters around Kudahuvadhoo have seen several shipwrecks, including the 1340-ton *Liffey*, which went down in 1879, and the *Utheem*, which hit the same reef in 1960.

In the north of the atoll are the so-called 'jewellers islands'. **Ribudhoo** (population 700) has long been known for its goldsmiths, who are believed to have learnt the craft from a royal jeweller banished here by a sultan centuries ago. Another version is that they developed their skills on gold taken from a shipwreck in the 1700s. The nearby island of **Hulhudheli** (population 720) is a community of traditional silversmiths. Most of the gold and silver work on sale in Male' now seems to be imported, though the gold chains and medallions worn by many children may be made in these islands. Many of the craftspeople here are now making jewellery, beads and carvings from black corals and mother-of-pearl. Ribudhoo is quite accessible from the resorts, but Hulhudheli would be a long day trip.

Sights & Activities

DIVING

A big attraction of these resorts is the access to infrequently explored dive sites.

A channel on the northern edge of the atoll, **Fushi Kandu** is a Protected Marine Area. Steps on the east side have eagle rays and white-tip reef sharks. Thilas inside the channel are covered with hard and soft corals, and are frequented by turtles, Napoleon fish and schooling snappers. Look for yellowmouth morays and scorpion fish in the crevices.

Macro Spot, a sheltered, shallow giri, makes a suitable site for snorkellers, novices and macrophotographers. Overhangs and nooks shelter lobsters, cowries, glassfish, blennies and gobies.

Resorts

A classy but reasonably priced resort is a rare beast in the Maldives and **Vilu Reef** (Meedhuffushi island; ☎ 6760011; www.vilureef.com; s/d/wb US$200/240/540; airport transfer by seaplane 35min, US$260; 101 rooms; 🗷 🖳 🖳) is regarded as a well-guarded secret by its many repeat visitors. It's small, with huge palms and great beaches almost all the way around the island, which are especially good on the lagoon side. The island itself is thick with trees and bushes and, despite being quite crowded, has been developed with considerable care.

The style is traditional on the outside (white walls, thatched roofs) and modern convenience inside. The rooms are round and have most mod cons (but no TV), as well as decent outdoor bathrooms.

The main Nautilus restaurant provides big buffets for every meal and they are of a high international standard. This is a quiet resort with the odd bit of live music, but Vilu is certainly not a place for kicking nightlife.

Some British guests on all-inclusive packages might also be up for the crab races, cultural shows and disco. Most guests are from Germany, and many of them are divers with little energy left to party. Tennis, badminton, volleyball and a gym cater for the more sports minded, and there's windsurfing, sailing and motorised water sports. The Amaan Spa offers the full range of treatments from massage to pedicure and has six treatment rooms.

On one side, a wide beach faces a lagoon that's perfect for sailing and sheltered swimming, while on the other side a nice but narrower beach fronts a house reef that offers excellent snorkelling. Divers are well catered for by **Sun International Diving School** (www.sundivingschool.com), which offers very reasonably priced dives and a full range of courses including nitrox.

Vilu Reef is a good choice – combining friendly informality with some class and style – and it's a great place to come for people looking for diving and pampering.

In 2005 **Velavaru Island Resort** (Velavaru island; ☎ 6760028; www.velavaru.com; s/d/t US$349/357/442; airport transfer by seaplane 35min, US$270; 84 rooms; 🗷 🖳) became the Banyan Tree hotel chain's third property in the Maldives, and it was a much needed post-tsunami boost to the country's shaky tourist industry when the Singapore-based luxury hotelier coolly announced that it had bought the property for US$20m. As well as shoring up the local travel industry, the information also answered, if in a gob-smacking kind of way, the question much-asked by holidaymakers in the Maldives: how much does one of these islands cost anyway?

Immediately the resort, which began operation in 1989, started a process of refurbishing itself along the lines of its now sister resorts Banyan Tree and Angsana Ihuru. The new-look accommodation has a strong Asian feel and the room categories are divided up into beach bungalows, deluxe beach bungalows and island bungalows (the highest category). Each is gorgeously attired in an effortlessly chic way.

Velavaru has wide sandy beaches where turtles once nested – Velavaru means turtle island. The wide lagoon is no good for snorkelling, but there are two free snorkelling trips every day. Dive sites in this atoll are not well documented, but the Velavaru Marine Centre is working on changing that. It charges US$60 for a boat dive with all equipment provided; an open-water course costs US$628. Two excellent restaurants, a bar and spa complete the picture of a modern high-end resort at reasonable prices.

Things have been changing fast at Velavaru, but if stylish seclusion, enormous natural beauty and great diving sound like things you're looking for, this is a very attractive resort.

THAA

Thaa administrative district, or Kolhu-madulu Atoll, is a large, slightly flattened circle about 60km across, and one of the major fishing regions of the country. It consists of 13 inhabited islands and is home to about 9300 people. The capital island is **Veymandhoo** (population 1800). All the islands are on the edges of the atoll, mostly clustered around the kandus, and they're quite densely settled. **Thimarafushi** (population 2300), near the capital, is the most populous island, and with two other islands makes up a sizable community. Ruins of a 25m-wide mound on the island of **Kibidhoo** show this group of islands has been populated for many years.

On **Guraidhoo** (population 1700), in another island group, is the grave of Sultan Usman I, who ruled the Maldives for only two months before being banished here. On **Dhiyamigili** (population 484) there are ruins of the palace of Mohammed Imaaduddeen II, a much more successful sultan who ruled from 1704 to 1721 and founded one of the Maldives' longest-ruling dynasties.

The northern island of **Buruni** (population 570) is a centre for carpenters, many of whom work elsewhere, building boats and tourist resorts. The women make coir rope and reed mats. Around the mosque are an old sundial and tombstones that have been dated to the late 18th century. The island of Kalhufahalafushi has been allocated but it is not yet operational.

LAAMU

Geographically known as Hadhdhun-mathee Atoll, Laamu administrative district has about 13,000 people living on its 12 inhabited islands, and it's one of the major fishing centres in the country. Freezer ships anchor near the former capital, **Hithadhoo** (population 930), collecting fresh fish direct from the dhonis.

The island of **Kadhoo** has an airfield (airport code KDO) that has five flights a week to/from Male'. Kadhoo is linked by causeways to the large island of **Fonadhoo** (population 1700) to the south, which is now the atoll capital. The causeway also goes north to the islands of **Maandhoo** (population 530) and **Gan** (population 2450), forming one of the longest stretches of road in the country – all of 12km. Maandhoo has a

government-owned STO (State Trading Organisation) refrigeration plant and a fish-canning factory.

There are numerous archaeological sites in Laamu, with evidence of pre-Muslim civilisations on many islands. At the north-eastern tip of the atoll, on **Isdhoo** (population 1100), a giant, black dome rises above the palms. Who built the ancient artificial mound, known as a *hawitta*, and for what reason, is not really known. Buddha images have been found on the island, and HCP Bell believed such mounds to be the remains of Buddhist stupas, while Heyerdahl speculated that Buddhists had built on even earlier mounds left by the legendary Redin people. For many years the mound was a landmark for boats navigating between the atolls, but it didn't save the British cargo ship *Lagan Bank*, which was wrecked here on 13 January 1938. The **Friday Mosque** on Isdhoo is around 300 years old. It was probably built on the site of an earlier temple because it faces directly west, rather than towards Mecca, which is to the northwest.

Bell also found quite a few mounds on Gan (also known as Gamu) island, which he also believed to be Buddhist stupas, and he found a fragment of a stone Buddha face, which he estimated was from a statue over 4m high. Almost nothing remains of these structures because the stones have been removed to use in more modern buildings. There are mounds on several other islands in Laamu, including Kadhoo, Maandhoo and Hithadhoo – one is over 5m high.

The island of Olhuveli has been allocated and will at some point become Laamu's first tourist resort.

GAAF ALIF

The giant Huvadhoo Atoll, one of the largest true coral atolls in the world, is separated from Laamu by the 90km-wide Huvadhoo Kandu. This stretch of water is also called the One-and-a-Half-Degree Channel, because of its latitude, and it's the safest place for ships to pass between the atolls that make up the Maldives.

Because Huvadhoo is so big, and perhaps as a response to the 'southern rebellion' (see p167), the atoll is divided into two administrative districts. The northern district is called Gaaf Alif, and it has 10 inhabited islands and about 8300 people. **Viligili**, the capital island, is also the most populated with about 2900 people. Just south, the island of **Kudhoo** has an ice plant and fish-packing works. The atoll also has some productive agriculture, much of it on **Kodey** (population 420). This island also has four *hawittas* – evidence of Buddhist settlement. Heyerdahl discovered a limestone carving here, which he believed to be of the Hindu water god Makara. The statue must have been here before the Buddhist period, and is perhaps 1000 years old.

In the centre of the atoll, **Dhevvadhoo** (population 970) is not well placed for fishing or farming, but the islanders are famous for their textile weaving and coir-rope making. There are also mosques from the 16th and 17th centuries.

There are two allocated islands for resort development here – Funamadhua and Hadahaa, which should be operational in the next few years.

GAAF DHAAL

Geographically isolated from Male', but strategically located on the Indian Ocean trade routes, Gaaf Dhaal – or Huvadhoo Atoll as it is geographically – had independent tendencies dating back many years. It had its own direct trade links with Sri Lanka, and the people spoke a distinct dialect almost incomprehensible to other Maldivians. The island of **Thinadhoo** was a focal point of the 'southern rebellion' against the central rule of Male' during the early 1960s. So much so, that troops from Male' invaded in February 1962 and destroyed all the homes. The people fled to neighbouring islands and Thinadhoo was not resettled until four years later. It now has a population of 4900. Huvadhoo Atoll was divided into two administrative districts, the southern part being Gaaf Dhaal, which now has nearly 12,000 people on 10 inhabited islands and Thinadhoo as its capital.

Though remote from any resorts, Gaaf Dhaal has a small but growing number of foreign visitors who make boat trips around the southeastern edge of the atoll to surf the uncrowded waves that break around the channel entrances (see p81). On the island of **Kaadedhoo**, near Thinad-

hoo, a small airport (airport code KDM) has daily connections to Male' with Island Aviation, and the surfing safari boats meet clients there.

On **Gadhdhoo** (population 2600), women make superb examples of the mats known as *tundu kunaa*, which are woven from special reeds found on an adjacent island. Souvenir shops in Male' and on some resorts sell these mats – those from Gadhdhoo are the softest and most finely woven.

Just southwest of Gadhdhoo, the uninhabited island of **Gan** has remnants of one the most impressive *hawittas*, originally a pyramid with stepped ramps on all four sides, like many Mexican pyramids. The ruin was 8.5m high and 23m square. Heyerdahl also found stones here decorated with sun motifs, which he believed were proof of a sun-worshipping society even older than the Buddhist and Hindu settlements.

In the south of the atoll, only about 20km from the equator, the island of **Vaadhoo** has two *hawittas*, and a mosque that dates from the 17th century. The mosque is elaborately decorated inside and has a stone bath outside, as well as ancient tombstones carved with three different kinds of early Maldivian script.

Now earmarked for development are the first two islands – Konottaa and Lonudhoohutta – which will open at some point as resorts.

GNAVIYANI

Gnaviyani administrative district is made up of just one island, intriguing **Foammulah** (sometimes called Fuamulaku). It's not an atoll, but rather a solitary island stuck in the middle of the Equatorial Channel with a population of around 10,000. About 5km long and 1km wide, it's the biggest single island in the country and one of the most fertile, producing many fruits and vegetables such as mangoes, papayas, oranges and pineapples. Yams grow so well here that they were once a dietary staple, though rice is now preferred. The natural vegetation is lush, and there are two freshwater lakes.

A beach goes around most of the island, but the fringing reef is quite narrow and is pounded by big waves on whatever side is exposed to the prevailing swells. The lack of

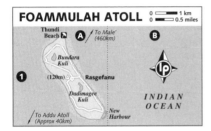

FOAMMULAH ATOLL

a safe anchorage has always limited fishing activity and made it difficult to get passengers and goods ashore. With help from the national government, a new harbour was completed at the eastern tip of the island in 2003, allowing Foammulah to join the modern world by enabling goods and equipment to be brought in easily and making development of some light industry feasible.

A new road links the harbour and the main village at the island's heart. New roads, wetland reclamation and infrastructure improvements are planned. A 120m-high telecommunications tower in the island's centre is visible from miles away. It makes the microwave connection north to Gaaf Dhaal and south to Addu Atoll, and has reduced the island's isolation, which now has an Internet café and well-used mobile-phone service.

Foammulah is officially divided into eight districts, but most of the people live around the north side and across the centre of the island in villages that appear to be a continuous settlement. Sandy roads crisscross the island, and there are lots of motorcycles and small pick-up trucks. Many of the people work in resorts in the tourism zone, and the money they send home partly accounts for the apparent affluence of the island.

Despite Foammulah's apparent isolation, navigators passing between the Middle East, India and Southeast Asia have long used the Equatorial Channel. Ibn Battuta visited in 1344, stayed for two months and married two women. Two Frenchmen visited in 1529 and admired the old mosque at the west end of the island. In 1922 HCP Bell stopped here briefly, and noted a 7m-high *hawitta*. Heyerdahl found the *hawitta* in poor condition, and found remnants of another nearby. He also investigated the nearby

mosque, the oldest one on the island, and believed it had been built on the foundations of an earlier structure built by skilled stonemasons. Another old mosque, on the north side of the island, had expertly made stonework in its foundations and in an adjacent stone bath.

Foammulah is not an easy destination for modern travellers. It has no hotels or guesthouses and only a couple of teashops, so you'll need an invitation from a local to get a permit. To get to Foammulah you go via Gan, which has several scheduled flights a day from Male'. From Gan it's 50km and you'll need to charter a speed boat or you may be able to take the passenger speed launch which carries about 20 people and takes just over an hour if the weather is OK. Unfortunately until the Maldives opens up to independent tourism, visiting fascinating places like Foammulah will be more trouble than it's worth to most people.

ADDU ATOLL

Definitely one of the best places for independent travellers to come, heart-shaped Addu Atoll is the most southern extreme of the country and has a very different feel to it for a number of reasons. It's good for so-called FITs (fully independent travellers), as from Equator Village, the charming budget resort on the former British naval base of Gan, you can cycle to three inhabited islands via a causeway – the only resort in the country where you have such access and freedom.

Addu Atoll is the main economic and administrative centre in the south of the country, and the only place to rival Male' in size and importance. Its 28,000 people spread out over seven inhabited islands is a huge number in the Maldives. With the airport being upgraded at the time of writing to accommodate long-haul flights and the huge, luxury Shangri-La resort being built on the nearby island of Viligili, the region will play an important role in the future development of the Maldives' travel market.

There is an independent streak in the Addu folk – they even speak differently from the people of Male'. Tensions came to a head in the 1960s under the leadership of Abdulla Afif Didi, who was elected president of the 'United Suvadiva Islands', comprising Addu, Foammulah and Hu-vadhoo. Afif declared independence from the Maldives, but an armed fleet sent south by Prime Minister Ibrahim Nasir quashed the short-lived southern rebellion. Afif fled the country, but is still talked about on his home island of Hithadhoo. He went to live in the Seychelles, where he ultimately rose to the position of foreign minister.

The biggest influence on Addu's modern history has been the British bases, first established on Gan during WWII as part of the Indian Ocean defences. In 1956, when the British could no longer use Sri Lanka, they developed a Royal Air Force base on Addu as a strategic Cold War outpost. The base had around 600 personnel permanently stationed here, with up to 3000 during periods of peak activity. The British built a series of causeways connecting Feydhoo, Maradhoo and Hithadhoo islands and employed most of the population on or around the base. In 1976 the British pulled out, leaving an airport, some large industrial buildings, barracks and a lot of unemployed people

who spoke good English and had experience working for Westerners. When the tourism industry took off in the late 1970s, many of the men of Addu went to Male' to seek work in resorts and tourist shops. They have never lost their head start in the tourism business and to this day, in resorts all over the country, there's a better than even chance that the Maldivian staff will be from Addu.

Tourism development in Addu itself has been slow to start, due to bad transport links. Now there are several flights a day to Male' and direct charter flights to Gan should be in operation from 2007.

Sights & Activities
DIVING

A particular highlight of Addu is the magnificent coral here, much of which escaped the widespread coral bleaching of 1998. If you go diving elsewhere in the Maldives and then come here you'll be amazed. On the northern edge of the atoll you can see huge table corals that might be hundreds of years old, and fields of staghorns that

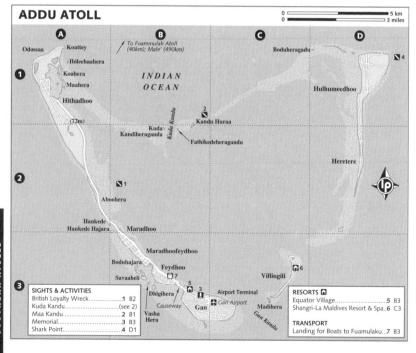

ADDU ATOLL

0 ——— 5 km
0 ——— 3 miles

SIGHTS & ACTIVITIES	
British Loyalty Wreck...............1	B2
Kuda Kandu...........................(see 2)	
Maa Kandu.............................2	B1
Memorial................................3	B3
Shark Point............................4	D1

RESORTS	
Equator Village..........................5	B3
Shangri-La Maldives Resort & Spa..6	C3

TRANSPORT	
Landing for Boats to Fuamulaku..7	B3

have all but disappeared in most parts of the country. It's not all good, though – corals inside the lagoon suffered as badly as anywhere else from coral bleaching.

The **British Loyalty Wreck** has a good covering of soft corals, and turtles, trevally and many reef fish inhabit the encrusted decks. This oil tanker was torpedoed in 1944 by the German submarine U-183, which fired through an opening in the antisubmarine nets at the entrance to Gan Kandu. The disabled ship stayed in the atoll until 1946 when it was towed to its present location and used for target practice by another British ship. The 140m wreck lies in 33m of water with its port side about 16m below the surface.

The northeastern edge of **Maa Kandu** has a wide reef top, between 5m and 7m, covered with live acrophora corals – big brain corals, long branching staghorns and table corals 3m across. White-tip reef sharks, eagle rays and sometimes mantas can be spotted, along with turtles and numerous reef fish. It's an excellent site for snorkelling.

Kuda Kandu is another superb sight near to Maa Kandu where a huge array of coral thrives between 5m and 15m. Currents can be strong here, so it's not for novices.

Off the northeast corner of the atoll **Shark Point**, sometimes called the Shark Hotel, is a plateau at about 30m. Grey reef sharks cruise around here, white-tip reef sharks lie on the sand and other sharks can be seen in deeper water further out.

GAN

Gan is atypical of the Maldives; it has a far more colonial feel and a refreshingly different atmosphere from anywhere else in the country. Even though you'll be staying at a resort here, there's much more to do and see here than at your standard Maldivian desert island.

Inhabited since ancient times, Gan was the site where HCP Bell excavated a large 9m-high mound. Bell believed it to be the ruins of a Buddhist stupa. His expedition made careful measurements of the site, took photos and made precise drawings that are published in his monograph. This was fortunate, as the archaeological sites and almost everything else on Gan were levelled to create the air-force base in 1956.

The British took over the entire island and constructed airport buildings, barracks, jetties, maintenance sheds, a Naafi (Navy, Army and Air Force Institutes) canteen, a golf course, tennis courts and a 2600m concrete runway. For more information about RAF Gan, go to www.gan .philliptsmall.me.uk. Many of these structures remain, some picturesquely run-down, others used for various purposes. Most of the island's lush native vegetation was cleared, but the British then landscaped with new plants – avenues of casuarinas, clumps of bougainvillea, swaths of lawn and even roses. It's much more spacious than most resort islands and it has a slightly weird and eerie atmosphere, but it's very peaceful and relaxed – like an old, abandoned movie set.

One sight is a low-key **memorial** to those who served on the base, including Indian regiments such as the 13th Frontier Force Rifles and the Royal Bombay Sappers & Miners. Dozens died here 'in the service of their country', though the atoll saw no action at all apart from the 1944 attack on the British Loyalty. Big guns, which were part of the WWII defences, now guard the memorial. Across the road are the post office, some telephones and a branch of the Bank of Maldives. The old Astra cinema, a fixture at all RAF bases, has a few nifty 1950s architectural touches. Several times a week it shows Indian and Sri Lankan movies to entertain the Sri Lankan garment workers who now work on the island and live in the former barracks. There are several pleasant cafés scattered around the island.

West of the Equator Village resort is a complex of buildings that used to be the officers' mess and living quarters. It's now the 'Dhoogas', a facility providing accommodation for visiting government officials, and off-limits to foreigners. A small and unimposing building here was once a chapel, but has been converted to a mosque. You can walk or cycle right around the island on narrow dirt roads, crossing the airport runway at each end. You'll see lots of trees and greenery, a couple of graveyards and a few incongruous buildings. There are no decent beaches and no surfable waves – just the Indian Ocean crashing on a broad, shallow reef.

FEYDHOO, MARADHOO & HITHADHOO

The causeways and the new road go from Gan to the atoll capital Hithadhoo via Feydhoo and Maradhoo as well as some other tiny islands that are now joined together. There are no spectacular attractions along the way, but the smaller villages are an absolute delight. Local teashops serve tea, cakes and 'short eats', and some will have a more substantial fish curry. Though you don't need a permit to visit, tourists are supposed to be back at Gan before dark. Remember that these villages are inevitably very conservative, so dress modestly.

Like most Maldivian villages they are laid out on a rectangular grid with wide, straight, sandy streets and white coral-stone houses. A few vehicles will be seen, but for most of the day the streets are empty. In the early morning, and especially the evening, locals will be out walking or cycling, sitting outside their houses or leaning against the low front walls. Shady trees overhang the streets and you can usually catch a glimpse of the sea at one end of the street or the other.

Most of the houses have corrugated iron roofs, but are otherwise traditional. Older buildings are made of coral-stone while newer ones are of concrete blocks. There's usually a courtyard or an open space with a shady tree and a *joli* or *undholi* providing a cool place to sit in the heat of the day. Notice the big, square chimney blocks – there are wooden racks inside where fish are hung to be smoked. Another distinctive feature can be seen at street junctions, where walls and buildings all have rounded corners.

You can easily walk from Gan to Feydhoo (population 4400), which has several mosques – a large, new white one, a small, pretty blue one, and several old ones on the sandy back roads that look a little like tiny churches. On the new lagoon-side road are several new buildings, like the modern petrol station, a big store and a teahouse/café with a Rf20 buffet. Boats to Foammulah use the small harbour here.

When the British took over, the villagers from Gan were resettled on Feydhoo, and some of the people from Feydhoo were then moved to the next island, Maradhoo, where they formed a new village. Maradhoo now has a population of 3000 in two villages that have run together – the southern one is called Maradhoo-Feydhoo. The first thing you'll see as you approach up the road is the boat-building activity on the lagoon side.

Further north, the road follows an isthmus that was once three narrow, uninhabited islands. One island used to house an ammunition bunker. After a few kilometres of palm tree–lined road you pass a recycling zone and a sports ground with several football pitches and a grandstand. You're on Hithadhoo, the Maldives' largest town outside Male', with a population of 13,000. The Dhiraagu office near the tower has pay phones and an Internet café. Further up the road are a new mosque and several schools – the high school is one of two outside Male' that teaches up to A level (matriculation). There's nothing in particular to see here, but there are a few shops and just wandering and seeing a real Maldivian town is quite something.

Near the main road there are several light-industry buildings and a power station, while a grid of streets with traditional houses extends to the western seashore. A few teashops and some quite big, new commercial premises are appearing here too. Beyond the built-up area, the tip of the island bends to the east, and is covered with coconut plantations, swampy lakes and a surprising amount of woodland. The coast is mostly too rocky or shallow for bathing, but there are some narrow beaches. Rough roads go right to the tip of the island at Koattey, also called Demon Point. It's said there was once a fort here, and later a British gun emplacement, but there's nothing left to see now. It feels like the end of the earth.

HULHUMEEDHOO

At the northeast corner of the lagoon, this island has two adjoining villages, Hulhudoo and Meedhoo, both known as Hulhumeedhoo, with a total population of about 5500. Local legend says that an Arab was shipwrecked here in about 872, and converted the islanders to Islam 280 years before the people of Male'. The cemetery is known for its ancient headstones, many of which are beautifully carved with the archaic Dhives Akuru script. A history on this remote little community can be seen on www.angelfire.com/country /addumeedhoo/gallery/album.html. You'll ncd to charter a dhoni to get here; inquire at Equator Village.

Resorts

For our money **Equator Village** (Gan island; ☎ 6898721; www.equatorvillage.com; all-inclusive s/d US$100/130; flight from Male' to Gan 1½hr, US$271, complimentary bus service from airport; 78 rooms; ☒ ☒) is one of the best resorts in the country and it's also one of the cheapest. The additional expense of flying to Gan from Male' is quickly offset by the low, low room rates and the all-inclusive packages they come with.

Equator Village is relaxed and friendly and more than a little bizarre. The rooms are actually the former barracks of the British Naval Base here – there's been an effort to disguise this but it's clear when you know the truth how little has really changed. Neat lines of rooms fan out from the main reception building, and are surrounded by extremely mature and well-tended gardens that overflow with exotic flowers and plants.

The rooms are modern, basic and thoroughly unromantic – this is not a honeymooners' destination. They are also spacious and have everything you need (although no TV or phone), including an en-suite bathroom and air-con.

The reception, bar and dining areas have been created from the old mess, thoroughly redecorated in very unmilitary pink, white and grey. These open-sided spaces with their cane furniture and ceiling fans look out onto a sizable free-form swimming pool and through palm trees to the blue sea beyond. The full-size billiard table is a handsome inheritance from the Brits, as are the first-class tennis courts.

The meals are all buffet with a limited selection and a British bias – expect fairly good curry, roast beef, mashed potatoes and tinned fruit for dinner; and sausages, eggs and cereal for breakfast. The Maldivian barbecue buffet is the best meal of the week. Most guests are on an all-inclusive package, and can wash it down with beer or house wine. There's not a lot of organised evening entertainment, but the bar is one of the friendliest and most fun in the Maldives.

Despite the British bias to the food, most of the guests are actually from Germany, although Brits make up the second biggest group along with a mix of other Europeans. More than half are divers, and from time to time ex-RAF personnel who were once stationed here come back for a nostalgic holiday. An RAF visitor's book at reception has more than 50 signatures, and some books and photo albums are also kept here (available on request).

Bicycles are available for exploring the neighbouring islands at $5/10 per half-/ full day, although they're free with the all-inclusive deal, along with an island-hopping excursion, night fishing trip and twice-daily boat to Viligili for snorkelling and beach time.

The only beach on Gan is a few hundred metres east of the resort, and it's not great – don't come here if you want to re-enact the Bounty advert. It's one of the few resorts in the country that doesn't provide the fabulous turquoise-water and white-sand combo. However, divers take note: the coral here is flabbergasting – and this should definitely jump high up the list of top diving resorts. The dive centre is a small but friendly operation run by **Diverland** (www.diverland.com) and includes the great dive sites in the area at very reasonable prices.

FITs and anyone else wanting to see something of the real Maldives will really appreciate Equator Village as it allows you to see much more of daily Maldivian life; you can cycle to Hithadoo via the new road and you generally enjoy a much higher level of freedom here.

Still a building site when we visited, **Shangri-La Maldives Resort & Spa** (Viligili Island; www.shangri-la.com; 184 rooms; ☒ ☒ ☒), the Shangri-La group's first venture in the Maldives, is a huge undertaking and is due to open in mid-2007. It will bring the high-end luxury market to the very southern tip of the Maldives and hopefully coincide with the opening of Gan International Airport.

The resort is to be split into three accommodation 'concepts' (their term, not ours) with the unbelievably pretentious names Lost Horizon, Whispering Palms and Windance (their spelling, not ours). Of course it will be magnificent when it's open, as any resort hoping to compete in the increasingly luxurious top-end hotel market here has to be. Watch this space.

Getting There & Away

Island Aviation flies from Male' to Gan and back two or three times a day. The standard fare for foreigners is US$271 return.

Private yachts should report by radio to the NSS in Gan or Hithadhoo to arrange security and customs clearance, but may have to continue to Male' for health and immigration checks to complete the 'clear-in' process.

Getting Around

The best way to get around Gan and over the causeway to neighbouring villages is by bicycle. Equator Village includes bicycle hire in its rates, but they aren't too comfortable for tall people. Taxis shuttle between the islands and around the villages; from Gan to Hithadhoo should cost about Rf100. Taxis wait at the airport and you can order one from Equator Village. The buses you see on the main road are only for workers in the Gan garment factories. Equator Village picks up guests by free minibus from the airport, though you may need to call at arrival.

Directory

CONTENTS

Accommodation	173
Business Hours	174
Children	174
Climate Chart	175
Courses	175
Customs	175
Dangers & Annoyances	175
Embassies & Consulates	176
Food	176
Gay & Lesbian Travellers	176
Holidays	176
Insurance	177
Internet Access	177
Legal Matters	177
Maps	177
Money	178
Post	179
Solo Travellers	180
Telephone	180
Time	180
Toilets	180
Tourist Information	180
Travellers With Disabilities	181
Travel Permits	181
Visas	182
Women Travellers	182

ACCOMMODATION

Ouch. That's most people's reaction to Maldivian resort prices, and it's fair to say this is not and will never be a cheap place to stay. Even budget hotels cost more than a top-end place in India or Sri Lanka, but quality in general is superior to elsewhere in Asia.

In this book we list accommodation for each chapter, divided into three groups: budget, midrange and top end. For each option a bed-and-breakfast room rate is quoted for the height of the season (December to April) unless otherwise stated. There are almost no single rooms, so singles are nearly always doubles for single occupancy.

Resorts

The vast majority of accommodation for travellers consists of the roughly 100 self-contained island resorts throughout the country. We list all the operating resorts in this book, as well as many that were refurbishing at the time of writing and those that are planned to open during the lifetime of this book.

The government's 'one island, one resort' policy means that development is contained and nowhere in the country feels crowded. Each resort provides rooms, meals and activities for its guests, ranging from the simplest beach huts with a buffet three times a day and a simple diving school to vast water villas with every conceivable luxury in them, à la carte dining and every activity from kiteboarding to big game fishing.

Most resorts have a large selection of room categories, so for the sake of ease we give the rate for the lowest category of room and for the lowest category of water bungalow (if available). These prices also include the US$8 per person per night government bed tax and a 10% service charge.

Also, be aware that these are rack rates, ie those given to fully independent travellers (FITs) who book direct with the resort. Any travel agency that has a contract with the resort will have access to far lower rates.

Budget resorts (up to US$240 per double room per night) tend to be busier and more basic in their facilities and sophistication than more expensive resorts. Few budget resorts are being built these days so those that do exist tend to be dated from the 1980s or '90s, and are often in need of a lick of paint.

Midrange resorts (from US$240 to US$500 per night) make up the majority of the Maldives accommodation options. They are noticeably slicker, better run and have a better standard of facilities and accommodation, all carried off with some style.

Top-end resorts (more than US$500 per night) are currently what the Maldives is all about. The world-class standards are uniform in this category and range from the very good to the mind-bogglingly luxurious.

Booking resorts through travel agents
is nearly always cheaper than doing so
directly. However, with the (slow) rise of
independent travel in the Maldives, some
resorts offer some great deals via their
websites.

Hotels

The only hotels in the country are located in the capital Male'. As these are far
cheaper than the island resorts, we've used
a separate price breakdown for the capital's hotels: budget (under US$50), mid-
range (US$50 to US$80) and top end (over
US$80). The choice is not inspiring and the
rooms are often cramped due to the shortage of space (see p98).

Safari Boats

Live-aboard safari boats allow you to travel
extensively throughout the country, visiting
great dive sites, desert islands and small
local settlements usually too remote to see
travellers. Live-aboards also range from
simple to luxury. The advantage is that you
can visit many places off-limits to resort
travellers, dive in pristine places and enjoy a
very sociable atmosphere. Prices range from
bargain basement to exorbitant depending
on the facilities available (see p58).

Inhabited Islands

There's no commercial accommodation in
the island villages, and visitors are not legally
permitted to pay for a place to stay. If for
whatever reason you do stay on an inhabited
island, you'll be put up in the house of the
kateeb (island chief), or a house maintained
for the purpose of accommodating guests.

BUSINESS HOURS

Male' is really the only place you have to
worry about business hours in the Maldives, the resorts being far more flexible

in these terms with hoards needing to be
catered for.

The working week elsewhere in the
Maldives runs from Sunday to Thursday.
Friday and to a lesser extent Saturday
are rest days and it's advisable to avoid
Male' and local islands on Fridays as they
become like ghost towns. On work days,
businesses operate from 8am or 9am until
5pm or 6pm, but this varies. Shops in
Male' will often stay open until around
10pm or 11pm, and some will shut in the
heat of the afternoon – from midday until
3pm or thereabouts. Nearly all Male' businesses stop several times a day for prayers,
which can be frustrating for shoppers, as
businesses suddenly close up for about
half an hour. Most banks in Male' are
open from about 8am to 1.30pm, Sunday
to Thursday, or 9.30am to 12.30pm during Ramazan.

Government offices are open Sunday
to Thursday from 7.30am to 2pm. During
Ramazan, hours are from 9am to 1.30pm.

Teashops can open very early or close
very late. During Ramazan the places
where locals eat will probably be closed
during daylight hours, but will bustle after
dark.

CHILDREN

Younger children will enjoy a couple of
weeks on a Maldivian resort island, particularly if they like playing in the water and on
the beach. Though exotic cuisine is sometimes on the menu, there are always some
pretty standard Western-style dishes that
kids will find OK.

Older children and teenagers could find
a resort a little confining after a few days
and they may get bored. Canoeing and
fishing trips might provide some diver-
sion, while a course in sailing or windsurfing could be a great way to spend a
holiday. Table tennis, tennis, volleyball or
badminton might also appeal. The minimum age for scuba diving is 16 years, but
most resorts offer a 'bubble blowers' introduction for younger kids, which is very
popular.

The main danger is sunburn, so bring
sun hats and sunblock. Lycra swim shirts
are an excellent idea – they can be worn on
the beach and in the water and block out
most UV radiation.

DIRECTORY

Practicalities

Be aware that many resorts do not encourage young children – check with the resort directly – and that children under five are often banned from honeymoon resorts. Where kids are welcome, it's no problem booking cots and organising high chairs in restaurants, and there's often a babysitting service and kids club in bigger, family-oriented resorts. Nappies are available in Male', but usually not in resorts, so bring all the nappies and formula you'll need for the duration of the holiday. Breast-feeding should only be done in private.

CLIMATE CHART

The Maldives has a tropical climate distinguished by two seasons, or monsoons: the dry northeast monsoon from December to March, and the wet southwestern monsoon from May to November, with more strong winds and rain. April is a transitional period noted for clear water and heat. The temperature remains remarkably consistent at around 30°C. For more on weather, see p12.

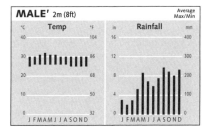

COURSES

Diving courses are a particular attraction for travellers to the Maldives. The standard learn-to-dive course is an open-water certificate, but the bigger dive centres offer a host of advanced and speciality courses, including advanced open water, divemaster, night diving and so on (see p66 for more information).

CUSTOMS

The immigration cards issued to you on your flight to Male' include a great list of items that are banned from the republic. Alcohol, pornography, pork, narcotics, dogs, firearms, spear guns and 'idols of worship' cannot be brought into the country and you're advised to comply. Baggage is always X-rayed and may be searched carefully, and if you have any liquor it will be taken and held for you till you're about to leave the country. This service will not extend to other prohibited items, and the importation of multiple bibles, pornography and in particular, drugs, will be treated very seriously.

The export of turtle shell, or any turtle-shell products, is forbidden.

DANGERS & ANNOYANCES

It's hard to imagine anywhere much safer than the Maldives. Theft from resorts is very rare, given that only staff and guests have access to the resort island; but still, make use of the safes in the rooms, keep your doors locked and don't leave cash around wherever you are.

The most likely danger is sunburn – don't ever underestimate the power of the equatorial sun at midday on a bright, cloudless afternoon. Sadly many people do, and receive bad burning and exposure to dangerous UV rays. Ensure you sunbathe with a high-factor lotion the first couple of days and be particularly careful when snorkelling or travelling by boat (when the breeze can make it seem far cooler than it is).

Second to the sun is the water. While it's true most diving accidents happen on the diving boat, it's extremely important to take diving seriously.

Don't touch coral, shells or fish. Beware of the possibility of strong currents and don't swim too far out from an island's fringing reef, or too far from a boat on a snorkelling trip. Don't try surfing unless you know where you are and what you're doing – the surf breaks over coral reefs and you could be badly grazed, or knocked unconscious.

It would be unlucky to be hit by a falling coconut, but it does happen, more so in windy weather. Imagine a 2kg coconut falling 15m onto your head. Check if a coconut tree is laden with big coconuts before lying underneath it.

Crimes of violence are very unusual, but there are burglaries and theft in the capital. There are very few cases of theft from resort rooms. Nevertheless, it's wise to deposit your valuables with the resort office, to keep your room locked and not leave cash lying around.

EMBASSIES & CONSULATES
Maldives Embassies & Consulates
Maldivian diplomatic representatives overseas include:

Australia (☎ 03-9349 1473; linton@iimetro.com.au; 164 Gatehouse Street Parkville, Vic 3052)

Austria (☎ 013-696 64 40; weidler.1882@magnet.at; Weima Rer Strasse 104, A-1190 Vienna)

Belgium (☎ 01 06 892 12; Clos des Genets 17, 1325 Chaumont Gistoux)

Germany (☎ 069-2740 44 20; info@visitmaldives.de; Bethmannstrasse 58, 60311 Frankfurt am Main)

Japan (☎ 033-94 26222; 1-26-1 Otowa, Bunkyo-ku, Tokyo 112-865)

Singapore (☎ 62258955; maldives@cyberway.com.sg; 10 Anson Rd, No 18-12 International Plaza)

Sri Lanka (☎ 015-516302; www.maldiveshighcom.lk; 23 Kavirathne Place, Colombo 6)

South Africa (☎ 021-797 9940; 69 Totnes Rd, Plumstead 7800, Cape Town)

UK (☎ 020 7224 2135; www.maldiveshighcommission .org; 22 Nottingham Place, London WIU 5NJ)

UN (☎ 212-599-6195; maldives@un.int; 800 Second Avenue, Ste 400-E, New York, NY 10017)

Embassies & Consulates in the Maldives
The foreign representatives in Male' are mostly honorary consuls with limited powers and often nobody in residence. If it's an emergency, then contact your country's embassy or high commission in Colombo, Sri Lanka.

Sweden, Denmark, Finland & Norway (Map p94; ☎ 3315174; Abdulla Saeed, Cyprea, 25 Boduthakurufaanu Magu)

Germany & Austria (Map pp90-1; ☎ 3322971; Ibrahim Maniku, Universal Enterprises, 38 Orchid Magu)

India (Map p94; ☎ 3323016; Ameer Ahmed Magu)

Italy (Map p94; ☎ 3322451; Bandhu Ibrahim Saleem, Cyprea, 25 Boduthakurufaanu Magu)

Netherlands (Map p94; ☎ 3323609; 1/1 Fareedhee Magu)

New Zealand (Map p94; ☎ 3322432; 30 Boduthakuru-faanu Magu)

UK (Map pp90-1; ☎ 3311205; c/o Dhiraagu, Majeedee Magu)

FOOD
See p84 for information about food in the Maldives.

GAY & LESBIAN TRAVELLERS
This is a grey area legally in the Maldives, where gay awareness can hardly be said to be very high. By Maldivian law all extra-marital sex is illegal although such mores are not applied to the resorts, where in practice anything goes as long as it is low key or behind closed doors. Same-sex couples will be able to book a double room with no questions asked (from budget to luxury, Maldivian hotel staff are the model of discretion) and it's common to see same sex-couples enjoying Maldivian holidays, although no resort here markets itself to the gay market specifically. Public displays of affection may embarrass Maldivian resort staff, but won't result in anything but blushes on their part. In Male' and on inhabited islands discretion is key and public displays of affection should not be indulged in by anyone, gay or straight – the Maldives remains an extremely conservative place.

HOLIDAYS
If you're in a resort, Maldivian holidays will not affect you – service will be as normal. If you visit Male' or an inhabited island on a holiday, you might see some parade or public celebration, shops may not open or may open late in the day, and government offices and most businesses will be closed. Christmas, New Year, Easter and European school holidays will affect you more – they're the busiest times for tourists and bring the highest resort prices, although locals don't celebrate them, of course.

If a holiday falls on a Friday or Saturday, the next working day will be declared a holiday 'on the occasion of' whatever it was. Most Maldivian holidays are based on the Islamic lunar calendar and the dates vary from year to year.

Ramazan Known as Ramazan or *roarda mas* in the Maldives rather than Ramadan, the Islamic month of fasting is an important religious occasion that starts on a new moon and continues for 28 days. Expected starting dates for the next few years are 13 September 2007, 2 September 2008, 22 August 2009, 11 August 2010. The exact date depends on the sighting of the new moon in Mecca and can vary by a day or so either way.

Kuda Eid Also called Id-ul-Fitr or Fith'r Eid, this occurs at the end of Ramazan, with the sighting of the new moon, and is celebrated with a feast.

Bodu Eid Also called Eid-ul Al'h'aa, the Festival of the sacrifice, 66 days after the end of Ramazan, this is the time when many Muslims begin the pilgrimage (hajj) to Mecca.

National Day A commemoration of the day Mohammed Thakurufaanu and his men overthrew the Portuguese on Male' in 1578. It's on the first day of the third month of the lunar calendar.

Prophet's Birthday The birthday of the Prophet Mohammed is celebrated with three days of eating and merriment. The approximate start dates for the next few years are: 31 March 2007, 20 March 2008, 9 March 2009, and 26 Feb 2010.

Huravee Day The day the Malabars of India were kicked out by Sultan Hassan Izzuddeen after their brief occupation in 1752.

Martyr's Day Commemorates the death of Sultan Ali VI at the hands of the Portuguese in 1558.

The following are fixed holiday dates:

New Year's Day 1 January

Independence Day Celebrates the ending of the British protectorate on 26 and 27 July.

Victory Day Celebrates the victory over the Sri Lankan mercenaries who tried to overthrow the Maldivian government in 1988. A military march is followed by lots of schoolchildren doing drills and traditional dances, and more entertaining floats and costumed processions on 3 November.

Republic Day Commemorates the second (current) republic, founded in 1968 on 11 November. Celebrated in Male' with lots of pomp, brass bands and parades. Sometimes the following day is also a holiday.

INSURANCE

A travel-insurance policy to cover theft, loss and medical problems is highly recommended. Some policies offer lower and higher medical-expense options; the higher ones are chiefly for countries which have high medical costs, and this would be a good idea for a Maldives trip. You may prefer to choose a policy that pays doctors or hospitals directly rather than your having to pay on the spot and claim later. If you have to claim later, make sure you keep all documentation. Some policies ask you to call back (reverse charge) to a centre in your home country where an immediate assessment of your problem is made.

Some policies specifically exclude 'dangerous activities', which can include diving, so check your policy carefully if you plan to dive. See p70 for information on insurance for divers.

Worldwide cover for travellers from over 44 countries is available online at www.lonelyplanet.com/travel_services.

INTERNET ACCESS

Most resorts have Internet access available for guests. In the top-end resorts this will typically be free and may include a wi-fi area for people with their own laptops and an airport card. In other resorts Internet use is paid for, and rates can vary enormously.

Elsewhere in the Maldives, Internet cafés and wi-fi hotspots provide customers with Web access. Prices are extremely low and in the case of wi-fi hotspots in Male', free.

LEGAL MATTERS

Alcohol is illegal outside resorts – you're theoretically not even allowed to take a can of beer out on a boat trip. Some foreign residents in the capital have a liquor permit, which entitles them to a limited amount per month, strictly for personal consumption at home.

Illicit drugs are around, but are not widespread. Penalties are heavy. 'Brown sugar', a semirefined form of heroin, has become a problem among some young people in the capital and even in some outer islands.

With a scattered island population and limited resources, the Maldivian authorities rely heavily on delegation. Apart from the police and the military, there is a chief on every atoll and island who must keep an eye on what is happening, report to the central government and be responsible for the actions of local people.

Every foreigner in the country has, in effect, a Maldivian minder who is responsible for him or her. Resorts are responsible for their guests and for what happens on their island. If a guest goes swimming in the nude, the resort can be fined as well as the visitor.

MAPS

Put simply, the Maldives is a nightmare to map. The islands are so small and scattered that the result is an extremely confusing one in which you're forever trying to distinguish between the tiny islands and the reefs that surround them. Another problem is scale – the country is over 800km from north to south, but the largest island is only about 8km long.

DIRECTORY

Several tourist maps are available in Male' and in resort shops, and while they rather misleadingly only feature the atolls in the tourist zone (ie not even half of the country) they are by far the most useful and practical for anyone travelling in the Maldives. The two standard issues are *Divers & Travellers Maldives Map* (Atoll Editions) and *Satellite Map of the Maldives* (Edition MM). The former is the better of the two, with far more detail and also including an overview map of all the atolls. The latter is good for locating resorts.

For anyone doing any serious amount of travel, especially diving, *Atlas of the Maldives* (Atoll Editions) is indispensable and in a very practical book form, alleviating the need to fold out a vast map. It includes everything from shipwreck sites to Protected Marine Area plans. It's on sale at the Novelty Bookshop (p89) in Male'.

MONEY

The currency of the Maldives is the rufiya, which is divided into 100 larees. Notes come in denominations of 500, 100, 50, 20, 10, five and two rufiya, but the last two are uncommon. Coins are in denominations of two and one rufiya, and 50, 25 and 10 larees. The value of the rufiya is pegged to that of the US dollar, so the exchange rate between the two currencies never changes. Most hotel and travel expenses will be billed in dollars. If you're staying in a resort, all extras (including diving costs) will be billed to your room, and you pay the day before departure. Resorts accept cash, credit cards or travellers cheques in all major currencies, although US dollars are preferred.

See the Quick Reference inside the front cover for other exchange rates. See also p13 for information on costs.

ATMs

There's a slowly growing number of ATMs in Male' – most of them (but not all) now allow you to withdraw funds from international accounts. Those that definitely do are those outside the major banks on Boduthakurufaanu Magu in Male'. Note that while you can do cash advances on credit cards over the counter at Male' airport and at most resorts, there are no ATMs outside Male'.

Cash

It's perfectly possible to have a holiday in the Maldives without ever touching cash of any sort, as in resorts everything will be chalked up to your room number and paid by credit card or travellers cheques on departure. However, it's a good idea to have some cash with you – small-denomination US dollars are most handy for tipping staff and buying sundries in transit. You won't need Maldivian rufiya unless you're using local shops and services. Even these will usually take dollars, but you'll be given change in rufiya.

There are no restrictions on changing money into rufiya, but there's no need to change a lot. Rufiya are not readily negotiable outside the country, so reconvert any leftovers at the bank counter in the airport when you leave.

Credit Cards

Every resort takes major credit cards including Visa, Amex and MasterCard. A week of diving and drinking could easily run up a tab over US$2000, so make sure your credit limit can stand it. The cashier may want 24 hours' notice to check your credit. Many resorts apply a surcharge of 5% to credit-card payments, so it may be best to have enough travellers cheques to cover the bulk of your extras bill.

International Transfers

Banks in the Maldives are not noted for their efficiency in international transactions. A transfer using the 'Swift' system seems to be the most efficient way to get money to the Maldives. Villa Travels is the agent for **Western Union** (Map p94; ☎ 3329990; moneytransfer@villatravels.com; Boduthakurufaanu Magu), one reliable but expensive way to transfer funds. The **HSBC Bank** (Map p94; Boduthakurufaanu Magu) might be your best bet. Try to have the money handed over to you in US dollars, not rufiya.

Tipping

Tipping is something of a grey area in the Maldives, where 10% service tax is added to nearly everything from minibar drinks to room prices. In many places this would mean that you don't need to tip in addition, but it's still the case that people serving you personally will often expect something. It's good form to leave a tip for your room staff and in smarter resorts, your *thakuru* (butler). Give any tips to the staff personally, not to the hotel cashier – US dollars, euros and local currency are equally acceptable. A few dollars a day is fine for room staff, while anyone carrying your bags might expect US$1 or so per bag.

In Male' the fancier restaurants usually add a 10% service charge, so you don't need to tip. Tipping is not customary in local teashops. Taxi drivers are not tipped, but porters at the airport expect Rf10 or US$1.

Travellers Cheques

Banks in Male' will change travellers cheques and cash in US dollars, and possibly UK pounds, euros, Japanese yen and Swiss francs. Most will change US-dollar travellers cheques into US dollars cash with a commission of US$5. Changing travellers cheques to Maldivian rufiya should not attract a commission.

Some of the authorised moneychangers around town will exchange US-dollar or euro travellers cheques at times when the banks are closed. You can always try some of the hardware shops, souvenir shops and guesthouses. Most tourist businesses will accept US dollars in cash at the standard rate, and euros at reasonable rates.

POST

Postal services are quite efficient, with mail to overseas destinations delivered promptly; mail from overseas, especially packets and parcels, is subject to customs screening and can take considerably longer. The new **main post office** (Boduthakurufaanu Magu; ☽ 8.15am-9pm Sun-Thu, 3-9pm Fri, 9.15am-9pm Sat) in Male' has a poste restante service.

To send a postcard anywhere overseas costs Rf10 and a standard airmail letter to most countries costs Rf12. A high-speed EMS service is available to many countries. Parcel rates can be quite expensive and will

---

PRACTICALITIES

NEWSPAPERS & MAGAZINES
The three Maldivian daily papers are Aufathis, Miadhu and Haveeru, all costing Rf2 and available from shops throughout the country, although rarely in resorts. They all have some pages in English, although there's nothing of much interest. The Evening Weekly (www.eveningweekly.com.mv) is the country's most popular English-language current-affairs magazine, but its articles are fairly uninspiring – this is hardly the home of crusading journalism. A smattering of international papers and magazines are available from bookshops in Male'.

RADIO & TV
TVM, the national TV station, is broadcast from Male' during the day, with regular breaks for prayer and much religious content. The rest of the schedule is made up of He-Man reruns, local news and CNN rebroadcasts in English.
Nearly all resorts and Male' hotels have satellite TV including BBC World, CNN, Star Movies and HBO alongside Sri Lankan, Indian and European channels.
The Voice of Maldives Radio (www.vom.gov.mv) is broadcast to the whole country for 11 hours each day on medium wave, 1449kHz, and also at 89MHz. The news, in English, is read at 6pm for 15 minutes.

ELECTRICITY
Electricity supply is 220V to 240V, 50Hz AC. The standard socket is the UK-style three-pin, although there are some variations so an international adaptor can be useful (or essential for non-UK travellers).

WEIGHTS & MEASURES
Although the Maldives is officially converting to the metric system, imperial measures are widely used. Metric measurements are used in this book.

DIRECTORY

have to clear customs at the main post office, where a bored-looking customs official will be stationed to inspect any packages you're sending home.

At the resorts you can buy stamps and postcards at the shop or the reception desk. Generally there is a mailbox near reception.

SOLO TRAVELLERS

While travelling on your own through the Maldives can feel akin to spending Valentine's Day alone in a romantic French restaurant, it's perfectly possible and many people do it. As there are almost no single rooms in the country's resorts and hotels, you'll find that you'll be paying much more than someone in a couple, as often the reductions for single occupation are tiny. However, if you can afford to, there's nothing stopping you, and if – like most single travellers in the country – you're here for a specific reason such as diving or surfing, you'll quickly meet up with kindred spirits in the resorts where these activities are most popular. Safari boats are likewise a great option as the sociable nature makes them good for making friends. Single women will find the Maldives a wonderful place to travel, completely free of the chauvinism that can so often be a deterrent. For more on independent travel, see p52.

TELEPHONE

There are two telephone providers operating in the Maldives: the relatively old-timer Dhiraagu, a joint venture of the government and the British Cable & Wireless company; and the newer Wataniya, a Kuwaiti provider that introduced some much-needed competition to the market in 2005.

Both providers operate somewhat patchy coverage, although given the unique geography of the country this is hardly surprising. Only in and around Male' are you 100% guaranteed a signal, where it's hit and miss elsewhere. You can buy a local SIM card for around US$15 and use it in your own phone if it's been unlocked at home (check with your provider) – this becomes worth the price almost immediately if you're using your phone much at all.

Every inhabited island now has a telephone connection, and very modern card-operated telephone boxes can be seen somewhat incongruously on the most traditional island

streets. Every business in Male' is on the phone, telephone cards are widely available, and card phones are numerous.

All resorts have IDD phones, either in the rooms or available at reception. Charges vary from high to astronomical, starting around US$15 for three minutes; our advice is never to use them outside of an emergency.

The international country code for the Maldives is ☎ 960. All Maldives numbers have seven digits and there are no area codes. If you find you have a six-digit number for a Male' business, add a 3 to the start and it should work. Operator and directory inquiry numbers are ☎ 110 for the Maldives and ☎ 190 for international inquiries. To make an international call, dial ☎ 00, then the country code, area code and number.

TIME

The Maldives is five hours ahead of GMT, in the same time zone as Pakistan. When it's noon in the Maldives, it's 7am in London, 8am in Berlin and Rome, 12.30pm in India and Sri Lanka, 3pm in Singapore and 4pm in Tokyo.

The majority of resorts operate one hour ahead of Male' time to give their guests the illusion of extra daylight in the evening and a longer sleep in the morning. This can make it tricky when arranging pick-up times and transfers, so always check whether you're being quoted a time in Male' Time or Resort Time.

TOILETS

Male's public toilets charge Rf2. On local islands, you may have to ask where the *fahana* is. In general you're better off using toilets in cafés and restaurants in Male' – they're usually cleaner and free.

TOURIST INFORMATION

The official tourist office is the **Maldives Tourism Promotion Board** (☎ 3323228; www.visitmaldives.com; Boduthakurufaanu Magu, Male'). Its office on the 4th floor of the Bank of Ceylon building has maps and other printed material, and can answer specific inquiries.

The Maldives has only one official tourist office abroad: the **Maldives Tourism Promotion Board** (☎ 69-2740-4420; info@visitmaldives.de; Bethmannstrasse 58, 60311 Frankfurt am Main, Germany). Most tourism promotion is done by private travel agents, tour operators and resorts.

TRAVELLERS WITH DISABILITIES

At Male' International Airport, passengers must use steps to get on and off planes, so contact your airline to find out what arrangements can be made. The arrivals area is all at ground level, but departure usually involves going up and down stairs.

Transfers to nearby resorts are by dhoni or speedboat and a person in a wheelchair or with limited mobility will need assistance. Transfer to more distant resorts is often by seaplanes, which can be more difficult to access, but staff are quite experienced in assisting passengers in wheelchairs or with limited mobility.

Most resorts have few steps, ground-level rooms and reasonably smooth paths to beaches, boat jetties and all public areas. Staff will be on hand to assist disabled guests. When you decide on a resort, call them directly and ask about the layout. It's usually a good idea for guests to advise the tour agency of any special needs, but if you want to find out about specific facilities, it's best to contact the resort itself.

Quite a few resort activities are potentially suitable for disabled guests, apart from the very popular sitting-on-a-beach-doing-nothing. Fishing trips and excursions to inhabited islands should be easy, but uninhabited islands may be more difficult to disembark on. Catamaran sailing and canoeing are possibilities, especially if you've had experience in these activities. Anyone who can swim will be able to enjoy snorkelling. The **International Association for Handicapped Divers** (www.iahd.org) provides advice and assistance for anyone with a physical disability who wishes to scuba dive. Resort dive schools should be able to arrange a special course or programme for any group of four or more people with a similar disability.

No dogs are permitted in the Maldives, so it's not a destination for anyone dependent on a guide dog.

TRAVEL PERMITS

Foreigners must have an Inter-Atoll Travel Permit to stay on any inhabited island other than Male' or a resort island, and permits are also required to visit all uninhabited islands outside the tourism zone. You don't need a permit for a day trip organised by a resort.

Permits are issued by the **Ministry of Atolls Administration** (Map p94; Boduthakurufaanu Magu) in Male' and cost Rf10. All foreigners must have a local sponsor who will guarantee their accommodation and be responsible for them. Note also that it is illegal for anyone to request payment for accommodation on an inhabited island.

Permit applications must be in writing, and include the applicant's name, passport number, nationality, the name of the island/atoll to be visited, dates of visit, name and address of sponsor, the name and registration number of the vessel to be used, and the purpose of the visit.

If you are going on a diving or sightseeing safari trip through the atolls in a registered vessel with a registered safari company, the company will obtain the necessary permits before you start. In effect, the company is acting as your sponsor and supplying accommodation on the boat.

Your sponsor should be a resident of the island you wish to visit, and must be prepared to vouch for you, feed you and accommodate you. This support must be given in writing, preferably with an OK from the *kateeb* and submitted with your application. It's best to have the sponsor submit the application on your behalf.

The most straightforward way to visit the outer atolls is with a registered safari boat, but a reputable tour company, travel agent or guesthouse proprietor may be able to help you make the necessary contacts to get a sponsor. Many Male' residents have friends or family in various outer atolls, but as they will be responsible for you when you visit the island, a great deal of trust is involved. Getting a letter of support-cum-invitation back from the island can take a couple of weeks if it's isolated from the capital.

The stated purpose of the visit can be something like visiting friends, sightseeing, photography or private research. The permit will specify which atolls or islands you can visit. Permits are issued only between 8.30am and 11am on all days except government holidays.

As soon as you land on an island you must go to the island office to present the permit. A foreigner travelling in the outer atolls without a permit, or breaching its conditions, can be fined Rf100.

DIRECTORY

VISAS

The Maldives welcomes visitors from all countries, issuing a 30-day stamp on arrival. Citizens of India, Pakistan, Bangladesh or Nepal are given a 90-day stamp. If you want to stay longer you'll either need to apply for a visa or leave the country when your 30 days is up, then return.

While officially you're supposed to show US$30 for every day's stay, this is not usually enforced, and showing a credit card will usually placate concerns. However, you should know the name of your hotel and be able to show a return air ticket out of the country, if asked by immigration officials.

Visa Extensions

To apply for an extension, go to the **Immigration Office** (Map p94; ☎ 3323913; ⏱ 8am-1pm Sun-Thu) in the Huravee Building next to the police station in Male'. You must first buy an Extension of Tourist Visa form (Rf10) from the ground-floor desk. You'll need a local to sponsor you. The main requirement is evidence that you have accommodation, so it's best to have your resort, travel agent or guesthouse manager act as a sponsor and apply on your behalf. Have your sponsor sign the form, and bring it back to the office between 7.30am and 9.30am, along with your passport, a passport photo, the Rf750 fee and your air ticket out of the country. You have to have a confirmed booking for the new departure date before you can get the extension – fortunately, the airlines don't ask to see a visa extension before they'll change the date of your flight. Proof of sufficient funds (US$30 per day) or a credit card may also be required. You'll be asked to leave the documents at the office and return

in a couple of days to pick up the passport with its extended visa (get a receipt for your passport).

Extensions are for a maximum of 30 days, but they give you only until the date on your ticket – the cost is the same, for one day or 30. Overstaying your visa (or extension), even by an hour, can be a major hassle as they may not let you board your flight, and you will have to go back to Male', book another flight, get a visa extension and pay a fine before you can leave.

WOMEN TRAVELLERS

Culturally, resorts are European enclaves and visiting women will not have to make too many adjustments. Topless bathing and nudity are strictly forbidden, but brief bikinis are perfectly acceptable on resort beaches.

Reasonably modest dress is appropriate in Male' – shorts should cover the thighs and shirts should not be very low cut. Women may be stared at on the street in Male', especially if their dress or demeanour is seen as provocative, but nothing more serious is likely to happen. Local women don't go into teashops in Male', but a foreign woman with a male companion would not cause any excitement.

In more out-of-the-way parts of the country, quite conservative dress is in order. It is very unlikely that a foreign woman would be harassed or feel threatened on a local island, as Maldivian men are conservative and extremely respectful. They are very closed, small communities and the fact that a foreign woman would be associated with a local sponsor should give a high level of security.

Transport

CONTENTS

Getting There & Away	**183**
Entering the Country	183
Air	183
Sea	184
Getting Around	**185**
Air	185
Boat	186
Car & Motorcycle	186

GETTING THERE & AWAY

Flights, tours and rail tickets can be booked online at www.lonelyplanet.com/travel_services.

ENTERING THE COUNTRY

Entering the Maldives is simple and hassle-free. However, you must know the name of your resort or Male' hotel, and if you are travelling independently and don't have one arranged, then be prepared to make one up – the immigration officials will view anyone just arriving in the country with great suspicion.

Passport

There are no restrictions on foreign nationals entering the country. Israelis and people who have Israeli stamps in their passports are perfectly welcome, which is rare in the Muslim world. Visas are not needed for visits of 30 days or less (see opposite). Theoretically travellers must have US$30 per day for the duration of their stay.

AIR
Airports & Airlines

At the time of writing there was only one international airport in the Maldives – **Male' International Airport** (MLE; ☎ 3322075; www.airports.com.mv), on the island of Hulhule', 2km across the water from the capital. It's a decent airport that was being upgraded to include new departure and arrival areas at the time

of research. The current domestic terminal on the southern island of Gan is also being upgraded to a new international airport, and should be taking international charter flights some time in the near future.

There is no national carrier; the carriers serving Male' can roughly be divided into scheduled and charter airlines. Some airlines only fly in certain seasons and the list of charter airlines changes frequently.

SCHEDULED AIRLINES

Austrian (OS; ☎ 3334004; www.aua.com)
Emirates (EK; ☎ 3315465; www.emirates.com)
Air India (Map p94; IC; ☎ 3310111; www.airindia.com)
Malaysian Airlines (MH; ☎ 3332555; www.malaysiaairlines.com)
Qatar Airways (Map p94; QR; ☎ 3334777; www.qatarairways.com)
Singapore Airlines (Map p94; SQ; ☎ 3310031; www.singaporeairlines.com)
Sri Lankan Airlines (Map p94; UL; ☎ 3310031; www.srilankan.aero)
Transaero (UN; www.transaero.ru; Male' airport)

CHARTERED AIRLINES

Note that most charter airlines don't have offices in Male' and should be contacted via the home country.
Britannia Airways (BY; www.thomsonfly.com)
Blue Panorama Airlines (BV; www.blue-panorama.com)
Condor (DE; www5.condor.com)
Corsair (SS; ☎ 3310111; www.corsair.fr)
Edelweiss (EDW; www.edelweissair.ch)
Eurofly (GJ; www.eurofly.it)

THINGS CHANGE...

The information in this chapter is particularly vulnerable to change. Check directly with the airline or a travel agent to make sure you understand how a fare (and ticket you may buy) works and be aware of the security requirements for international travel. Shop carefully. The details given in this chapter should be regarded as pointers and are not a substitute for your own careful, up-to-date research.

TRANSPORT

First Choice (FCA; www.firstchoice.co.uk)
LTU (LT; ☎ 3334004; www.ltu.com)
Martinair (MP; ☎ 3323069; www.martinair.com)
Monarch (MON; www.flymonarch.com)
Neos Spa (NO; www.neosair.it)

Tickets

If you're on a package you'll usually have no choice about the airline you fly, as it will be part of the package. Fully independent travellers (FITs) should shop around for both scheduled and charter deals. More and more chartered airlines are selling flight-only seats and these can be good deals. The other advantage of charter flights is that you can fly direct from Western Europe to Male', without the usual change in the Middle East or Sri Lanka common for scheduled airlines.

Australia

Australians usually reach the Maldives via Singapore or Kuala Lumpur on Singapore Airlines, Malaysia Airlines, Qantas or a combination. The few Australian visitors to the Maldives make this an expensive flight. There are no chartered flights currently operating between Australia and Male'.
Flight Centre (☎ 131-600; www.flightcentre.com.au)
STA Travel (☎ 1300-733035; www.statravel.com.au)

France

Charter flights operate between Charles de Gaulle and Male' on Star Airlines and from Paris Orly on Corsair International during high season. The rest of the year Emirates, Qatar and Sri Lankan offer the best connections and prices.
OTU Voyages (☎ 0 820 817 817; www.otu.fr)
Nouvelles Frontières (☎ 0 825 000 825; www.nouvelles-frontieres.fr)
Voyageurs du Monde (☎ 01 42 86 16 40; www.vdm.com)

Germany

Germany has a huge number of charter airlines bringing huge numbers of visitors to resorts year-round. Direct flights from Dusseldorf, Frankfurt and Munich as well as from other cities are available on a number of chartered airlines.

Italy

There is an excellent charter choice available from Italy to Male' – most are nonstop flights, although some pick up in two or more Italian cities en route. For scheduled flights, Emirates followed by Sri Lankan and Qatar have the best connections from Rome and Milan. **CTS Viaggi** (☎ 840 501150; www.cts.it) is a recommended travel agency.

Other Europe

There's a weekly flight on Austrian Airlines from Vienna, a twice-weekly flight from Moscow on Transaero, flights from Amsterdam on Martinair and from Switzerland on Edelweiss.

Japan

Japanese travellers usually fly via Sri Lanka or Singapore, though some travel on Thai Airways via Bangkok and Colombo, for a lower price. Chartered flights are not in operation.

UK & Ireland

British travellers have a choice of several charter flights from London and Manchester that go direct to Male' and scheduled flights from London via Doha (Qatar Airways), Dubai (Emirates) and Colombo (Sri Lankan).
Bridge the World (☎ 0870-4447447; www.bridgetheworld.com)
Ebookers (☎ 0800-0823000; www.ebookers.com)
Opodo (☎ 0871-2770091; www.opodo.co.uk)
STA Travel (☎ 0870-1600599; www.statravel.co.uk)
Trailfinders (☎ 020-79383939; www.trailfinders.co.uk)

USA & Canada

The sheer distance involved in travelling between North America and the Maldives makes the US and Canadian tourism market minuscule. People travelling from North America will usually fly via London and then continue by Qatar Airways, Emirates or Sri Lankan. From the West coast travel via Singapore makes most sense.

SEA
Sri Lanka

Despite the obviousness of this route, it is currently impossible to travel between Sri Lanka and the Maldives by boat. There are no scheduled ferries operating, nor do cargo ships generally take paying passengers. You might be lucky if you ask around in Colombo, but we don't recommend this.

Yacht

Yachts and super yachts cruise Maldivian waters throughout the year – this is after all one of many playgrounds for the rich and famous. However, with the Maldives being somewhat out of the way, this is not a standard port of call. The Maldives has not been a popular stop for cruising yachties, but more are coming through and official policy is becoming more welcoming. The negatives include: the maze of reefs that can make it a hazardous area; the high fees for cruising permits; the officialdom; the restrictions on where yachts can go; and the absence of lively little ports with cheap cafés and waterfront bars.

A new 100-berth marina has been built at Island Hideaway in the far north of the country (see p148), and this is the only place currently set up for servicing yachts in a professional way. Addu, in the far south, has a sheltered anchorage, a tourist resort and refuelling and resupply facilities.

The three points where a yacht can get an initial 'clear in' are Uligamu (Haa Alif) in the north, Hithadhoo/Gan (Addu Atoll) in the south, and Male'. Call in on VHF channel 16 to the National Security Service (NSS) Coastguard and follow the instructions. If you're just passing through and want to stop only briefly, a 72-hour permit is usually easy to arrange. If you want to stay longer in Maldivian waters, or stop for provisions, you'll have to do immigration, customs, port authority and quarantine checks, and get a cruising permit. This can be done at any of the three clear-in facilities.

If you want to stop at Male', ensure you arrive well before dark, go to the east side of Viligili Island, between Viligili and Male', and call the coastguard on channel 16. Officially, all boats require a pilot, but they don't usually insist for boats under 30m. Carefully follow the coastguard's instructions on where to anchor, or you may find yourself in water that's very deep, or too shallow. Then contact one of the port agents, such as **Island Sailors** (☎ 3332536; www .islandsailors.com) or **Century Star** (☎ 3325353). A full list of agents can be found at www .customs.gov.mv/agents.htm.

Port agents can arrange for port authority, immigration, customs and quarantine checks, and advise on repairs, refuelling etc. They'll charge about US$175 for a two-week stay, including all government charges – it would be a nightmare to do it all without an agent's help. After the initial checks you'll be able to cross to the

lagoon beside Hulhumale', the reclaimed land north of the airport. This is a good anchorage. The bigger stores, like STO People's Choice and Fantasy, have quite a good range of provisions at reasonable prices. The port agents can advise on other necessities such as radio repairs, water and fuelling. Diesel fuel is about Rf5 per litre.

The cost of a cruising permit increases greatly with the length of stay – the first two weeks are free, the first month is US$200, and the second month US$300. Customs, port and inspection charges increase with the size of the boat. If you go cruising in the tourism zone, you'll be able to stop at many of the resorts to eat, drink, swim, dive and spend your money, but you should always call the resort first. Usually you have to be off the island by sunset.

Before you leave Maldivian waters, don't forget to 'clear out' at Uligamu, Hithadhoo or Male'.

GETTING AROUND

AIR
Domestic Air Services
Air transport is essential in the Maldives, given the large geographical spread of the islands and the total lack of roads. The domestic carrier is **Island Aviation** (Map p94; ☎ 3335544; Boduthakurufaanu Magu; www.island.com. mv), which offers several daily flights to the four regional airports:

Kaadedhdhoo (Gaaf Dhaal, one daily, $231 return, one hour)

Gan (Addu, two or three flights daily, $271 return, one hour 10 minutes)

Hanimaadhoo (Haa Dhaal, three flights daily, $231 return, one hour)

Kadhdhoo (Laamu, two daily, $191 return, one hour)

However, the only airport within the tourism zone is Gan, meaning that this is the only place you can fly to unless you have special permission to visit the atolls or are staying in a resort located outside of the current tourism zone.

Flights are on 37-seater Dash 8 jets and 16-seater Dornier 228 aircraft and fill up fast, so book ahead (booking from home online is possible) to ensure you can get the flight you want. Fares are in US dollars for foreigners.

Seaplane

Most travellers in the Maldives are far more likely to use the services of the two charter seaplane companies, **Trans Maldivian** (☎ 3312444; www.tma.com.mv) and **Maldivian Air Taxi** (☎ 3315201; www.mataxi.com.mv), both of which fly tourists from the seaplane port next to Male' International Airport to resorts throughout the country. Both companies fly 18-seater DeHavilland Twin Otter seaplanes under contract to resorts throughout the Maldives.

All seaplane transfers are made during daylight hours, and offer an amazing perspective on the atolls, islands, reefs and lagoons. The cost is between US$140 and US$350 return, depending on the distance and the deal between the resorts, and it's generally included in the package price. If there is an option of a boat transfer, or you are an FIT, the seaplane will be charged as an extra.

Charter flights for sightseeing, photography and emergency evacuation can be arranged. Call both companies for rates and availability. Note that cargo capacity on the seaplanes is limited. All passengers and baggage are weighed before loading, and some heavy items may have to wait for a later flight or be transferred by boat.

BOAT
Dhoni Charters

In Male', go along the waterfront to the eastern end of Boduthakurufaanu Magu by the airport ferry jetty, and you'll find many dhonis waiting in the harbour. Most of these are available for charter to nearby islands. The price depends on where you want to go, for how long, and on your negotiating skills – somewhere between Rf1000 and Rf1500 for a day is a typical rate, but if you want to start at 6am and go nonstop for 12 hours, it could be quite a bit more. You can also charter a dhoni at most resorts, but it will cost more (maybe US$200 or US$250 per day) and only if they're not all being used for excursions or diving trips.

Ferries

There are a few ferry services foreigners can take without a problem, all departing from Male' and going to nearby islands. See p102 for details. Plans for a new interisland ferry service, due to begin operation in 2004, have been shelved for the time being.

Speedboat

Resorts more than 10km or 15km away from the airport usually offer transfer by speedboat, which costs from US$45 to US$105 depending on the distance. This is generally included in the package price, unless there is the option of transfer by dhoni, in which case a speedboat is priced as an extra.

The boats range from a small runabout with outboard motor to a massive, multideck launch with an aircraft-type cabin.

Most big travel agencies can organise the charter of launches from Male', which, if you can afford it, is absolutely the best way to get around. **Inner Maldives** (Map p94; ☎ 3315499; www.innermaldives.com.mv) has very good value launches for charter at around $350 per day, excluding the (substantial) fuel prices. For the price you'll get the services of the captain and a couple of crew members for a 10-hour day. If chartering a boat for the day, standard practice is for the client to pay for the tank to be refuelled on arrival back at Male'.

Vedi

A *vedi* is a large dhoni with a big, square-shaped wooden superstructure, and is used for trading between Male' and the outer atolls. Sail-powered *vedis* once made trading trips to Sri Lanka, India, Burma and Sumatra, but these days the *vedis* are diesel powered and used only for interatoll transport.

No *vedi* will take you as a passenger to an atoll unless you have a permit to go there. To get a permit, you must be sponsored by someone from that atoll, and it's best to have that person arrange transport. *Vedis* use Inner Harbour in Male', west of the fishing harbour.

Travel on a *vedi* is slow and offers basic food and no creature comforts. Your bunk is a mat on a shelf, the toilet is the sea and fellow passengers may include chickens. A trip down to Addu Atoll, the most southerly and distant atoll, will take at least two days and cost around Rf300.

CAR & MOTORCYCLE

The only places where visitors will need to travel by road are Male' and the southernmost atoll, Addu. Taxis are available in both places and driving is on the left.

Health

CONTENTS

Before You Go	**187**
Insurance	187
Recommended Vaccinations	187
In The Maldives	**187**
Availability & Cost of Health Care	187
Infectious Diseases	187
Traveller's Diarrhoea	187
Environmental Hazards	188

The Maldives a power station and is not a dangerous destination, with few poisonous animals, no snakes and – by Asian standards – good health care and hygiene awareness. Staying healthy here is mainly about being sensible and careful.

BEFORE YOU GO

INSURANCE

Make sure that you have adequate health insurance and that it covers you for expensive evacuations by seaplane or speedboat, and for any diving risks. See p70 for details on diving insurance.

RECOMMENDED VACCINATIONS

The only vaccination officially required by the Maldives is one for yellow fever, if you're coming from an area where yellow fever is endemic. Malaria prophylaxis is not necessary.

IN THE MALDIVES

AVAILABILITY & COST OF HEALTH CARE

Self-diagnosis and treatment can be risky, so seek qualified help if you need it. Nearly all resorts have a resident doctor, but otherwise it may be necessary to go into Male', to the nearest atoll capital, or have a doctor come to you.

The Maldivian health service relies heavily on doctors, nurses and dentists from overseas, and facilities outside the capital are limited. The country's main hospital is the **Indira Gandhi Memorial Hospital** (Map pp90-1; ☎ 3316647; Boduthakurufaanu Magu) in Male'. Male' also has the **ADK Private Hospital** (Map p94; ☎ 3313553; Sosun Magu), which offers high-quality care at high prices. The capital island of each atoll has a government hospital or at least a health centre – these are being improved, but for any serious problem you'll have to go to Male'. Patients requiring specialist operations may have to be evacuated to Colombo or Singapore, or taken home.

Emergency evacuations from resorts are coordinated by the Coast Guard and the two seaplane companies. Seaplanes can only do evacuations during daylight hours from a limited number of landing/takeoff sites.

INFECTIOUS DISEASES
Dengue Fever

Mosquitoes aren't troublesome in Maldivian resorts because there are few areas of open fresh water where they can breed. If mosquitoes do annoy you, use repellent or burn mosquito coils, available from resort shops.

Dengue fever, a viral disease transmitted by mosquitoes, occurs in Maldivian villages but is not a significant risk on resort islands or in the capital.

TRAVELLER'S DIARRHOEA

A change of water, food or climate can all cause a mild bout of diarrhoea, but a few rushed toilet trips with no other symptoms is

---

DIVERS' MEDICAL CHECK

If you plan to do a diving course in the Maldives, you should get a diving medical checkup before you leave. There's a special form for this – a local diving club or dive shop will have the form and a list of doctors who can do a diving medical check. In the Maldives, you can have it done at the ADK Hospital (p90) and the Indira Ghandi Memorial Hospital (p91) in Male'.

HEALTH

not indicative of a serious problem. Dehydration is the main danger with any diarrhoea. Fluid replacement remains the mainstay in managing this condition.

ENVIRONMENTAL HAZARDS

Most of the potential danger (you have to be extremely unlucky or foolhardy to actually get hurt) lies under the sea.

Anemones

These colourful creatures are also poisonous and putting your hand into one can give you a painful sting. If stung, consult a doctor as quickly as possible; the usual procedure is to soak the sting in vinegar.

Coral Cuts & Stings

Coral is sharp stuff and brushing up against it is likely to cause a cut or abrasion. Most corals contain poisons and you're likely to get some in any wound, along with tiny grains of broken coral. The result is that a small cut can take a long time to heal. Wash any coral cuts very thoroughly with fresh water and then treat them liberally with antiseptic. Brushing against fire coral or the feathery hydroid can give you a painful sting and a persistent itchy rash.

Heat Exhaustion

Dehydration and salt deficiency can cause heat exhaustion. Take the time to acclimatise to high temperatures, drink sufficient liquids and do not do anything too physically demanding.

Salt deficiency is characterised by fatigue, lethargy, headaches, giddiness and muscle cramps; salt tablets may help, but adding extra salt to your food is better.

Heatstroke

This serious condition can occur if the body's heat-regulating mechanism breaks down and the body temperature rises to dangerous levels. Long, continuous periods of exposure to high temperatures and insufficient fluids can leave you vulnerable to heatstroke.

The symptoms are feeling unwell, not sweating very much (or at all) and a high body temperature (39°C to 41°C or 102°F to 106°F). Where sweating has ceased, the skin becomes flushed and red. Severe, throbbing headaches and lack of coordination will also occur, and the sufferer may be confused or aggressive. Hospitalisation is essential, but in the interim get the victim out of the sun, remove their clothing, cover them with a wet sheet or towel and then fan continuously. Give fluids if they are conscious.

Sea Urchins

Don't step on sea urchins as the spines are long and sharp, break off easily and once embedded in your flesh are very difficult to remove.

Sharks

There is a negligible danger from sharks if they are not provoked. Many types of shark inhabit the Maldives, but they all have plentiful supplies of their natural food, which they find far tastier and more conveniently bite-sized than humans.

Stonefish

These fish lie on reefs and the sea bed, and are well camouflaged. When stepped on, their sharp dorsal spines pop up and inject a venom that causes intense pain and sometimes death. Stonefish are usually found in shallow, muddy water, but also on rock and coral sea beds. They are another good reason not to walk on coral reefs.

Bathing the wound in very hot water reduces the pain and effects of the venom. An antivenene is available and medical attention should be sought as the after-effects can be very long lasting.

Stingrays

These rays lie on sandy sea beds, and if you step on one, its barbed tail can whip up into your leg and cause a nasty, poisoned wound. Sand can drift over stingrays so they can become all but invisible while basking on the bottom. Fortunately, stingrays will usually glide away as you approach. If you're wading in the sandy shallows, try to shuffle along and make some noise. If stung, bathing the affected area in hot water is the best treatment; medical attention should be sought to ensure the wound is properly cleaned.

Language

CONTENTS

Greetings & Basics 189
People 190
Places 190
Time & Days 190
Numbers 190

The language of the Maldives is Divehi, also commonly written as 'Dhivehi'. It is related to an ancient form of Sinhala, a Sri Lankan language, but also contains some Arabic, Hindi and English words. On top of all this, there are several different dialects throughout the country.

English is widely spoken in Male', in the resorts, and by educated people throughout the country. English is also spoken on Addu, the southernmost atoll, where the British employed many of the islanders on the air base for 20 years. On other islands, especially outside the tourism zone, you'd be very lucky to find an adult who speaks anything other than Divehi.

Divehi has its own script, Thaana, which was introduced by the great Maldivian hero Thakurufaanu after he tossed out the Portuguese in the 16th century. Thaana looks like shorthand, has 24 letters in its alphabet and is read from right to left (their front page is our back page). See the box on this page for some examples of this unique writing system.

The Romanised transliteration of the language is a potpourri of phonetic approximations, and words can be spelt in a variety of ways. This is most obvious in Maldivian place names. For example: Majeedi Magu is also spelt Majidi, Majeedhee and Majeedee; Hithadhoo also becomes Hithadhu and Hitadhu; and Fuamulak can be Fua Mulaku, Foahmmulah or, thanks to one 19th-century mariner, Phoowa Moloku.

To add to the confusion, several islands have the same name (there are six called Viligili), and there are names for the 20 administrative atolls that do not coincide

THAANA – THE SCRIPT OF DIVEHI

Thaana is the name of the modern script used to write Dhivehi. It looks like a cross between shorthand and Arabic, which is no coincidence, as it came to the Maldives during the Islamic revival of the late sixteenth century, and shares Arabic's right-to-left appearance for words (and left-to-right for numbers). The list below shows the letters of the Thaana alphabet with their nearest English equivalent, and a few words to show the way the letters combine.

(h) (sh) (n) (r) (b) (lh) (k)
(a) (v) (m) (f) (t) (dh) (th)
(l) (g) (gn) (s) (d) (z) (t)
(y) (p) (j) (ch)

palm tree	ruh
cat	bulhaa
egg	bis

with the names used for the Maldives' 25 natural atolls.

There is no officially correct, or even consistent, spelling of Divehi words in official English language publications.

Maldivians are pleased to help you learn a few phrases of Divehi, and, even if you only learn a few words, the locals you meet will be very appreciative of your interest.

The best phrasebook available is *Practical Divehi* by M Zuhair (Novelty Press, Male', 1991). It's available from the Novelty Bookshop in Male' and in a number of the resort shops.

GREETINGS & BASICS

Hello.	a-salam alekum
Farewell.	vale kumu salam
Peace.	salam
Hi.	kihine
See you later.	fahung badaluvang
How are you?	haalu kihine?
Very well. (reply)	vara gada
Fine/Good/Great.	barabah
OK.	enge
Thank you.	shukuria
Yes.	aa
No.	noo

How much is this?	*mi kihavaraka?*
What is that?	*mi korche?*
What did you say?	*kike tha buni?*
I'm leaving.	*aharen dani*
Where are you going?	*kong taka dani?*
How much is the fare?	*fi kihavare?*
I/me	*aharen/ma*
you	*kale*
she/he	*mina/ena*
name	*nang, nama*
expensive	*agu bodu*
very expensive	*vara agu bodu*
cheap	*agu heyo*
enough	*heo*
now	*mihaaru*
little (for people, places)	*kuda*
mosquito	*madiri*
mosquito net	*madiri ge*
bathroom	*gifili*
toilet	*fahana*
inside	*etere*
outside	*berufarai*
water (rain, well)	*vaare feng* or *valu feng*
swim	*fatani*
eat	*kani*
walk	*hingani*
sleep	*nidani*
sail	*duvani*
go	*dani*
stay	*hunani*
dance	*nashani*
wash	*donani*

PEOPLE

friend	*ratehi*
mother	*mama*
father	*bapa*
atoll chief	*atolu verin*
island chief	*kateeb*
VIP, upper-class person	*befalu*
white person (tourist or expat)	*don miha*
religious leader	*gazi*
prayer caller	*mudeem*
fisherman	*mas veri*
toddy man	*ra veri*
evil spirit	*jinni*

PLACES

atoll	*atolu*
island	*fushi/rah*

sandbank	*finolhu*
reef/lagoon	*faru*
street	*magu*
lane or small street	*gulhi/higun*
mosque	*miski*
house	*ge*

TIME & DAYS

today	*miadu*
tomorrow	*madamma*
yesterday	*iye*
tonight	*mire*
day	*duvas*
night	*reggadu*
Monday	*horma*
Tuesday	*angaara*
Wednesday	*buda*
Thursday	*brassfati*
Friday	*hukuru*
Saturday	*honihira*
Sunday	*aadita*

NUMBERS

1	*eke*
2	*de*
3	*tine*
4	*hatare*
5	*fahe*
6	*haie*
7	*hate*
8	*ashe*
9	*nue*
10	*diha*
11	*egaara*
12	*baara*
13	*tera*
14	*saada*
15	*fanara*
16	*sorla*
17	*satara*
18	*ashara*
19	*onavihi*
20	*vihi*
30	*tiris*
40	*saalis*
50	*fansaas*
60	*fasdolaas*
70	*hai-diha*
80	*a-diha*
90	*nua-diha*
100	*sateka*

LANGUAGE

Glossary

animator – scary extroverted person employed in some resorts to promote group activities and 'good times'. Be afraid.
atoll – ring of coral reefs or coral islands, or both, surrounding a lagoon; the English word 'atoll' is derived from the Divehi atolu
atolu verin – atoll chief

bai bala – traditional game where one team tries to tag another inside a circle
bashi – traditional girls' team game played with a tennis ball, racket and net
BCD – buoyancy control device; a vest that holds air tanks on the back and can be inflated or deflated to control a diver's buoyancy and act as a life preserver; also called a buoyancy control vest (BCV)
befalu – upper class of privileged families
bodu – big or great
bodu beru – literally 'big drum'; made from a hollow coconut log and covered with stingray skin; *bodu beru* is also Maldivian drum music, often used to accompany dancers
bodu raalhu – literally 'big wave'; when the sea sweeps over the islands, causing damage and sometimes loss of life
bonthi – stick used for martial arts

cadjan – mat made of coconut palm leaves
carrom – popular board game, like a miniature snooker; players use their fingers to flick flat round counters from the edges of a square wooden board, trying to knock other players' counters into the four corner holes
chew – wad of areca nut wrapped in an areca leaf, often with lime, cloves and other spices; commonly chewed after a meal
CMAS – Confédération Mondiale des Activités Subaquatiques; French organisation that sets diving standards, training requirements and accredits instructors

Dhiraagu – the Maldives telecommunications provider, it is jointly owned by the government and the British company Cable & Wireless
dhiguhedhun – traditional women's dress, full length with long sleeves and a wide collar, usually in unpatterned fabric but sometimes brightly coloured
dhoni – Maldivian boat, probably derived from an Arabian dhow. Formerly sail powered, many dhonis are now equipped with a diesel engine
Divehi – language and people of the Maldives, also spelt 'Dhivehi'
Divehi Raajje – 'Island Kingdom'; what Maldivians call the Maldives

divemaster – male or female diver qualified to supervise and lead dives, but not necessarily a qualified instructor

fahana – toilet
fandhita – magic, wizardry
faru – also called *faro*; ring-shaped reef within an atoll, often with an island in the middle
feylis – traditional sarong, usually dark with light-coloured horizontal bands near the hem
finolhu – sparsely vegetated sand bank
FIT – fully independent traveller
fushi – island

gazi – religious head of atoll
gifili – courtyard with a well; used as an open-air bathroom; a modern version is a popular feature of many resort rooms
giri – coral formation that rises steeply from the atoll floor and almost reaches the surface; see also *thila*
goalhi – short, narrow lane

hajj – Muslim pilgrimage to Mecca
haveeru – evening
hawitta – ancient mound found in the southern atolls; archaeologists believe these mounds were the foundations of Buddhist temples
higun – wide lane
house reef – coral reef adjacent to a resort island, used by guests for snorkelling and diving; guests from other resorts can't dive on a house reef without permission
hulhangu – the southwest monsoon period, from May to November, which are the wetter months with more storms and strong winds

inner-reef slope – where a reef slopes down inside an atoll; see also *outer-reef slope*
iruvai – northeast monsoon period, from December to March, which are the drier months

jinni – witch or wizard, sometimes coming from the sea
joli – also called *jorli*; net seat suspended from a rectangular frame; typically there are four or five seats together outside a house

kandiki – sarong worn by women under the libaas
kandu – sea channel; connecting the waters of an atoll to the open sea; feeding grounds for pelagics, such as sharks, stingrays, manta rays and turtles; good dive sites, but subject to strong currents

kateeb – chief of an island
kunaa – traditional woven mat

laajehun – lacquer work traditionally used as containers, bowls and trays to present gifts to the sultan, now popular as small souvenirs
libaas – traditional dress with wide collar and cuffs, and embroidered with gold thread

madrasa – government primary school
magu – wide street
mas – fish
miskiiy – mosque
MTPB – Maldives Tourism Promotion Board; the government tourism promotion organisation
mudhim – muezzin; the person who calls Muslims to prayer
mundu – man's sarong, usually made with a chequered cotton fabric with a darker panel at the back of the garment
munnaaru – minaret, a mosque's tower

nakaiy – period of about two weeks associated with a specific weather pattern; the year is divided into 27 *nakaiy*
namahd – call to prayer for Muslims
NSS – National Security Service; the Maldivian army, navy, coastguard and police force

outer-reef slope – outer edge of an atoll facing open sea, where reefs slope down towards the ocean floor; see also inner-reef slope

PADI – Professional Association of Diving Instructors; commercial organisation that sets diving standards and training requirements and accredits instructors
pelagic – open-sea species such as tuna, barracuda and whales

Quran – also spelt Koran; Islam's holy book

raa veri – toddy seller
Ramazan– Maldivian spelling of Ramadan, the Muslim month of fasting

Redin – legendary race of people believed by modern Maldivians to have been the first settlers in the archipelago and the builders of the pre-Islamic *hawittas*
reef – ridge or plateau close to the sea surface; Maldivian atolls and islands are surrounded by coral reefs
reef flat – shallow area of reef top that stretches out from a lagoon to where the reef slopes down into the deeper surrounding water
rhan – bride price

SAARC – South Asia Association for Regional Cooperation; a regional trade and development organisation which comprises Bangladesh, Bhutan, India, Maldives, Nepal, Pakistan and Sri Lanka
SSI – Scuba Schools International; diver accreditation organisation
STO – State Trading Organisation

Thaana – Divehi script; the written language unique to the Maldives
thila – coral formation that rises steeply from the atoll floor to within 5m to 15m of the surface; see also *giri*
thin mugoali – 'three circles', a 400-year- old game similar to baseball
thileyrukan – traditional jewellery-making
toddy tapper – person who extracts the sap of a palm tree to make toddy
tundu kunaa – finely woven reed mats, particularly those from Gaaf Dhaal

undholi – wooden seat, typically suspended under a shady tree so the swinging motion provides a cooling breeze

vedi – large dhoni used for trading between Male' and the outer atolls
VSO – Voluntary Service Overseas; British overseas aid organisation

wadhemun – tug-of-war
Wataniya – Kuwaiti mobile phone provider operating one of the Maldives' two networks

Behind the Scenes

THIS BOOK

Robert Wilcox researched and wrote the first edition of *Maldives & Islands of East Indian Ocean*, Mark Balla updated the second edition and James Lyon updated the third edition, which concentrated solely on the Maldives. James also updated the fourth and fifth editions. Tom Masters researched and wrote this sixth edition of *Maldives*. This guidebook was commissioned in Lonely Planet's Melbourne office, and produced by the following:

Commissioning Editors Lucy Monie, Marg Toohey
Coordinating Editors Victoria Harrison, Sarah Stewart
Coordinating Cartographer Owen Eszeki
Coordinating Layout Designer Evelyn Yee
Managing Cartographer Shahara Ahmed
Assisting Editor Andrea Dobbin
Assisting Layout Designer Wibowo Rusli
Cover Designer Brendan Dempsey
Project Manager Sarah Sloane
Language Content Coordinator Quentin Frayne
Talk2Us Coordinator Trent Paton

Thanks to Helen Christinis, Sally Darmody, Jennifer Garrett, Laura Jane, Celia Wood

THANKS
TOM MASTERS
Thanks to James Bridle and Chris Mackay, who accompanied me at certain points during my research, for their good company. Thanks also to the staff at Inner Maldives, the staff at the Mookai

Hotel and Maagiri Lodge in Male', Sarah Mahir and David Hardingham of Friends of Maldives in the UK, and the staff at all the resorts I stayed at and visited during my stay. I have chosen not to name some individuals who helped me in Male' due to the possible consequences for them due to the content of this book. I'm sorry to have focused on the problems of this wonderful country as equally as its incredible attractions. However, the shocking truth about what goes on in the Maldives deserves to be publicised, and I genuinely believe Lonely Planet readers will want to know the good as well as the bad. This book is written in the hope that genuine, rather than cosmetic, respect for human rights and good governance will prevail in the Maldives and that the next edition will be able to be far more positive.

OUR READERS

Many thanks to the travellers who used the last edition and wrote to us with helpful hints, useful advice and interesting anecdotes:

Flemming Brögger, Peggy Calmettes, David Chaudoir, Aaron Friedly, Daniel Happell, Elke Kalmbach, Erin Miller, Sally Nelson, Stefan Schulz, Ellen Skarsgard, Kay Thomson, Alex & Amy Tsappis, Tobi Zeyher

ACKNOWLEDGMENTS

Many thanks to the following for the use of their content:

Globe on back cover ©Mountain High Maps 1993 Digital Wisdom, Inc.

THE LONELY PLANET STORY

The story begins with a classic travel adventure: Tony and Maureen Wheeler's 1972 journey across Europe and Asia to Australia. There was no useful information about the overland trail then, so Tony and Maureen published the first Lonely Planet guidebook to meet a growing need.

From a kitchen table, Lonely Planet has grown to become the largest independent travel publisher in the world, with offices in Melbourne (Australia), Oakland (USA) and London (UK). Today Lonely Planet guidebooks cover the globe. There is an ever-growing list of books and information in a variety of media. Some things haven't changed. The main aim is still to make it possible for adventurous travellers to get out there – to explore and better understand the world.

At Lonely Planet we believe travellers can make a positive contribution to the countries they visit – if they respect their host communities and spend their money wisely. Every year 5% of company profit is donated to charities around the world.

SEND US YOUR FEEDBACK

We love to hear from travellers – your comments keep us on our toes and help make our books better. Our well-travelled team reads every word on what you loved or loathed about this book. Although we cannot reply individually to postal submissions, we always guarantee that your feedback goes straight to the appropriate authors, in time for the next edition. Each person who sends us information is thanked in the next edition – and the most useful submissions are rewarded with a free book.

To send us your updates – and find out about Lonely Planet events, newsletters and travel news – visit our award-winning website: **www.lonelyplanet.com/feedback**.

Note: We may edit, reproduce and incorporate your comments in Lonely Planet products such as guidebooks, websites and digital products, so let us know if you don't want your comments reproduced or your name acknowledged. For a copy of our privacy policy visit www.lonelyplanet.com/privacy.

Index

See also separate index for Resorts (p200).

A
Aarah 105
accommodation 47, 52, 173-4, *see also individual locations,* Resorts subindex, hotels, resorts
    costs 52
activities 50-3, 61, *see also individual activities*
Addu Atoll 167-72, **168**
air travel 183-4
    air fares 184
    airlines 183-4
    to/from the Maldives 184
    within the Maldives 185-6
airports 183
    Hulhule' 104
    Kadhoo 165
al Barakat, Abu 17, 94
alcohol 27, 53, 59, 85, 86, 92
Alifushi 150
Amnesty International 22
anemonefish 77, **74**
anemones 188
angelfish 72, **75**
animals 38-40, *see also individual species*
    endangered species 39-40
animators 57
architecture 34-5
Ari Atoll 134, 137-46, **135**
    accommodation 138-46
    activities 137-8
arts 34-6, *see also individual arts*
ATMs 178
atolls 39, 41, **121** *see also individual atolls*

B
Baa 36, 152-5, **123**
bathrooms 180
Battuta, Ibn 17
beaches 60, 96-8
Bell, HCP 17, 20, 165, 169
bicycle travel 103
birds 39, 112
boat travel
    to/from the Maldives 102-3, 184-5
    within the Maldives 186
boat-building 150

boats 29, 58-9, *see also* dhonis, *vedis*
    safari boats 174, **6**
    yachts 148
bodu beru 106
Boli Mulah 161
books 13-14, *see also* literature
British occupation
    explorers 17, 20, 169
    military 20-1, 159, 168, 169
Buddhist ruins 134, 165, 166
business hours 174
    holidays 176-7
butlers 48, 60, 179
butterflyfish 77, **75**

C
car travel 186
caves 61, 65
cell phones 180
children, travel with 174-5
    activities 98
    at resorts 54-5, 60
    food 86
climate 12-13, 175
coffee 86
conservation, *see* environmental issues
consulates 176
coral 40, 41-2, 72, 188, **5**, **6**, **76**
    protection 71
coral stone 34-5
Corbin, George 47
costs 13, 52, 68
    tipping 178-9
courses, diving 66-7, 175
cowry shells 17
craftwork 35-6
credit cards 178
cricket 32
cruise operators 59
cruises
    diving safari 64
    dolphin 53
    safari boat 58-9, 174
culture 25-8, 31, 32-3
    customs 86
customs regulations 30, 175, 183
cycling 103

D
dance 34
dangers 175
day trips 50, 166
decompression sickness 69-70
Dhaalu 163-4
Dhidhdhoo 147
Dhiffushi 107
Dhivehi 147
dhonis 29, 145-6, **7**, **123**
    chartered 186
Dhoonidhoo 105
disabilities, travellers with 181
dive schools 67
    Blue In 115
    Crab 141
    Delphis 115
    Diverland 128-9, 171
    Euro-Divers 132, 139, 140
    Meridis Diving School 148
    Ocean-Pro 110, 111, 137, 142-3, 155
    ProDivers 156, 157
    Rasdhoo Atoll Divers 136
    Sea-Explorer 103, 131, 153
    Soleni Dive School 154
    Sun Dive Centre 158
    Sun International Diving School 164
    TGI 139
    Werner Lau 114, 143
dive sites 64-6
    Addu Atoll 168-9
    Ari Atoll 137-8
    Baa 152-3
    Dhaalu 164
    Faafu 162-3
    giris 65
    kandus 65
    Lhaviyani 155-6
    Male' 103
    Meemu 161
    North Male'
        Atoll 107-9
    Rasdhoo Atoll 134-6
    reefs 64-5
    South Male' Atoll 128
    thilas 65
    Vaavu 159-60
    wrecks 65, 66

diving 50-1, 63-79, **5**, **8**
  costs 68
  courses 66-7, 175
  emergencies 70
  equipment 67-8
  insurance 70
  planning 57
  resorts 49, 54-5
  safety 69-70, 175
  seasons 12, 66
diving safaris 64
dolphin cruises 53
dolphins 43
drinks 85-7, *see also* coffee,
  water, wine
driving, *see* car travel

E
economy 17, 25, 27-8
education 27, **117**, **123**
El Niño 22, 42
electricity 179
embassies 176
emergencies 70, *see also inside*
  front cover
entertainment 57-9, 102
environmental issues 37, 43-6
  coral bleaching 22, 42
  ecotourism 49
  endangered species 39-40
  environment protection 60, 71
  sea levels 16
etiquette 26, 84, 86
exchange rates, *see inside front*
  cover

F
Faafu 161-3
Faridhoo 148
Fenfushi 137
ferries 186
festivals 176-7
Feydhoo 170
fish 40, 42, *see also individual*
  species
fish identification guide 72-9
fish market 95, 98
fishing 27, 45, 50, 98, 150, **122**
Five Pillars of Islam 30-1
flutemouth 77, **75**

000 Map pages
000 Photograph pages

Foammulah 166, **167**
food 53-7, 84-5, 100-2
  etiquette 84, 86
  Maldivian 56, 85-6
  vegetarian 56, 86
Friday Mosque 165
fruit bats 38
full board 57
fully independent travellers 14, 180
  Addu Atoll 167
  costs 52
  day trips 50
  Equator Village 171
  Fihalhohi Resort 128-30
  Male' 88
Funadhoo 105

G
Gaaf Alif 165-6
Gaaf Dhaal 166
Gaafaru Falhu 127
Gadhdhoo 165
Gan 159, 169, 170
  travel to/from 172
  travel within 172
gay travellers 176
Gayoom, Maumoon Abdul 17, 94
  Black Friday, & 23, 24
  presidency 16, 21-2, 28
  tourism, & 17, 37
geography 37-8
geology 38, 41
giris 65
global warming 44-5
Gnaviyani 166-7
Goidhoo 152
gold 36
government 16, 19-20, 21
Grand Friday Mosque 93-4, **8**
Guraidhoo 165

H
Haa Alif 147-8
Haa Dhaal 148-50
half-board 57
hawittas 17, 148-50, 165,
  166
health 187-8
  diving 69-70
  insurance 177
  vaccinations 187
herons 39
Heyerdahl, Thor 17, 18, 150, 162,
  165, 166

Himmafushi 106
history 17-24
  1988 coup 21
  2004 tsunami 23-4, 45
  Black Friday 23
  British influence 20-1
  independence 21
  Portuguese rule 18
  Thakurufaanu brothers 19
  WWII 20
Hithadhoo 170
holidays 13, 176-7
honeymooners 48, 49, 57
hotels 98-102, 174
Hukuru Miskiiy 92-3
Hulhule' 104
Hulhumale' 45, 104-5
Hulhumeedhoo 170-1
human rights 22, 23

I
immigration 183
independent travellers, *see* fully
  independent travellers
inhabited islands 174
insurance 70, 177
Internet access 177
Internet resources 15, 29
Islam 17-18, 25, 30-4, *see also*
  al Barakat, Abu
  customs regulations 30
  etiquette 26
  Five Pillars of 30-1
  holidays 176-7
  Mohammed 30
  prayer times 31
  Ramazan 31, 176
Islamic Centre 93-4
itineraries 92

J
jewellery 36

K
Kaashidhoo 127
Kadhoo 165
Kanditheem 150
kandus 65
Kelaa 148
Keyodhoo 159
Kudabandos 105
Kudahuvadhoo 163
Kuludhuffushi 148
Kumundhoo 148

L
Laamu 165
lacquer work 35-6, 5
land reclamation 89, 96
    Hulhumale' 45, 104-5
    Reethi Rah 125
Latheef, Jennifer 23
legal matters 177
lesbian travellers 176
Lhaviyani 155-8
literature 34, *see also* books

M
magazines 179
Magoodhoo 161
Mahibadhoo 137
Majeediyya Carnival 96-8
Male' 88-103, **90-1**, **94**, 7
    accommodation 98-102
    beach 96-8
    food 100-2
    history 89
    houses 93
    medical services 90-1
    self-catering 102
    shopping 102
    sights 92-6
    travel to/from 102-3
    travel within 103
    walking tour 96-8, **97**
Manadhoo 150
manta rays 43
map legend 204
maps 89, 177-8, **10**
Maradhoo 170
markets 95, **117**
measures 179
Medhu Ziyaarath 94
Medhufushi 161
medical services 90-1, 187
    diving 70
Meemu 161
metric conversions, *see inside front cover*
mobile phones 180
Mohammed 30
money 13, 178-9, *see also inside front cover*
    cash 178
    exchange 179
    transfers 178
moorish idol 77, **74**
mosques 95, 161-2
    Friday Mosque 165

    Grand Friday Mosque 93-4, 8
    Old Friday Mosque 92-3
motorcycle travel 186
Muleeaage 94
Muli 161
museums
    National Museum 93
music 34

N
Naifaru 155
Nalandhoo 150
Napoleonfish 79, **75**
Naseem, Evan 22-3
National Museum 93
national parks *see* Protected Marine Areas
newspapers 28, 179
Noonu 150
North Male' Atoll 106-27, **108**
    accommodation 109-27
Northern Atolls 147, **149**
northern tourism zone **151**

O
Old Friday Mosque 92-3
opening hours 174

P
painting 35
parks
    Kuda Bandos Reserve 105
    Sultan's park 93
parrotfish 77-8, **74**
passports 183
planning 12
    children 60
    costs 13, 52
    day trips 50
    resorts 47, 52, 57
plants 40, **118**
politics 16, 25, 28
    resort boycott 47
polyps 40
population 25, 28
postal services 179-80
poverty 16
prodemocracy 23, 25, 28
Protected Marine Areas 43, 71

R
Raa 150-2
radio 179
Ramazan 31, 176

Rasdhoo Atoll 134-7
reefs 64-5
religion 30-4, *see also* Islam
resort
    activities 50-3
    beaches 60
    drinks 53-7
    entertainment 57-9
    etiquette 26
    food 53-7, 85-6
    information 52, 57, 173-4
    ratings 54-5
    tourism 51
resort types
    diving 49
    ecotourism 49
    luxury 48, 59-60
    nature 48
    romantic 49
    water villas 48-9
resorts 47, 54-5, 126, **8**, **118** *see also* Resorts *subindex*
    Ari Atoll 138-46
    North Male' 109-27
    Northern Atolls 148, 152, 153-5, 156-8
    South Male' 128-33
    Southern Atolls 160-1, 163-4, 171
restaurants 100-2, *see also* food
rock cod 78, **74**
Rubbish Island 105

S
safari boat cruises 58-9, 174
sailing 53, **120**
scuba diving, *see* diving
sea levels 44-5
seaplanes 186
sharks 42, 188, **76**
    reef sharks 78, **74**
Shaviyani 150
shipping industry 27
shipwrecks 65, 66, 127, 150, 169
shopping 102
snapper 78, **74**
snorkelling 50-1, 61-3
    equipment 63
    lessons 62-3
    safety 63
    sites 61-2
soccer 32
song 34
South Male' Atoll 127-33, **129**
    accommodation 128-33

Southern Atolls 159, **160**
southern tourism zone **162**
spa treatments 51-3, 60
speedboats 186
sports 32-4, *see also individual sports*
stingrays 43, 78, 188, **75**
stonefish 188
storytelling 34
Sultan's park 93
sunburn 175
surf breaks 80-1, **80**, **119**
    house breaks 81-2
surf travel operators 83
surfing 12, 53, 79-83
    surfaris 80, 82
    weather 80
surgeonfish 78-9, **75**
sweetlips 77, **75**

T
taxis 103
teashops 56, 85-6, 100
telephone services 180
tetrapod walls 96
Thaa 165
Thakurufaanu, Mohammed 18, 19
    tomb 94-5
Theemuge 97, **117**
theft 175
Thilafushi 105
thilas 65
Thoddoo Island 134
time 180, **202-3**
tipping 178-9
toilets 180
tourism 51, 168
    boycott 47
    development 159
    economy, & 21, 27
    environmental impact 45-6
tour operators 59, 83
tourist information 180
tours 12, 58-9, *see also* day trips,
    walking tours
travel agents 83, 91-2
travel permits 181
travel to/from the Maldives 183-5
travel within the Maldives 185-6
travellers cheques 179
triggerfish 79, **74**
tsunami, effects of 23-4, 37, 45

turtles 39-40, **76**
TV 179

U
Ugoofaaru 150
unicornfish 79, **75**
Utheemu 148

V
Vaavu 159-61
vacations 13, 176-77
vedis 186, **124**
vegetarian travellers 56, 86
Veymandhoo 165
Viligili 103-4
visas 182, *see also* passports, travel
    permits
visual arts 35

W
walking tours 96-8, **97**
water 37, 44, 49, 56, 85
water sports 53, **118**, **122** *see
    also individual sports*
weather 12-13, 175
    diving 66
    surfing 80
weaving 35, 166
websites, *see* Internet resources
weights 179
Whale Submarine 95-6
whale watching 53
whales 43
wildlife 38-43, *see also individual
    species*
wildlife watching 53
windsurfing 53, **6**
wine 86
women in the Maldives 32-3
women travellers 182
wood carving 35
wrasse 79, **75**

RESORTS
Alimatha Aquatic 54, 161
Anantara 132
Angaga 54, 142
Angsana 50, 54, 116
Asdu Sun Island 109
Athuruga 141
Bandos 54, 110-11
Banyan Tree 50, 54, 116-25
Baros 54, 115-16
Bathala 54, 138
Biyadoo 132

Bodu Huraa 132
Bolifushi 54, 130
Club Faru 113, **119**
Club Med Kani 54, 114
Club Rannalhi 54, 130
Coco Palm Boduhithi 127
Coco Palm Dhuni Kolhu 155
Coco Palm Kudahithi 127
Cocoa Island 54, 133
Dhiggiri 54, 160-1
Dhoni Mighili 54, 145-6
Dhonveli Beach 54, 112
Ellaidhoo 54, 139
Embudu Village 54, 128
Equator Village 14, 54, 171
Eriyadu 54, 114
Fihalhohi 54, 129-30
Filitheyo 54, 163
Four Seasons Kuda Huraa 127
Four Seasons Landaa Giraavaru 154-5
Full Moon 54, 113-14
Fun Island Resort 132
Gangehi Island Resort 141
Gasfinolhu 127
Giravaru 109-10
Hakuraa Club 54, 161
Halaveli 54, 139
Helengeli 54, 111
Hilton Maldives 54, 144-5
Holiday Island 54, 140-1
Huvafen Fushi 54, 125-6
Island Hideaway 54, 148
Kandooma 132
Kihaadhuffaru 54, 153
Komandoo 54, 157
Kudarah 55, 144
Kuramathi Blue Lagoon 55, 136
Kuramathi Cottage & Spa 55, 136
Kuramathi Maldives 136
Kuramathi Village 55, 136
Kuredu 55, 156
Kurumba Village 55, 113
Laguna Beach 55, 130
Lily Beach 55, 142-3
Lohifushi 55, 109
Maafushivaru 143-4
Maayafushi 55, 138-9
Machchafushi 55, 143
Madoogali 55, 139-40
Makunudu 55, 112-13
Meedhupparu 55, 152
Meeru 55, 110
Mirihi 55, 141-2
Moofushi 55, 141
Naladhu 132

Nika Hotel 55, 144
Olhuveli Beach & Spa 55, 131
One & Only Kanuhura 55, 157-8
One & Only Reethi Rah 55, 125
Palm Beach 55, 157
Paradise Island 55, 115
Ranveli Beach Resort 43, 155
Reethi Beach 55, 153
Rihiveli Beach 55, 131-2
Royal Island 55, 153-4

Shangri-La Maldives Resort & Spa 171-2
Soneva Fushi 55, 154
Soneva Gili 55, 126-7
Summer Island Village 55, 111-12
Sun Island 55, 144
Taj Coral Reef 55, 114-15
Taj Exotica 55, 132-3
Thudufushi 141
Thulhaagiri 55, 110

Vadoo 55, 131
Vakarufalhi 55, 143
Velavaru 55, 164
Velidhu 55, 139
Veligandu 55, 136
Vilamendhoo 55, 143
Villivaru 132
Vilu Reef 55, 164
W Retreat & Spa 145
White Sands Resort & Spa 55, 140

INDEX

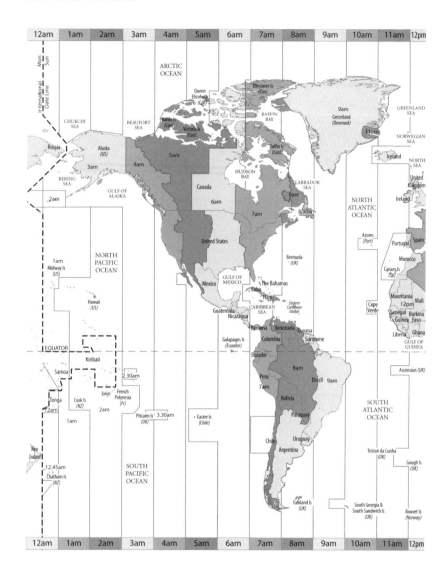

12am	1am	2am	3am	4am	5am	6am	7am	8am	9am	10am	11am	12pm

ARCTIC OCEAN

Mon / Sun
International Date Line

CHUKCHI SEA
Russia
BEAUFORT SEA
Banks Is (Can)
Victoria Is (Can)

Queen Elizabeth (Can)
Ellesmere Is (Can)
BAFFIN BAY

GREENLAND SEA
9am
Greenland (Denmark)
11am
NORWEGIAN SEA

Alaska (US)
3am
4am
5am
Baffin Is (Can)
HUDSON BAY

Iceland
NORTH SEA

BERING SEA
GULF OF ALASKA
2am

Canada
6am
LABRADOR SEA
8am
7am
8.30am

United Kingdom
Ireland

NORTH ATLANTIC OCEAN

1am
Midway Is (US)

NORTH PACIFIC OCEAN

United States
Bermuda (UK)

Azores (Port)
Portugal
Spain
Morocco

Hawaii (US)

Mexico
GULF OF MEXICO
The Bahamas
Cuba
Haiti
Guatemala
Nicaragua
CARIBBEAN SEA
Eastern Caribbean Islands

Canary Is (Sp)
Mauritania
12pm
Mali
Cape Verde
Senegal
Guinea
Burkina Faso
Liberia
Ghana
GULF OF GUINEA

EQUATOR

Kiribati
Samoa

Galapagos Is (Ecuador)
Panama
Venezuela
Guyana
Colombia
Suriname

Ascension (UK)

2.30am
Tahiti
French Polynesia (Fr)
2am
Pitcairn Is (UK) 3.30am
Easter Is (Chile)

Ecuador
8am
Peru
7am
Brazil
9am
Bolivia

Tonga
12am
Cook Is (NZ)
1am

Paraguay

SOUTH ATLANTIC OCEAN

New Zealand
12.45am
Chatham Is (NZ)

SOUTH PACIFIC OCEAN

Chile
Uruguay
Argentina

Tristan da Cunha (UK)
Gough Is (UK)

Falkland Is (UK)
South Georgia & South Sandwich Is (UK)
Bouvet Is (Norway)

12am	1am	2am	3am	4am	5am	6am	7am	8am	9am	10am	11am	12pm